Communications
Policy and the
Political
Process

Recent Titles in
Contributions in Political Science

Series Editor: Bernard K. Johnpoll

Communications Policy and the Political Process

EDITED BY
JOHN J. HAVICK

CONTRIBUTIONS IN POLITICAL SCIENCE, NUMBER 101

GREENWOOD PRESS
Westport, Connecticut • London, England

Library of Congress Cataloging in Publication Data

Main entry under title:

Communications policy and the political process.

(Contributions in political science, ISSN 0147-1066 ;
no. 101)
  Bibliography: p.
  Includes index.
  1. Telecommunication policy—United States—Addresses,
essays, lectures.   I. Havick, John J.   II. Series.
HE7781.C644   1983   384′.068   83-1673
ISBN 0-313-23234-2 (lib. bdg.)

Library of Congress Catalog Card Number: 83-1673
ISBN: 0-313-23234-2
ISSN: 0147-1066

First published in 1983

Greenwood Press
A division of Congressional Information Service, Inc.
88 Post Road West
Westport, Connecticut 06881

Printed in the United States of America

10 9 8 7 6 5 4 3 2 1

Contents

Figures

Tables

Preface

CHANGES in communications are transforming society and underscoring the importance of public policies dealing with communications. Notably, political analysts have not spent much time studying communications policy. Although books in print discuss the policy process, drawing upon illustrations and cases from areas such as energy, health, pollution, and welfare, communications policy is not usually included. A considerable amount has been written about communications but much of this material focuses on such matters as the choice of a particular communications policy rather than the political process that makes the policy. What has been written about the communications policy process has seldom been underpinned by much theoretical explanation from the work of political analysts. There is very little attempt to relate the communications policy process to a more general understanding of the policy process so, consequently, very little material is available regarding the political process for communications policy.

The role of politics in the making of communications policy is this book's primary concern. While not being encyclopedic, it represents research and thought on specific, focused topics. At least one paper deals with the making of communications policy in nearly every major policy arena of American politics including Congress, the executive branch, the courts, elections, and interest groups. The papers vary in scope and method, but they share a common interest in communications policy, and add information to the slim holdings in this area.

PART ONE

Communications Policy and Political Institutions

1

JOHN J. HAVICK

Introduction

TECHNOLOGICAL CHANGE AND POLICY DILEMMAS

SOCIETY is in the midst of a communications revolution. Live television programs from Europe via satellite and cable television only partially reveal the future shape of mass communications. Because the full range of communications possibilities is still unknown, communications is the latest frontier. The fact is that "we are at an interesting juncture of history—the transition from the transportation age to the age of communications."[1]

The technologies that make the communications revolution possible are, for the most part, available. Among the existing technologies are cable systems with a two-way, interactive capability, and satellite communications. The computer, a technology that in the past has been less associated with communications, gives the new communications systems vast capacity to manage, initiate, and respond to information. Indeed, the computer's role in communications is so pervasive that there is a blurring and merging of what once were thought to be separate industries—computers and communications.

Most homes, in the future, will have a cable with a two-way communications capability. The cable will connect the homes to a myriad of economic, recreational, and civic activities and possibilities. A variety of applications for cable are still being developed and tested to determine their profitability and appeal. Cable systems are currently marketing or test marketing such services as transactional banking, electronic mail, information retrieval, daily news, video games, burglary systems, and fire protection. Also the cable systems hold promise for coverage of local political meetings and the

The author thanks the National Endowment for the Humanities for financial support to study public policy theories.

instant measurement of viewers' opinions on a range of topics. Although most cable systems currently are co-axial cable, at some future date optical fiber will become conventional because it is much lighter, can carry more channels, and is less prone to interference.[2]

The principal benefits of cable currently are better television reception, access to recent movies, several additional channels (such as stations from other cities), an all news channel, and a much greater variety of sporting events than are carried by the network channels. The typical cable system currently being installed also has public access channels to give individuals and groups the opportunity to communicate with the entire cable audience if the audience chooses to tune in the access channel.

Satellite communication offers another dimension of the new era since, unlike cable, no connecting wire is needed. Information is sent to a satellite that is fixed in space, and the satellite in turn sends signals to land-based receiving stations. Dish-like mechanisms called earth stations serve as the sending and receiving antennae. Thus, television signals originating hundreds and thousands of miles away are sent to the satellite and these signals from the satellite are received by anyone possessing a receiving dish. Businesses can hold conferences using such systems; programming can be distributed to cable systems or local broadcasters; and individual homes, if they have the proper antenna, can receive satellite communications. Even Fidel Castro admits owning a receiving dish and watching American television programs via satellite communications. Once the entire communications system is developed and available, the result will be "an entirely new pattern of living . . . a change that will have a greater impact on our lifestyle than the impact of the automobile on the living habits of [our] ancestors."[3]

How United States society controls and shapes its communications system is crucial. Already people fear that the new communications era may provide opportunities for egregious abuses.[4] Any effort to establish legal parameters and safeguards for this communications era is complicated by the fact that the existing law, the 1934 Communications Act, is out of date, and two powerful interests, AT&T and the network television broadcasting industry, have benefited from the law. Presently AT&T and the broadcasters are scrambling to adjust to the new technologies that threaten to encroach upon their established positions in American communications. Considering the stakes, the interests of the average citizen and the entire nation could easily become lost in the politics of the revision of an antiquated law. Communications policy and its revision is clearly important since it will influence society for decades. Because of the role communications will play in the future, it is important to understand the political process in which communications policy is made. This book focuses on the political aspects of the policy process that shapes communications policy.

The Political Environment

In the 1950s and 1960s communications policy was relatively stable and the policy process was free of sweeping divisiveness. The network broadcasters and AT&T dominated the policy process. Few proposals became policy when the dominant interests opposed the proposal. In the sixties the broadcasting industry basked in the knowledge that President Lyndon Johnson and his wife owned a substantial broadcasting system.[5]

The shift in communications policy began under the Nixon administration. Nixon believed that he had been unfairly treated by a media largely dominated by the three major television networks.[6] Nixon's anti-broadcasting policy carried over to his key appointments on the Federal Communications Commission (FCC) and the creation of the Office of Telecommunications Policy within the Executive Office of the President. The Nixon attack on the nation's network broadcasters included appointments of officials who were not afraid to make decisions contrary to the interests of the networks. The Nixon administration policy was an effort to diversify the information alternatives of average citizens. At this time an expansion of information alternatives to the networks included a policy favorable to cable television.[7]

The new communications technologies were given a second boost when the movement to deregulate swept Washington in the mid-seventies. Under President Carter, communications policy followed the trend to deregulate other sectors of the economy, such as the airlines. Many communications policymakers may have embraced deregulation as a convenient means of extricating themselves from what seemed to be a hostile regulatory environment. As under Nixon, a major step for setting the policy tone was through appointments to the FCC. Broadcasters believed that Charles Ferris, Carter's choice for FCC chairman, was very anti-broadcasting. Ferris advocated an expansion of communications alternatives and reliance on market forces to dictate the communications choices available to citizens. Broadcasters countered the Ferris approach by contending that they were hemmed in by numerous constraints on their activity while the new technology communications industries, such as cable television, had an increasingly free reign to flourish, unfettered by government restrictions, and often at the expense of broadcasters.

The broadcasting industry even is divided on some issues. Regarding matters of media access most broadcasters agree on a policy of deregulation, but on other issues there is disagreement. For example, network broadcasters in 1983 are lobbying for the repeal of network syndication and financial interest rules. These rules have prevented networks from owning, programming or participating in the ownership of independently produced programming. The impact of the rules has been to eliminate network control of programming, and this in turn is believed to have given independent television stations greater access to better programming. Independent broadcasting stations have an easier time today purchasing popular network reruns for their programming than they did before 1971 when the networks controlled the ownership of some of their programming. However, network broadcasters faced with increased competition from independent stations and from the new technologies believe the existing rules put them at an unfair disadvantage. Network broadcasters want the same rules to apply to them that apply to other media.

Cable Issues

At the moment the leading competitor to free broadcasting is cable television. Cable television policy is complicated and only a few of the major issues will be addressed here.[8] Much of the debate about cable television policy concerns "distant signals," signals not initiated in the immediate vicinity but usually imported from at least several hundred miles away. In the 1950s distant signals played a very minor part in cable television: cable was chiefly a means of providing people, particularly in rural areas, with better reception of the broadcasting stations in the immediate area. However, cable companies soon realized their product could be more attractive to subscribers if stations from distant cities were offered in a package along with the local channels. The controversy over carrying the distant signals developed when local broadcasters contended the signals would decrease their audience and thus directly conflict with the FCC's established policy of encouraging local broadcasters.

A second aspect of the importation of distant signals involved the viewing of programs by larger audiences than the market where the distant signal originated. Since program producers were usually paid on the basis of audience share, the owners of the program who had contracted with the distant signal station probably were being insufficiently compensated for the use of their program since the actual audience was greater than that in the local community. Moreover, stations in the communities in which the distant signal was being imported found themselves in a situation in which their programming was no longer exclusive in their communities, but instead was competing for viewers with a distant signal.

To deal with these problems in the 1960s the FCC developed "syndicated exclusivity" rules and restrictions on the importation of distant signals. During the 1970s the FCC slowly relaxed its restrictive policy with respect to distant signals, and in 1976 Congress responded to the more lenient rules on distant signals by creating a Royalty Tribunal whose five members are appointed by the president. The Royalty Tribunal's function is to assess the cable systems for their use of programming, and then to redistribute the money to the owners of the programs. The Royalty Tribunal has met with considerable criticism, particularly for the level of compensation and percentage distribution to the various program owners. For example, big cable operators were paying to the Royalty Tribunal less than 1 percent of their gross income for each independent distant signal station carried. The Royalty Tribunal raised the fee to 3.75 percent beginning in 1983. The immediate impact of the Tribunal's ruling is that fewer cable operators are carrying distant signals and those operators who do continue carrying such signals will pay substantially more for these signals. Cable operators and distant signal stations are unhappy with the decision, but local broadcasters and copyright holders are elated. The fight over a proper settlement between the cable operators and the owners of the programming is likely to persist in Congress and the courts. Moreover, Congress will be slow to act because they usually do not take official action until a compromise has been worked out agreeable to all the opposing interests.

What are the impacts of policies that encourage the new communications technologies? One negative impact of a policy permitting cable and other pay television systems to flourish is that the quality of free programming over the airwaves offered by the existing stations and networks may erode. It is very likely that as the percentage of people watching the networks declines, and more and more people turn to other communications alternatives, the networks will cut the cash outlays for programming. Then as the quality of programming declines the percentage of viewers will erode further. Moreover, as the relative quality of pay communications services improves, more people will be lured away from the free over-the-air stations. In short, the change in viewer habits will set in motion a downward spiral in the quality of free programming. It is not likely that the new technologies will drive the free broadcasters out of business, but they can severely change the future economic prospects of free over-the-air broadcasters.

AT&T Issues

The potential of new communications technologies has motivated AT&T, which has held a virtual monopoly on the wire leading into most American homes (until the advent of cable television), to push for a revision of its arrangement with the government. Specifically, AT&T has sought to change a 1956 consent agreement made with the Justice Department in which AT&T agreed not to get into the business of enhanced services. Enhanced services involve providing an entire communications system rather than simply the wire over which the communications travel. In 1956 the agreement may have appeared favorable to AT&T because the government dropped its antitrust suit but by the 1980s the opportunities for communications had become so great that AT&T wanted to change the agreement. Advanced computers and numerous types of hardware that process and store information for business and the home have made communications much more than simply a telephone wire. The distinction between computer processing of information and the transmission of information has become blurred.

AT&T has pressed its case to void the 1956 consent agreement and seems to have been successful. AT&T has persuaded the FCC to agree to an arrangement which allows them to organize a profit-making subsidiary that deals in enhanced services. This FCC policy is known as Computer Two and pundits have termed the subsidiary "baby Bell." Before the FCC arrangement was under way the Republican Justice Department reached an agreement with AT&T which gave Bell the right to engage in non-regulated enhanced services, and in return Bell agreed to divest itself of all local telephone companies in the United States. This new agreement meant that Bell retains Western Electric, Bell Laboratories, Bell Long Lines, and the recently structured baby Bell, giving up its most stable but least profitable business.

The reaction to the restructuring of Bell has been mixed. Critics say that Bell has built up a substantial capability because of its regulated and protected position. Most of the future promise of AT&T is lodged in Bell Laboratories where a considerable number of research devices will be quickly brought into production. An unregulated Bell may derive enormous profits from its research component, and therefore the new agreement is very attractive to AT&T.

A number of arguments can be made to support changing the regulatory arrangement for AT&T. First, the technological changes in communications make it impractical and unrealistic to compartmentalize communications activity. Second, it is very clear that the government is virtually incapable of actually regulating AT&T. A General Accounting Office (GAO) report has shown that the FCC is hopelessly unable to control AT&T:

A 15 year effort at the FCC has failed to produce a uniform system of accounts for monitoring AT&T's costs of operation, and thus, the FCC is not prepared to protect the public's interest by preventing AT&T from unfairly subsidizing its nonregulated services with revenues from its basic, regulated services. Although Computer Two is scheduled to go into effect on March 1, 1982, the FCC has allocated almost no staff or resources toward implementing that program.[9]

Thus, since regulation of AT&T is extremely difficult, if not impossible, it could be argued that a structural agreement that would reduce the need for regulation is a more practical solution. A third reason given for deregulation of AT&T, expressed by such people as MIT economist Lester Thurow, is that for the United States successfully to compete in world markets American firms must not have their hands tied with regulations.

Other Issues

There are a number of other critical issues in addition to the policy struggle between the established interests and the newcomers of which only a sample will be provided here. One issue that strikes at the very underpinnings of a free society is the vast amount of information likely to be on record about people. As people begin to use their home communications systems to do such activities as banking, shopping, responding to public issues, and ordering a variety of entertainment, a clear profile of each person could be developed and recorded. It is likely that additional legislation will be required to protect the privacy of individuals in this communications era.

A second issue involves the potential danger to people from the non-ionized electromagnetic radiation caused by communications waves. Most experts are not worried about the effects of low levels of non-ionized radiation, while the danger of ionized radiation from nuclear energy is widely recognized; however, the city of Onondaga, New York, on the advice of its Environmental Advisory Council halted construction of a station because of the potential health hazard. Clearly some people are concerned about the effects of radiation caused by communications.[10]

A third issue deals with the awarding of cable television franchises in communities. Typically numerous private companies compete for a franchise issued by a local government. The franchise amounts to a monopoly in all, or part, of a community. The competition to win the franchise often becomes so intense that both city officials and the competing companies are tempted to operate dishonestly. Moreover, charges and counter charges are often made about a franchise decision so that this community decision-making process is usually discredited. For example, the mayor of Council Bluffs, Iowa, while still serving out his term, accepted a job as general manager of the local cable franchise winner.[11] Also, a number of franchise decisions are under investigation or in court, such as the decisions of Houston, Texas, and Prince George County, Maryland.

A fourth issue deals with satellite communications—a technology even less developed than cable television but with perhaps even greater future potential.[12] Presently broadcasters and cable companies use satellites as a mechanism for distributing their signals to many parts of the world, but there is a limited amount of room in the sky for satellites and as the use of communications satellites proliferates, control of this relatively scarce resource could provoke increased controversy. Since existing technology limits the availability of satellite communications, its use is regulated by the FCC. At the present time companies such as Home Box Office, which chiefly provides movies for cable television systems, or the Cable News Network (CNN), must rent transponders on a satellite. Obtaining a satellite transponder is by no means a certainty, and at present a shortage of transponders seems likely to persist. With more companies requesting transponder space on satellites, such as RCA's SatCom 4, satisfactory methods of awarding this scarce service are yet to be developed. In 1981 RCA auctioned transponder space to the highest bidder, raising 90.1 million dollars from the sale of seven transponders, but the FCC voided this auction procedure.

The Extent of Regulation

The growth of different communications alternatives, such as cable television, satellite broadcasting, and video discs, has caused some observers, including broadcasters, to argue that the rationale for the existing laws is no longer valid. Indeed, the government has justified its control of broadcasting through granting licenses for a limited duration, monitoring broadcaster's programming, and requiring broadcasters to give all political candidates equal time and to give alternative viewpoints access on the premise that electronic media are scarce. Broadcasters argue that electronic media alternatives are no longer scarce. They point out that the newspapers which are protected by the First Amendment from government control are actually much scarcer. In many communities there are numerous television and radio stations but only one newspaper, yet the newspaper is unregulated and broadcasting is regulated.

Counter arguments contend that to promote a diverse communications environment, the new technologies need assistance and protection. In an unregulated environment the established, powerful communications interests would remain dominant and real diversity could not be achieved. Therefore, completely deregulating all communications would in the long run actually narrow the diversity of communications sources and limit public access to communications. A second counter argument is that access, even in a more abundant media environment, is still largely limited to those few with a government franchise. Samuel A. Simon of the National Citizens Committee for Broadcasting made the point as follows: "The ultimate prior restraint on a speech is one that absolutely prohibits it, and . . . the Communications Act prohibits absolutely all electronic speech except by the privileged few who hold federal licenses"[13] Moreover, the scarcity argument seems still to have powerful supporters in Congress. John Dingell, Chairman of the House Energy and Commerce Committee, which is a crucial hurdle for many communications bills, said in 1981: "We should never lose sight of the fact that spectrum space is limited and broadcasters are privileged to operate over this most precious public resource."[14]

A third argument for retaining some regulation is the intrusive nature of electronic communications. Television seems always to be on, and in many families children have free access to the television. Scenes from programs may flash on the screen before the viewer has time to react. In short, individuals lose some of their capacity to avoid and choose what programs are viewed. It is simply a fact that the printed word takes longer to transmit and lacks the transmission speed of electronic communications.

A fourth reason often given to retain regulation of broadcasting is the enormous power of electronic communications. Television has become the primary source of information for most Americans, and it has the highest credibility. Currently three networks still attract most of the viewing audience while Public Broadcasting and channels that might permit greater diversity and access languish with limited audiences. The fact is that the power of the electronic media, particularly television, depends on the number of viewers. Thus, if the masses persist in watching only a few channels, the power of the media will be very concentrated. To preserve the public interest some control over this powerful societal force seems likely.

The political aspects of deregulation have taken a decidedly Republican bent since Ronald Reagan assumed the presidency. Republicans are not interested in turning the clock back to the time in which broadcasters had a favored position and the newer technological communications systems were at a disadvantage. But the Republicans want to give the broadcasters and AT&T something in return for the emergence of the powerful new competitors. The Republican-dominated FCC, and the Reagan FCC chairman, Mark Fowler, have advocated removing many of the FCC monitoring requirements placed on broadcasters and propose giving the broadcasting industry the type of First Amendment freedom that newspapers have; such deregulation implies that broadcasters would have greater control over what they do over the air and greater control over the access of others to their air time. It seems hardly an accident that the Republican Reagan administration rather than a Democratic administration was the one in which the Justice Department dropped its pursuit of AT&T in return for a settlement that seemed favorable to AT&T. In sum, the precise course of deregulation depends on which political party is in control of the government.

Communications issues are simply too myriad and intricate for encyclopedic coverage here, but several conclusions about communications policy can be made. First, it should be clear that communications is not what it was when the 1934 Communications Act was written; communications today are vastly more sophisticated. Second, the future developments of communications are enormous, but it is difficult to predict precisely all of the applications and innovations likely to occur. Third, with such potential for change and expansion, the stakes are substantial. Powerful interests are struggling for a role in the future communications society. Fourth, the government needs to protect the public and the state from the possibility of the erosion of constitutional rights associated with the use of new communications.

THEORETICAL EXPLANATIONS OF POLICY

There is little doubt that communications are important or that a number of critical communications issues are still to be resolved. Therefore, explaining government communications decisions is a matter that deserves attention. Rather than considering individual communications issues in a vacuum—separate and unique—we now generalize about the political forces that control the decision-making process and the characteristics of the policy process. In short, knowledge about the policy process is applied to the understanding of communications policy. In the sections below, several possible explanations for policy outcomes are discussed. These theoretical perspectives serve as a basis to consider how communications policy is made and which explanations are more or less plausible. Later different types of issues will be distinguished as a further means of generalizing and understanding policy.

Economic-Regulatory

One explanation of policy origination and outcome stems from economic theory. The essence of this theory is that government institutions which are intended to regulate industry actually serve the economic interest of the industry. Regulation helps the industry in a variety of ways, including keeping competitors out of the marketplace and maintaining a price rate that guarantees a profit. The dominance of industry over the government regulatory process occurs in several ways. George Stigler argues that industries desire and seek regulation—"Every industry or occupation that has enough political power to utilize the state will seek to control entry."[15]

A variant of the theory of industry dominance of the regulatory process argues that such dominance develops gradually as the regulatory agency matures and ages. At the outset the regulatory institutions are not dominated by the industry, but have the public's interest in mind. Over time the client industry develops influence over the agency: Marver Bernstein, for one, has depicted such a "life cycle" for regulatory institutions. But whether industry dominates from the outset or slowly gains dominance, the result is believed to be that industry captures the government regulatory institutions.[16]

Neo-pluralism

The neo-pluralist perspective maintains that interest groups are very powerful, concentrated, and influential. Some analysts believe interest group power is so pervasive that government does not control public policy; the government-interest group relationship is distorted, and it is, from a normative view, pejoratively called "interest group liberalism." Theodore Lowi and Grant McConnell argue that interest groups have a virtual monopoly over public policy. Interest groups are included in government decision-making to such a degree that government decisions are little more than reflections of powerful interest group preferences.[17] Lowi draws upon the following statement of Arthur Schlesinger, a Kennedy advisor, to explain how the interest groups obtain such access and power within government: "The leading interests in society are all represented in the interior processes of policy formation—which can be done only if members or advocates of their interests are included in key positions of government."[18]

Lowi sees interest groups, then, as not just having input into the policy-making process, but as dominating that process. While different interests may dominate different policy areas, ultimately relevant government institutions and leaders are controlled by the industry that is the subject of regulatory policy. Interest group control of policy is indifferent to what might be termed "liberal" or "conservative" policy; rather government makes policy in response to the preferences of entrenched, status quo interests, regardless of whether such interests are liberal or conservative.

Neo-pluralist theory is somewhat more general than an economic theory of regulation because the economic explanation seems to describe policy control in the hands of what is likely to be the more conservative interests. For our purposes the major reference point will be the more general explanation of neo-pluralist theory, rather than the more specific explanation of economic capture theory.

The critics of interest group power frequently mention communications policy as a classic example of what they refer to as interest group liberalism. For example, Lowi writes:

Whatever power was held by the networks was based largely on the commitment of the FCC implied in the original grants of licenses. Having granted exclusive privileges to private groups in the public domain (in this case the original assignment of frequencies) without laying down practical conditions for perpetual public retention of the domain itself, the FCC had actually given over sovereignty. The companies acquired property rights and legally vested interests in the grant that interfere enormously with later efforts to affect the grant. Thus, any FCC attempt to expand the communications business through FM would deeply affect the positions and "property" of the established AM companies and networks. Issuing FM licenses to new organizations would have required an open assault on property as well as the established market relations.[19]

Pluralism

Not all political observers believe that interest groups dominate policy decisions to the extent Lowi does. Analysts who believe government decisions are made in a pluralist fashion admit that interest groups are important; indeed, for pluralists it is difficult to describe politics apart from interest groups.[20] But the pluralist concept of the government decision-making process emphasizes the following points: (1) Pluralists believe different groups tend to be active in different issue areas so that no single group dominates all or most of the government decisions so that interest group power is muted. (2) For any policy area several interests are likely to compete with each other rather than one interest dominating, and this competition among groups tends to cancel out the power of any single interest.

(3) Groups form easily and virtually every person and every interest can be represented by groups. (4) The government remains on the sidelines, acting chiefly as a referee or broker while the interest groups debate and negotiate a policy. The government policy that emerges is "the resultant of effective access by various interests."

Critics of pluralism dispute the pluralist view of the policy process by saying that groups do not cancel out each others' power, but that particular interests tend to dominate the policy process. The fact that interest group power is parceled out across a number of issue areas and to a number of interest groups tends to conceal the full power and scope of interest group influence. Moreover, all individuals are not represented effectively by groups, and even if everyone could be represented by groups, the entrenched interests have an enormous advantage in maintaining government policy that is favorable to them. Finally, the government, rather than acting as a broker or referee, behaves more as a cipher that has been captured and infiltrated by interests.

State Autonomy

The state autonomy perspective offers yet another explanation of government decision-making. Both the above explanations, neo-pluralism and pluralism, maintain that interest groups in the society make public policy; however, the state autonomy perspective contends that government can act, independent of the preferences and desires of interests in the society. From a state autonomy perspective it is possible for government preferences to dominate society rather than society preferences dominating government policy.[21]

A crucial point necessary to accept the possibility of a state autonomy explanation involves the origin of government preferences. One must recognize that officials representing government can have views and beliefs different from societal interests. Independent preferences of government officials can occur because of their personalities, professional goals, or career objectives. It is very possible that office-holders have preferences in particular issue areas that diverge from societal interests, because a narrow range of issues are important during elections and because numerous issues arise during a term of office that are not discussed during an election. Saying this, however, does not imply that government is constantly going against the preferences of society and the major interest groups; the state autonomy perspective simply says that it is possible for government officials to act in a fashion contrary to the preferences of powerful interests.[22]

The characteristics and assumptions behind society-dominated decision-making explanations can be used to make a logical argument for a state autonomy perspective. For example, from a pluralist perspective, groups compete and tend to check each other and balance each other out while the government is acting as a referee. Instead, government could gain autonomy in such situations by using its power to tip the balance in the direction of its preferences. Also, in the neo-pluralist explanation, groups enter into close working relationships with government, and it could be that rather than the interest groups capturing government, the government could end up influencing interest groups. There is evidence that governments do influence interest groups and exercise independent preferences. Paul Sacks, reviewing a set of books about British policy, concludes that government can influence interest group preferences and can pursue an agenda independent of societal interests.[23] With respect to United States policy, Stephen Krasner, studying raw material policy, reaches a similar conclusion to Sacks.[24]

Policy Types

An inspection of a range of issues usually reveals that none of the above explanations accurately applies for every issue. James Q. Wilson, after analyzing a number of regulatory policy areas (excluding communications) concludes that "a single explanation theory of regulatory politics is about as helpful as a single explanation of politics generally, or of disease."[25]

One means of restoring some systematic understanding to this varied policy process is to consider the possibility that there are particular policy types, and that these particular types of policy will evoke certain types of political characteristics. Theodore Lowi, for example, believes that the policy types depend upon the impact of the policy. James Q. Wilson has offered a policy typology that builds on the work of Lowi.[26] Wilson's policy types depend upon whether the impact of policy results in widely or narrowly distributed losses or benefits. Wilson, then, develops four policy types based upon these impacts.

Concentrated Costs/Concentrated Benefits—When the benefits are concentrated and the costs of a policy are also narrowly concentrated, interests stand to gain or lose a great deal. Therefore, interest groups become locked in intense competition and protracted conflict. Issues frequently are of low visibility since few people will benefit or lose. This policy type is termed *interest group politics*.

Widely Distributed Costs/Widely Distributed Benefits—Issues in which both the benefits and costs are widely distributed have very little interest group activity associated with them; public opinion is important in determining the fate of such issues, and the issues tend to be visible. This policy type is termed *majoritarian politics*.

Narrowly Concentrated Benefits/Widely Distributed Costs—For this issue type the costs are so widely distributed that the cost to individuals or groups is small, but the benefits, because they accrue to a much smaller group, are quite substantial. According to Wilson these issues are of low visibility and high interest group activity; the interest groups have substantial control over this type of policy, and it is termed *client politics*.

Narrowly Concentrated Costs/Widely Distributed Benefits—For this issue type a few interests stand to lose a great deal while many interests stand to gain only a little. Thus, the interests of the few are likely to present stiff political opposition. Likewise, since no single individual is likely to gain very much there is little individual reason to become politically active on the issue. Wilson believes the policy entrepreneur, an individual capable of articulating and stimulating the policy preferences of the general public, represents a substantial force to countervail and overcome the narrowly concentrated interests. This policy type is termed *entrepreneurial politics*.

A Revised Policy Typology

A perspective that builds upon the above work is now developed by making several modifications or changes in emphasis in Wilson's policy types. First, radically new policy or redirection of old policy is sufficiently unique, in terms of the politics of such issues, to justify its own policy type. Wilson, in fact, makes this point when he writes that "a distinction should be made between the adoption of a new policy and the amendment of an existing one."[27] The forces for change in policy direction may be events, such as a war, charismatic political leaders, a new political elite, or new ideas spread through the media. The impetus for change may vary, and the policy types are "less important than the fact that they represent major redefinitions of the proper role and powers of government."[28]

A second modification deals with the two policy types, widely distributed benefits/narrowly concentrated costs, and narrowly concentrated benefits/widely distributed costs. In both of these policy types the incentive seems to be the same, that is, to avoid a narrowly concentrated cost or to insure a narrowly concentrated benefit. The crux of the argument in either case is that an interest group will work very hard on the issue because it has a great deal to lose or gain; however, for a widely distributed benefit or cost the incentive of any single individual is minimal because the benefit or cost is minimal. Therefore, these two policy types can be joined into one category called *preferential politics*.

What is most unique about the preferential politics of unequally dispersed benefits and costs is that for some issues the entrenched interests have prevailed, largely sustaining a neo-pluralist explanation of policy, but for other issues significant policy change has come about at the expense of the entrenched interests. The salient explanation in most cases is that the forces for change were mobilized, particularly those forces within the government. It seems quite likely that for new policy directions to occur, the various government officials and institutions must be substantially weighted (by their power and agreement on the issue) on the side of change. If the government institutions and officials are solidly in favor of the policy change, it is difficult for the entrenched interests to preserve the status quo.

A new policy direction may be proposed, but not be successful. In such cases, it is likely that the government officials and institutions were not sufficiently unified and weighted in favor of change. Thus, the political characteristics of the issue, such as the level of visibility and the location of the decision within the government (for example, a congressional committee on the floor or Congress), may resemble that of a new policy thrust, but the outcome may resemble that of a status quo policy with the key interest groups in control.

This modified conceptualization of policy types represented in Figure 1-1 should be understood to represent a tendency rather than a one hundred percent certainty. Indeed, the policy dimensions could be portrayed in a continuum, suggesting the probabilistic nature of each policy type. Since virtually all social science research reflects probabilities rather than total certainties, the political activity associated with these policy types must be viewed in a probabilistic manner. Therefore, while it is more likely that substantial policy change will occur, if the vector of government forces is substantially on the side of change, change can occur on occasion with other patterns of political activity.

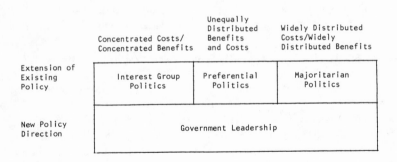

Figure 1-1. A Policy Typology

COMMUNICATIONS ISSUES AND POLICY EXPLANATIONS

Communications issues, while varied, tend to have some common characteristics. For example, it could be argued that communications issues are all low visibility; even very important communications decisions do not receive the attention given to such matters as the MX missile and nuclear power plants, or such general concerns as inflation and balancing the budget. Nevertheless, some communications issues have greater visibility than others, and depending on the issue, different political forces may be present. Thus, communications issues seem to vary; this variation is examined by policy type below.

Interest Group Politics

Communications issues that have narrowly concentrated benefits and costs are such matters as competition for licenses, and cable television interests versus broadcasting interests. When these issues do not involve a dramatic change of policy, the process seems to conform to Wilson's description: low visibility, protracted conflict, and substantial interest group activity. Frequently the political activity and conflict occurs in congressional subcommittees and at the FCC, which are institutions of low visibility.

An important distinction should be made between issues that involve a substantial redirection of policy and issues that involve status quo-type policy. Issues with narrowly concentrated benefits and costs that advocate a major shift in policy are unlikely to be settled in the subcommittees of Congress or at the FCC, unless other factors are present; usually other political institutions would be drawn into the conflict. For policy change to occur the powerful established interests must be countered, partially neutralized, and circumvented. The most likely route for policy change under these circumstances is for other government officials and institutions to intervene forcefully on the side of change. For example, a president can apply pressure for change in policy through his influence over the budget and the activities of the bureaucracy. Also, the president can exercise care in appointments to the FCC and other key posts. Although frequently these appointments to the FCC are not made with great care or future policy in mind, the fact is that a few presidents have made appointments to the FCC to achieve a particular policy emphasis.[29] There can be little doubt that Nixon's anti-network views led to an FCC chairman with a sympathy for cable television growth, even if such growth came at the expense of network broadcasters. Thus, issues processed in a climate that does not challenge the status quo are likely to appear to be neo-pluralist decisions. When a change in policy is seriously considered, a state autonomy explanation is likely.

Preferential Politics

Communications issues in which the costs and benefits are unequally distributed are illustrated by restraint upon the broadcasters, such as the fairness doctrine and equal time standards. Such requirements, in general, provide the public with certain access rights to the privately owned broadcasting stations' air time. The costs, then, are narrowly concentrated with the broadcasters, but the benefits of such rules are broadly dispersed to the public. From another perspective, if these constraints on the broadcasters were not present, the benefits would be narrowly concentrated while the costs would be widely distributed among the public.

Although issues of unequal cost and benefit may attract more attention because of the number of people affected, the benefit or cost to the public is not great, and therefore such issues usually will not reach a high level of visibility; however, visibility is usually higher for issues of unequal costs and benefits than for issues in which both costs and benefits are narrowly concentrated. When issues of unequal costs and benefits do become more visible it is often because a public interest group or policy entrepreneur has mobilized public awareness.

Issues of unequal costs and benefits seem to be characterized by a high degree of interest group control, and thus fit the neo-pluralist explanation of decision-making. However, if the issue involves a substantial policy redirection, then a somewhat different pattern is likely. For the powerful interest groups to lose on an issue, to either absorb a concentrated cost or lose a concentrated benefit, the issue must be somewhat visible; often this means that group opposition to the entrenched interests has intensified, possibly with the aid of policy entrepreneurs, and government officials have asserted their preferences. In short, it is very difficult to set out new policy directions that run counter to the established communications interests unless countervailing interests are active and unless the preponderance of government institutions supports the change. Thus, when a redirection of preferential policy occurs there is a blurring of the likely explanations, but usually the state autonomy perspective can find considerable support from a study of the events and activities associated with the decision.

Majoritarian Politics

Widely distributed benefits and costs are less frequent in communications policy because many of the issues seem to involve concentrated, narrow interests, such as the interests of the broadcasting industry and AT&T. Occasionally, however, policies that could be characterized as majoritarian do occur. Two such policies are public broadcasting and citizens band (CB) radio. Many people benefit from each policy, although the benefits are not substantial. Likewise, the costs are widely distributed. Public broadcasting was seen as a substantial enhancement for the education of Americans. In the mid-sixties the Carnegie Commission on Educational Television stated in its report that "a well-financed and well-administered educational television system serving the entire United States had to be created if the needs of the American people were to be served."[30] Substantial support for the concept of public broadcasting was present among political leaders, private organizations, and interest groups. For a small cost spread among many people, public television was organized and begun so that many individuals could receive the small but widely distributed benefits.

In the instance of CB radio the FCC changed its policy in 1975 and 1976 by first permitting CB radio to be used as a hobby (prior to 1975 CB radio was not mandated for recreational purposes by the FCC) and then later adding more channels for CB users. Millions of CB users and the CB radio industry benefited from the expansion of CB use; the benefits were widely dispersed. The costs of the change in policy were also widely dispersed. CB radio did cause some interference problems, but often the interference was not constant and was often correctable.[31]

Issues of widely dispersed benefits and costs seem to be characterized by less interest group activity and conflict, and public opinion seems important. The policies on CB radio and public broadcasting represent new directions or departures from existing policy. The various governmental institutions were not all involved in these issues, but the main vectors of government preferences were in favor of change. For example, the FCC was unanimous in its decision to expand the use of CBs while other government institutions were inactive. In short, government supported the change.

Clarifying Policy Types

Occasionally a policy is difficult to classify according to type. Obviously typologies serve as heuristic devices, and most real world situations do not conform precisely to ideal types. One recent issue that illustrates this point involves the bandwidth for radio spectrum spaces. If the bandwidth were shortened, then additional stations could be added in the United States and around the world. The Carter administration supported a narrowing of the radio bandwidth. The controversy over this policy position was that present broadcasters would have considerable expense to make the change, with the prospect of more radio stations on the air competing with them. Nevertheless the Carter administration was committed to a market force approach to policy rather than regulation. It was believed that more radio stations would simply enhance market competition. Obviously the expansion of stations and the cost to broadcasters to make bandwidth adjustments were narrowly concentrated. The benefits were less clearly determined. It could be argued that benefits might fall widely to the public, which would enjoy more programming choices, or it could be argued that the benefits would be narrowly concentrated in the hands of the new stations obtaining licenses. Unquestionably the Carter policy was unpopular with the established interests, yet Carter adhered to this policy proposal.

THE PAPERS IN THIS BOOK

The papers in this book range over a number of sub-arenas typically associated with American politics. C. Anthony Broh's paper deals with President Carter's re-election campaign effort to buy air time from the networks. Carter's dispute with the networks was first handled by the FCC and then later in the federal courts. The paper suggests the enormous potential of communications to dominate, control, and set the tempo of party politics and elections.

Florence Heffron, in a paper of wide scope, traces FCC policy from the tranquil and stable situation in the 1950s to the turbulent ear of the 1960s and 1970s. In so doing she finds an FCC that is largely responsive to the established, powerful interests. She illustrates that the FCC responds to its environmental pressures in bureaucratic fashion, ultimately trying to restore order in its relationship with the environment through deregulation.

Michael J. Stoil examines the formulation of United States policy preferences advocated at the International Telecommunications Union's World Administrative Radio Conference (WARC). Stoil demonstrates the substantial role of the government—particularly the executive branch— and the major interest groups in shaping United States communications policy.

Steven Weinberg traces the political forces at work in the United States Congress during a protracted effort to comprehensively rewrite the 1934 Communications Act. Weinberg shows the important influence upon the policy process of staff members in Congress, the structure of Congress, and changes in leadership in Congress. His paper demonstrates the great power of entrenched interests to block policy initiatives.

Sarah Slavin and M. Stephen Pendleton provide an in-depth analysis of one interest group's struggle to influence communications policy. They find an FCC interested mostly in symbolic gestures rather than meaningful material policy change.

Jan Linker, in a quantitative analysis, examines the influence of such factors as the type of interest group and the type of issue on FCC policy decisions. She concludes that the public-spirited interest groups may have actually had the reverse impact they intended. In FCC cases in which public intervenors were present, the FCC actually was more likely to rule in favor of client groups, such as broadcasters.

Jon S. Crane investigates the Supreme Court cases dealing with communications in which the term *public interest* has been used. He locates many different types of issues to which public interest has been applied, and he shows that the concept's application follows two distinct eras of communications policy.

The last two papers offer a more forward-looking perspective about communications policy. Grover Starling describes the role government can play in establishing policies that stimulate or impede the innovation and development of communications. Joey Reagan, Thomas Baldwin, and John Abel provide information about the impact of cable television upon political behavior. As the new communications technologies become more common, it will be important that political analysts have information about how the electoral process is impacted.

The papers offer evidence that can be applied to the theoretical questions of policymaking discussed earlier in this chapter. A number of the papers suggest an interest group liberalism explanation for communications policy. Heffron, Weinberg, Stoil, Slavin and Pendleton, and Linker find that the narrow interests dominate the decision-making process. Crane demonstrates a shift in the issues before the Supreme Court that tends to support a capture theory. However, Broh, Starling, and Stoil demonstrate, at least in part, evidence that a state autonomy explanation may be present. Several of the papers offer insight regarding how a state autonomy perspective is important for a change in policy direction. For example, Weinberg describes the restructuring of congressional committees, the expansion of committee staff, and the personal interests of key congressmen as crucial to the effort to change communications laws. The Broh, Starling, and Stoil papers also suggest the resources available to government officials in affecting policy. Many of the papers suggest the power of broadcasting interests to block policy change, especially when government officials do not oppose the powerful interests. As a group, the papers reveal that explanations of policy are complex, requiring specification of political circumstances to explain outcomes.

NOTES

1. "What's Ahead in Communications," *Broadcasting* 101 (September 28, 1981): 26. (September 28, 1981): 26.

2. See Glen O. Robinson, ed., *Communications for Tomorrow* (New York: Praeger, 1978).

3. "What's Ahead," p. 26.

4. John Wicklein, *Electronic Nightmare: The New Communications and Freedom* (New York: Viking Press, 1981).

5. Louis M. Kohlmeier, Jr., *The Regulators* (New York: Harper and Row, 1969), pp. 219-28.

6. William E. Porter, *Assault on the Media: The Nixon Years* (Ann Arbor, Mich.: The University of Michigan Press, 1976).

7. Thomas Will, *Telecommunications Structures and Management in the Executive Branch of Government, 1900-1970* (Boulder, Colo.: Westview Press, 1978).

8. Richard O. Berner, *Constraints on the Regulatory Process: A Case Study of Regulation of Cable Television* (Cambridge, Mass.: Ballinger Press, 1976); Don R. LeDuc, *Cable Television and the FCC: A Crisis in Media Control* (Philadelphia: Temple University Press, 1973); Martin H. Seiden, *Cable Television U.S.A.* (New York: Praeger, 1972).

9. "GAO Says FCC's Not Up to Regulating AT&T," *Broadcasting* 101 (September 28, 1981): 23; also see Comptroller General Report to the Congress of the United States, *Legislative and Regulatory Actions Needed to Deal with a Changing Domestic Telecommunications Industry* (Washington, D.C.: General Accounting Office, 1981).

10. "Radiation Fears Stymie Station," *Broadcasting* 101 (December 14, 1981): 68.

11. *Broadcasting* (October 19, 1981): 57.

12. Benno Signitzer, *Regulation of Direct Broadcasting from Satellites* (New York: Praeger, 1976); Jonathan Galloway, *The Politics and Technology of Satellite Communications* (Lexington, Mass.: Lexington Books, 1972); Lloyd D. Musolf, ed., *Communications Satellites in Political Orbit* (San Francisco: Chandler Publ. Co., 1968).

13. "Dingell Puts Brakes on Deregulation," *Broadcasting* 101 (December 14, 1981): 28.

14. Ibid., p. 27.

15. George J. Stigler, "The Theory of Economic Regulation," *Bell Journal of Economics and Management Science* 2 (Spring 1971): 3.

16. Marver H. Bernstein, *Regulating Business by Independent Commission* (Princeton, N.J.: Princeton University Press, 1955), pp. 74-95.

17. Theodore Lowi, *The End of Liberalism*, 2d ed. (New York: Norton, 1978); Grant McConnell, *Private Power and American Democracy* (New York: Knopf, 1966).

18. Theodore Lowi, "The Public Philosophy: Interest Group Liberalism," in William E. Connolly, ed., *The Bias of Pluralism* (New York: Atherton Press, 1969), p. 101.

19. Ibid., p. 112.

20. See Robert Dahl, *Who Governs?* (New Haven: Yale University Press, 1961); David B. Truman, *The Governmental Process: Political Interests and Public Opinion*, 2d ed. (New York: Alfred A. Knopf, 1971).

21. For the most complete statement about this perspective, see Eric Nordlinger, *On the Autonomy of the Democratic State* (Cambridge, Mass.: Harvard University Press, 1981).

22. For suggestions of how independent preferences can occur, see James Q. Wilson, *The Politics of Regulation* (New York: Basic Books, 1980), pp. 372-82.

23. Paul M. Sacks, "State Structure and the Asymmetrical Society: An Approach to Public Policy in Britain," *Comparative Politics* 12 (April 1980): 349-76.

24. Stephen D. Krasner, *Defending the National Interest* (Princeton, N.J.: Princeton University Press, 1978).

25. Wilson, *The Politics of Regulation*, p. 393.

26. Theodore J. Lowi, "American Business, Public Policy Case Studies and Political Theory," *World Politics* 16 (July 1964): 677-715; James Q. Wilson, *Political Organizations* (New York: Basic Books, 1973), pp. 327-37; Wilson, *The Politics of Regulation*, pp. 364-72.

27. Wilson, *Political Organizations*, p. 330.

28. Ibid.

29. Lawrence W. Lichty, "The Impact of FRC, and FCC Commissioners' Backgrounds on the Regulation of Broadcasting," *Journal of Broadcasting* 6 (Spring 1962); Wenmouth Williams, Jr., "Impact of Commissioner Background on FCC Decisions: 1962-1975," *Journal of Broadcasting* 20 (Spring 1976).

30. George H. Gibson, *Public Broadcasting: The Role of the Federal Government, 1912-76* (New York: Praeger, 1977), p. 125.

31. Erwin G. Krasnow and Lawrence D. Longley, *The Politics of Broadcast Regulation*, 2d ed. (New York: St. Martin's Press, 1978).

2

C. ANTHONY BROH

Reasonable Access to the Airwaves: A Struggle Between Partisan Politics and the Mass Media

THE tension between the partisan arena and the mass media recently culminated in a legal struggle between the Carter-Mondale campaign and the commercial television networks. At issue was the power to determine when a campaign begins. The legal dispute took place over the "reasonable access" clause of the Federal Communications Act of 1934. This article examines that conflict and its implications for the nominating process.

THE TWO ARENAS

The November election for president of the United States takes place in two arenas, the political parties and the mass media. In the partisan arena, presidential candidates struggle for support of the party faithful through local campaign activities conducted by the precinct, county, and state party organization. The main objective of the campaign in the partisan arena is to activate voters with a predisposition to support the party nominee, that is, to activate the party in the electorate.

The mass media provide a second arena for the general election. In this arena, presidential candidates struggle for the support of the entire electorate through advertising activities conducted by campaign managers and media consultants. The main object of the campaign in the mass media arena is to create a favorable image for the candidate.[1]

Successful candidates generally have a winning campaign in both arenas.

The author acknowledges support for this project from the General Motors Corporation. The manuscript evolved from reading and research in conjunction with the Business Understanding Program of General Motors while the author was at Columbia University. The author also thanks the Eagleton Institute of Politics and the Department of Political Science at Rutgers University for research support in preparing the manuscript.

In 1960, for example, John Kennedy took advantage of his handsome, boyish looks to create an image of innovation and vigor in the mass media arena. He also mobilized the party organization in Chicago, Philadelphia, Massachusetts, and other crucial areas. Jimmy Carter was similarly successful in his 1976 campaign for the presidency. He used his Democratic Party strength in the industrial Northeast and his native South and a favorable media image as an honest, moral "Washington-outsider" to win a decisive victory over incumbent Gerald Ford in the November election.

On the other hand, the partisan arena and the mass media may compete for the attention of presidential candidates. The party regulars may require presidential contenders to attend private campaign dinners, while journalists and reporters may require presidential contenders to attend media events and public rallies. Fund-raising for the party coffers may require the time a presidential contender could use constructing an organization of volunteers or generating publicity for television. In 1960, Richard Nixon traveled to Alaska in the last days of the campaign to fulfill his earlier promise to the party organizations that he would visit all fifty states. In so doing, he sacrificed resources that could have been used in the mass media arena. Narrow defeats in Illinois and New York suggest that Nixon should have concentrated his time during the last few days of the campaign in getting publicity in these highly competitive states.

Not all candidates win in both arenas. In 1968, for example, Hubert Humphrey won the Democratic nomination in the partisan arena while his image in the mass media was damaged beyond recovery. In 1972, George McGovern, on the other hand, pursued a successful strategy in the mass media. His electoral success in primary states like Wisconsin and California generated publicity and popularity, but he never gained support of leaders like Mayor Richard Daley of Chicago in the partisan arena. Barry Goldwater's 1964 campaign exploited a similar nominating strategy by gaining mass media coverage in key primary states, but alienated the entire moderate wing of his party.

The Humphrey, McGovern, and Goldwater cases are particularly instructive because they demonstrate the linkage between nominating and electoral strategies. In each case the candidate's nominating strategy affected the selection of an arena to contest the general election in November. McGovern's success in obtaining the nomination without the help of the party organization required that he conduct his electoral campaign outside the partisan arena. His disastrous efforts at leading the party during the convention polluted the media arena as well; but his strategy for November was the only possibility—appeal to the people directly through television.

Hubert Humphrey's 1968 campaign illustrates the connection between nominating and electoral strategies in the partisan arena. Having lost his popular media image as a liberal crusader, and having been labeled a proponent of an unpopular war in Vietnam, Humphrey won the party nomination by activating support from the party faithful. But the press could not forgive him. His electoral strategy took place in the partisan arena, relying on traditional Democratic support from ethnic groups, minorities, and the poor. The campaign in the media arena showed demonstrations and confrontations between candidate and audiences. Furthermore, Humphrey appeared indifferent to direct confrontation between Mayor Daley's politicized police force and the television networks' highly visible news correspondents.

Of course strategies to win the nomination in the partisan arena are usually compatible with strategies to win the nomination in the mass media. The party organization wants to nominate a person who can win the general election.[2] The best tests for such a nominee are the many state contests. A presidential contender must demonstrate an ability to raise money, win voter support, organize a campaign, and convince the party faithful if he is to gain the nomination. In 1960, for example, John Kennedy performed these tasks in both the partisan arena and the mass media. He used presidential primary victories to raise funds which provided more media coverage, etc. Jimmy Carter's 1976 campaign was similarly successful in both the partisan arena and the mass media. Carter used his organizational strength in Iowa to get media coverage in the Maine caucuses. With victories in both states, he became the "front runner" in New Hampshire, which produced more money, delegate strength, popularity, and media coverage. Both candidates went on to conduct successful electoral campaigns in both the partisan and the mass media arenas.

"REASONABLE ACCESS" AT THE FCC

Section 312 (a) (7) of the Federal Communications Act provides that:

(a) the [Federal Communications] commission (FCC) may revoke any station license or construction permit—
    (7) for the willful or repeated failure to allow reasonable access or to permit purchase of reasonable amounts of time for the use of a broadcasting station by a qualified candidate for Federal elective office on behalf of his candidacy.[3]

Section 312 (a) (7) was enacted as an amendment to the Communications Act by the Federal Election Campaign Act of 1971. One of the primary purposes of this legislation was "to give candidates for public office greater access to the media so that they may better explain their stand on issues and thereby more fully and completely inform the voters."[4]

Prior to the adoption of Section 312 (a) (7), broadcasters were left with considerable discretion to decide what political programming to air, based on the reasonable good faith judgment about the relative importance and interest within the confines of each political race. No candidate had, pursuant to Section 312 (a) (7), any specific right of access to a broadcasting station, just as no broadcaster had a special obligation to provide that access.[5] However, since the adoption of Section 312 (a) (7), the FCC has interpreted the section as imposing an additional obligation, a general broadcasters mandate to operate in the public interest. Licensees were specifically required to afford reasonable access or to permit the purchase of reasonable amounts of broadcast time for "use" by Federal candidates.

On October 11, 1979, the Carter-Mondale campaign committee advised each of the three networks that it desired to purchase a thirty-minute time-period on one of the networks on December 4, 5, 6, or 7 for a documentary on President Carter that would be shown in connection with the President's announcement of his candidacy for renomination and reelection. The plan was to tie the television program to more than 2,000 grass roots fund-raising gatherings around the country. In response, all three networks declined to grant the thirty-minute time-period on any of these dates. ABC declined to offer any alternative time, stating that it had not decided when it would begin selling political time. NBC also declined to offer time on the grounds that it was too early in the political season to provide nationwide broadcasts for political purposes, and that it would be swamped with a "multiplicity" of candidates seeking equal time, thus disrupting the holiday season scheduling. CBS relented somewhat and offered to sell the committee five minutes on Saturday, December 8, from 10:55 to 11:00 P.M. This time slot immediately followed the show "Paris," the network's lowest-rated program. CBS stated that it could not sell thirty minutes of time for the same reasons given by NBC.[6]

These were the partisan demands and subsequent media responses. Both the Carter-Mondale campaign committee and the networks had strong supporters. In the partisan arena were both congressional parties, as represented by Barry Goldwater who served notice in the *Congressional Record* on October 30, 1979, that if the FCC and the networks did not produce a "satisfactory" resolution of the issue, "it would be incumbent on the Congress to attempt to solve the access question once and for all."[7] He also noted that the networks had turned down requests for half-hour periods of time from Republican presidential contenders John Connally and Ronald Reagan. Goldwater wrote the campaign managers of the presidential candidates and the chairmen of the Republican and Democratic committees to solicit their recommendations for a legislative solution.

Another political force supporting the Carter-Mondale campaign committee was the National Citizens Committee for Broadcasting (NCCB), a citizen's lobby generally antagonistic to the media corporate interests. Sam Simon, NCCB executive director, stated: "If the networks so brazenly refuse to provide paid access upon request by the nation's President, Democratic and Republican challengers and third party candidates are even less likely to be able to share their views with the public. And it is the public's right to hear those views that is at stake here."[8] Simon had clearly articulated the partisan interests represented by the president and other candidates.

Supporting the networks were most of the industry interest groups led by the National Association of Broadcasters (NAB), which filed a brief with the FCC on behalf of the networks and warned the commission not to "take any action which would unduly circumscribe the reasonable good faith judgment of the broadcast licensees."[9] The NAB based its claim on the commercial broadcasters' First Amendment rights to free speech.

On October 29, 1979, the Carter-Mondale campaign filed a complaint with the FCC alleging that the networks had violated the obligation imposed by Section 312 (a) (7) by rejecting committee requests to buy time. The committee reiterated that President Carter would be appearing as a candidate and that none of the reasons advanced by the networks for their refusal to sell the requested time was sufficient to deny access. The committee stated that the network actions constituted a "blatant denial" of the reasonable access provision and "denie[d] the public the opportunity of hearing and seeing the candidates in the manner the candidates chose."[10]

In a brief given to the FCC in defense of their actions, the networks cited three major reasons for their refusal of time:

(1) The time of the request—The networks argued that it was too early to begin selling time for political programs since the national political conventions were more than eight months away and the election still a year away.

(2) Multiplicity of candidates—Each network also stated that the unusually large number of candidates would obligate broadcasters, because of the equal time provision,[11] to make available large blocks of network time.

(3) Disruption of regular programs—Providing equal time to the multiplicity of candidates would disrupt the regular program schedule.

A fourth but unstated problem in providing political access was the necessity of giving the time to the candidates at the lowest per unit cost as stated in the Federal Elections Act. The networks stood to lose a substantial amount of advertising money since the request for time came at the height of the Christmas season. This is the time of year most sought after and most expensive for advertisers and the most important from a financial aspect for the networks. To sell time to candidates at the lowest unit rate would potentially cost the networks valuable air time.

The most important consideration was the tension between the two arenas of the nominating process. Application of the reasonable access clause to the Carter-Mondale request would mean that the presidential candidate and his party organization could determine when the campaign begins. Refusal to apply the rule would mean that the television networks could determine when the campaign begins. The major political institutions from each arena of the nominating process had locked horns over the timing of the campaign.

The institutions in the partisan arena had considerable influence when the debate reached the FCC. The executive and legislative branches nominate and appoint the commissioners, and the FCC had already received a direct threat of legislative action from Senator Goldwater. Futhermore, Commissioner James C. Quello was up for reappointment in June 1980. Though normally a supporter of industry demands and a former broadcaster himself,[12] Quello joined three other Democrats in a straight party vote supporting the Carter-Mondale position.

Reaction to the decision was immediate. All three networks sought reconsideration of the decision, but on November 28, 1979, the commission denied the three petitions and reiterated the decisions that were issued a week earlier. Chairman Charles Ferris, a Carter appointee, former staff member for House Speaker Thomas P. O'Neill, and a Democrat, criticized what he called the networks' "meat-ax approach" in deciding when a campaign should or should not begin. He further stated that the FCC had previously determined that "there are needs more than those of the broadcasters, there are the needs of the candidates and the public, and all three of those need to be balanced." Commissioner Joseph Fogarty stated, "We have no alternative but to find the networks' response inadequate and unreasonable. It's only 30 minutes of 5,400 in a month." Commissioner Quello questioned the constitutionality of Section 312 (a) (7), but commented that "it's our job to enforce it."

Of the dissenting commissioners, Robert E. Lee stated, "I don't think we should run political campaigns. I don't think we should run the networks either." Commissioner Abbott Washburn added what was perhaps the strongest statement of either side, that "the consequences of this precedent will rise to haunt the commission and the public in future campaigns."[13]

After the FCC rejected petitions for reconsideration, it asked the networks to state how they intended to fulfill their obligations regarding Section 312 (a) (7). But in doing so, the FCC clearly tried to give the networks an out by offering advice on how to settle the matter. The FCC stated, "One conceivable method of trying to act reasonably and in good faith might be for the licensees, prior to an election campaign in a federal office, to meet with candidates in an effort to work out the problems of reasonable access for them on their stations. We (the FCC) believe that good faith negotiations are to be preferred and urge that course."[14] This statement reflected FCC uncertainty about the constitutionality of its decision and interpretation of Section 312 (a) (7), and its hope that reasonable access questions could be worked out before judicial review became necessary. But the FCC ordered the networks to provide access within two days or else further FCC action would be taken.

The FCC made it clear that the contesting sides in the decision should meet and work things out. As negotiations between the Carter-Mondale campaign committee and the three networks began, the U.S. Court of Appeals granted the networks a stay in implementing the FCC order. Negotiations were unproductive for several reasons. First, NBC management was at an affiliate meeting in Puerto Rico which was interpreted as an attempt to buy time and moot the case. Second, rumors circulated that Democratic Commissioner Tyrone Brown might change his vote, swinging the decision in favor of the networks. Negotiations were unproductive primarily because the Iranian crisis began President Carter's "rose garden" strategy. The fact was that now Carter and Mondale really did not want or need the television time to announce their candidacy. They were gaining popularity as president and vice-president without campaigning.

A second stay was granted by the District of Columbia Court of Appeals, but two days later the FCC issued an order that the three networks "have now had two opportunities to justify their refusal of the requested time. Continued delay by them threatens to moot the candidate's complaint now before us. . . . If a judicial stay is not obtained, we will expect that they will forthwith meet their . . . obligations."[15]

The irony of this situation is clear. The Carter-Mondale campaign committee had won the decision rendered by the FCC, but because of the Iranian situation, now did not want the access granted to them. The networks did not want to grant the time, but were being told by the FCC to grant access before the complaint became moot. As negotiations broke down, prospects of another stay dimmed and with the FCC demanding action, the networks appealed the decision to the District of Columbia Court of Appeals in hopes of resolving the reasonable access issue through the judicial branch.

REASONABLE ACCESS AT THE DISTRICT OF COLUMBIA COURT OF APPEALS

The events leading up to the appeal provided a twist to the position of each campaign arena. The networks felt the decision could be reversed by the U.S. Court of Appeals. The Carter-Mondale campaign committee wanted the court to uphold the FCC decision but to spare it the humiliation of turning down television time offered by the networks.[16] The delay in granting time was consistent with Carter's pledge not to campaign during the Iranian crisis. Judicial review would grant the president a reprieve against an embarrassing offer.

The list of supporters of the Carter-Mondale position grew at the appellate stage. On the side of the FCC were eleven individuals and groups that submitted briefs to the court. Among them were the liberal Americans for Democratic Action, Conservative James L. Buckley, presidential candidates

Edward Kennedy and John Anderson, the National Education Association, the National Black Media Coalition, and other congressmen and interest groups generally associated with partisan activity. Supporters for the networks were the same groups represented in the first round at the FCC, groups associated with media interests.

The persons making the decision on jurisdiction of Section 312 (a) (7) were now three judges of the District of Columbia Court of Appeals. President Carter's original request for a half-hour of network prime time was no longer at issue, as he had already announced his candidacy. The Christmas season had passed and the networks no longer faced substantial monetary loss by granting prime time to presidential candidates. But all sides agreed that the issue of reasonable access was not moot. The issues involved had gone from specific to general. In fact, the networks stated in their brief to the court that the issues addressed by the commission and the court "are bound to recur in this and other elections." Accordingly, they said, the order is one which, "by agreement of all parties, warrants and requires prompt appellate review."[17] Thus, it became increasingly clear that the case would resolve the dispute over which institution has the power to decide when campaigns begin—the political party leadership or the mass media networks. The winning institution would incrementally increase its ability to determine the arena for nominating strategies.

The networks, the FCC, the Carter-Mondale campaign committee, and the eleven signers of the friend-of-the-court brief all filed opinions. The networks and the FCC gave oral arguments on January 14, 1980. After two months of deliberation, the District of Columbia Court of Appeals reached a decision. The court held that candidates for federal office have the right of "affirmative access" to broadcast media under the reasonable access provision of the Communications Act. Moreover, the court affirmed the standards the FCC had adopted for implementing the statute.

The networks may have lost more than just the case before the court. The decision appeared to have extended FCC jurisdiction over the networks. The court, in rejecting the networks' argument that Section 312 (a) (7) applied to licensees and not to the networks, used sweeping language. It supported the argument that the commission has "direct regulatory authority over networks in areas where such regulation is 'reasonably ancillary' to the commission's performance of its responsibilities."[18] And it stretched the jurisdiction of "reasonable access" to the point of "affirmative access." These policies are far-reaching.

The FCC and the advocates of the Carter-Mondale position in the case viewed the decision with tremendous pleasure. It was regarded as a mandate for the candidates to have greater authority in deciding when a federal campaign is to be launched. On the other hand, broadcast industry lawyers viewed the decision as a serious defeat, not only for the networks but for mass media generally.

REASONABLE ACCESS AT THE SUPREME COURT
AND AFTERMATH

The Supreme Court upheld the ruling of the Appeals Court on July 1, 1981. Chief Justice Warren Burger's opinion of the court stated that Section 312 (a) (7) "created a new, affirmative right of access to the broadcast media for individual candidates for Federal elective office."[19] This right belongs to the public, which can now be guaranteed the receipt of information "necessary for the effective operation of the democratic process."[20] The Court was, in effect, denying the mass media's right to decide when campaigns for elective federal officials begin and upholding the political party's traditional role in providing an arena for the early stages of the nominating process.

The media responded strongly to the decision. *Broadcasting* magazine, the trade journal of the commerical television industry, reported the decision as a "big blow for broadcasters" by the "bad news bench."[21] The magazine vowed to overturn the ruling through deregulation currently on the Reagan administration's political agenda. On July 17, 1981, FCC Chairman Mark Fowler, a Reagan appointee who leads the administration's and the industry's efforts to deregulate commercial broadcasting, mustered the necessary votes at the commission to recommend repeal of Section 312 (a) (7).

The proposal has received a cool reception on Capitol Hill. Both Democrats and Republicans share the desire to control their own political strategies. The "reasonable access" clause gives these partisan congressional candidates, as well as presidential candidates, the power to select the arena for pursuing elective office.

DISCUSSION

What are the implications of this struggle over the power to decide when a presidential campaign begins? In the first place, the parties to the conflict, the Carter-Mondale committee and the commercial television networks, symbolize the main arenas of the presidential nomination. The president is the leader of his party, especially when he is eligible for renomination. No president in the twentieth century has been denied the nomination of his party.[22] President Carter was no exception, even though he began the campaign with a huge deficit in the public opinion polls. The president controls the party machinery and consequently he remains an important figure in the partisan arena even if he is challenged in another arena. At the minimum he is the "candidate to beat."

The networks are the leaders of the mass media. ABC, CBS, and NBC have such control over the broadcast industry that Congress and the Federal Communications Commission felt compelled to conduct several inquiries into network dominance.[23] For example, in 1976 the networks accounted for over one-third (36 pecent) of all television industry profits. But network dominance is easier to see at the local level. Few television markets have more than three television stations and no market with three or less stations has a station that is unaffiliated with a network. The economics of the television industry show that a station can make a profit, even in small markets, by broadcasting popular network programming; and only a few stations in very large markets can make a profit by not broadcasting network programming. Incidentally, a few stations in very large markets can make very large profits by broadcasting network programming; they are owned and operated by the networks, the so-called O and O's!

The presidency and the networks, then, are powerful institutions in the main arenas of the nominating process. Since each institution claims to be the mouth-piece of public opinion, each believes it alone should decide what constitutes reasonable access to the airwaves.

A second implication of this study is that the political parties and the mass media want to make decisions about the nominating process in their arena. Traditionally, the main function of political parties is to recruit and select persons for political office. The legal procedures and the means of communication for performing this function provide the main, if not the only, structure for the party organization.[24]

On the other hand, the general trend of nominating politics in the United States is to include an expanding group of people. The nominating process has changed from elite domination by a few bosses to mass participation by a broad base of primary voters and caucus participants. The latter reforms require an equally broad base of communication among voters. Consequently, mass media perform the function of providing information to the decision-makers in the nominating process. Obviously, the media want to set guidelines for the candidates, but doing so intrudes on decision rules generally performed by the parties.

Jimmy Carter's and Edward Kennedy's struggle for the 1980 Democratic nomination illustrates this conflict over the arena for nomination. On June 3, 1980, Jimmy Carter had "won" the struggle in the partisan arena. According to most estimates, Carter had over 1,900 delegates pledged to him with only 1,666 needed for nomination. But Carter had not clearly won the struggle in the mass media. Inflation and unemployment, both Kennedy issues, dominated the news. Kennedy's June 2 victory in five of the eight "Super Tuesday" primaries could only be a defeat for the president. Furthermore, Carter failed to win a majority of delegates in California, New York, New Jersey, Massachusetts, and Pennsylvania—all key industrial states important to any Democratic coalition. Edward Kennedy's success in the media arena encouraged continued campaigning until the convention.[25] Jimmy Carter's failure to gain the support of traditional Democrats proved fatal in the general election.

The third implication of the reasonable access decision is that the political party ultimately decides the arena in which the nominating process takes place. The Carter-Mondale committee used the regulatory process, the courts, and the power of appointment to get access to the airwaves. The outcome is clear. When the stakes are as high as control of the nominating process itself, political parties will use their resources to insure the performance of their legitimate function. Parties nominate; the mass media communicate. An intrusion of one into the function of the other is sure to meet resistance.

Finally, the starting date for the presidential campaign of 1984 remains unfixed at the networks. At this writing, executives from the communications industry focus more attention on the repeal of FCC rules for political broadcasting than on reasonable application of the rules in campaigns.[26]

Political parties have taken the initiative to define, indeed to make shorter, the length of presidential campaigns. Rule 10 of the Commission on Presidential Nomination, adopted by the Democratic National Committee in March, 1982, sets limitations on the beginning of delegate selection procedures for the states. The rule defines an acceptable period of time for primaries and first-tier caucuses. When exemptions for Iowa and New Hampshire are added to the DNC nominating calendar, February 27 becomes the first day for delegate selection in the 1984 presidential election. Filing procedures will, of course, precede this date; but all steps in the delegate selection process must take place within 1984.[27] At a minimum, then, the 1980 conflict, which began in November the year before the election, has been delayed until after New Year's. Since January is a slower advertising period than December, the commercial dynamics of television seem compatible with the reform judgements of political parties. Consequently, the struggle between partisan politics and the mass media will probably shift to other issues of conflict.

NOTES

1. Unless otherwise noted, the partisan arena refers to the party in the electorate (V. O. Key, *Parties, Politics and Pressure Groups*). Thus presidential contenders compete for the nomination—ultimately decided by the party organization—in the partisan arena and in the mass media arena.

2. Nelson W. Polsby and Aaron B. Wildavsky, *Presidential Elections* (New York: Charles Scribner's Sons, 1973).

3. Harvey L. Zuckman and Martin J. Gaynes, *Mass Communications Law* (St. Paul, Minn.: West Publishing Co., 1977).

4. U.S. Congress, Senate. *Federal Elections Campaign Act of 1971*. S. Rpt. 92-96, 92d Congress, 1st Session, 1971.

5. FCC, "CBS, Inc., et al. Petitioners v. FCC and United States" (1980), Brief for the Respondents.

6. Ibid.

7. *Congressional Record* 125 (daily ed., October 30, 1979): S15461.

8. "Carter Campaign Argues Number of Candidates Means It's Best Networks Start Selling Early," *Broadcasting* 97 (November 19, 1979): 70.

9. Ibid.

10. "Reasonable Access Battle Joined," *Broadcasting* 97 (October 29, 1979): 31.

11. Section 315 of the Federal Communications Act states: "If any licensee shall permit any person who is a legally qualified candidate for any public office to use a broadcasting station, he shall afford equal opportunities to all other such candidates for that office in the use of such broadcasting station." See 47 U.S.C. 315.

12. For a discussion of Quello's broadcasting career and its influence on his voting, see William T. Gormley, "A Test of the Revolving Door Hypothesis at the FCC," *American Journal of Political Science* 23 (November, 1979): 665-83.

13. All quotes of commissioners from U.S. Federal Communications Commission. *FCC News Release*, no. 17183, November 28, 1979.

14. "Party Lines," *Broadcasting* 97 (November 26, 1979): 82.

15. "More Tangles in Carter-Mondale Case," *Broadcasting* 97 (December 3, 1979): 33-34.

16. The Carter-Mondale committee purchased five minutes of time from CBS on December 4 and a half-hour from ABC on January 6; but at the time of purchase, the networks had appealed the FCC decision to the U.S. Court of Appeals. The CBS purchase was not prime time and the thirty-minute spot at ABC ran opposite "60 Minutes," television's top-rated show. Carter spared himself the humiliation of turning down television time by purchase of time few would see!

17. "More Tangles in Carter-Mondale Case," *Broadcasting* 97 (December 3, 1979): 33-34.

18. "Double Jeopardy for Networks in C-M Decision," *Broadcasting* 98 (March 17, 1980): 29. Technically, the FCC has no direct jurisdiction over the networks since it only licenses broadcast stations. However, the FCC regularly regulates the contracts that an affiliated station may enter. Also the FCC can regulate the network's owned and operated stations. Consequently, the FCC has indirect jurisdiction over the networks. The FCC considered equal employment opportunity requirements for the networks. The question of direct jurisdiction was an issue in these proceedings.

19. Quoted in Linda Greenhouse, "Court, 6-3, Rules TV Must Sell Time in Federal Races," *New York Times*, July 2, 1981.

20. Ibid.

21. "Big Blow for Broadcasters from Supreme Court," *Broadcasting* 101 (July 6, 1981): 27; "The Bad News Bench," *Broadcasting* 101 (July 6, 1981): 96.

22. The last president to be denied his party's nomination was Chester A. Arthur in 1884. On the question of reelection Hamilton Jordan advised Jimmy Carter that reelection is not assured. When Jordan wrote his memo, half of the twentieth-century Presidents had been reelected and half (counting Carter) had not. On the other hand, Jordan's advice was misleading since only two of the previous seven presidents had not been reelected, the deceased John Kennedy and the unelected Gerald Ford. Jordan's warning now appears prophetic.

23. The FCC issued a preliminary report of its network inquiry special staff which stated that "the three commercial television networks and their affiliates are so successfully entrenched in their economic structure that any attempt by the FCC to regulate . . . would prove fruitless." See "First Word out of FCC Network Inquiry

Box: Encourage New Program Sources," *Broadcasting* October 22, 1979. See U.S. Federal Communications Commission, *An Analysis of Television Program Production, Acquisition and Distribution*, Preliminary Report of the Network Inquiry Special Staff (June 1980), and also the two sections of the same report entitled *The Determinants of Television Station Profitability* and *The Market for Television Advertising*.

24. The main decision body of political parties in the United States is the quadrennial nominating convention. Party rules explicitly state that the convention even supersedes state laws. This point was tested at the 1980 Democratic Convention when the Carter-Mondale campaign tried to get the Convention to adopt a rule that would bind delegates to candidates beyond the requirements of state laws.

25. This victory in the mass media is ironic since one of Kennedy's campaign problems was decentralized and unorganized media advice.

26. The FCC has proposed legislation that would eliminate the fairness doctrine, the equal time provision, and the reasonable access clause. If our analysis is correct, one might speculate that the forces of incumbency will defeat repeal of the equal time provision, partisan forces will defeat repeal of the reasonable access clause, and the politics of deregulation will make the fairness doctrine vulnerable to repeal. See "School Days at NAB on Political Broadcasting," *Broadcasting* 101 (April 12, 1982): 64.

27. See *Report of the Commission on Presidential Nomination*, Charles T. Mannatt, chairman (Washington, D.C.: Democratic National Committee, 1982), pp. 19-20, 43-44.

3

FLORENCE HEFFRON

The Federal Communications Commission and Broadcast Deregulation

DEREGULATION has rapidly become a major theme of contemporary American politics as political and business officials clamor for lifting a vast variety of governmental restrictions on the conduct of major segments of the American economy. The term "deregulation" has multiple meanings: "the removal of choice restriction," "the removal of governmental restrictions on economic activity," the elimination of specific regulations, or the reduction in the effectiveness of a specific program.[1] All of these meanings, however, support the view that deregulation is a process of organizational reduction which results in the restriction of bureaucratic power. Since the "power motive is to bureaucracy what the profit motive is to business,"[2] it seems logical to expect that the bureaucrats who administer the regulations "will almost always oppose deregulation."[3]

Although an agency might be expected to accede reluctantly to deregulation that has been legally mandated, one would not expect an agency to launch a sweeping program of deregulation in the absence of such compulsion. That, however, is exactly what the Federal Communications Commission (FCC) has done. The process of deregulation which began in the late 1970s accelerated in 1980. In March the FCC announced its decision to deregulate a major portion of the telecommunications industry; in April the Commission proposed rules for the international communications by satellite industry that de-emphasized regulation in favor of increased competition. In July the Commission substantially deregulated the cable television industry by lifting the distant signal and syndicated exclusivity rules. In December an FCC staff study called for the repeal of rules limiting the number of television stations a firm can own and prohibiting network ownership of cable television systems, recommending repeal of the prime time access rule and most of the rules governing network affiliate contract relationships. Proposed rulemaking for children's television programming was dropped from the FCC's 1981 agenda and in January 1981 the Commission signed rules which substantially deregulated radio broadcast licensees. None of these changes had been mandated by statute, many of them were of questionable legality without such authorization, and all of them were opposed by important actors in the FCC's environment. The combined impact of the actual and proposed deregulation measures was to restrict significantly the agency's power.

The FCC's deregulation efforts provide an excellent example of the general circumstances under which voluntary deregulation and reduction of power emerge as a rational organizational strategy for survival in a hostile environment. This chapter examines the changes that occurred in the FCC's environment in the 1960s and 1970s that compelled the agency to alter long-established policies and procedures in an attempt to accommodate these changes. The primary focus will be on deregulation of the broadcast industry, but, as indicated, the Commission was also following substantially the same policies in telecommunications regulation. The deregulation measures will be viewed as the most recent outcomes of a lengthy process through which the Commission had attempted to re-establish equilibrium within an environment that changed from one of relative homogeneity and placidity to one of heterogeneity, complexity, and constant conflict.

ORGANIZATIONS AND THEIR ENVIRONMENT

The basic theoretical framework that will be used is the open-systems approach to organizational analysis. Open-systems theory views organizations as adaptive systems which must continuously interact with their environments and which are totally dependent on successful interactions with their environment for survival.[4] As open systems, organizations seek equilibrium or a stable state wherein those actors in the environment who seek change are counterbalanced by those who desire either no change or a change in the opposite direction.[5] When the organization's environment changes sufficiently to unhinge the established equilibrium the organization will modify its behavior in an attempt to re-establish equilibrium.

An organization's environment may be broken into two basic components: the general environment or the broad societal conditions that are potentially relevant for organizational functioning, and the specific environment which is composed of those organizations, groups, and individuals with which the organization is in direct interaction. The general environment includes technological, legal, political, economic, demographic, ecological, and cultural conditions.[6] Changes in the general environment may affect the organization both directly and indirectly by modifying the complexity and intensity of the specific environment.

Shirley Terreberry has classified organizational environments into four basic types. Type I is a Placid-Random environment characterized by a low degree of change and low interconnection between environmental parts and actors. Type II environments are Placid-Clustered: composed of stable environmental actors that are divided into recognizable and potentially powerful coalitions. Type III environments are Disturbed-Reactive, and Type IV environments are Turbulent, marked by accelerating change and complexity that exceed the organization's ability to predict and control the consequences of its actions. A Type IV environment puts extreme pressure on organizational decision-makers, reduces their freedom of choice, and decreases their ability to anticipate the behavior of other organizations and actors.[7] Turbulence compels the organization to search constantly for methods to establish an equilibrium.

Organizational reponses to turbulence include inspirational efforts, attempts to decrease the complexity of the environment, compartmentalization of the environment, development of routines to formalize relations with and among environmental actors, and domain modification. Domain modification is a dominant strategy for managing organization-environment relations. Its use depends on the organization's domain choice flexibility—the extent to which the organization is free to alter its domain by determining "what aspects of the environment are to be of concern, what phenomena should be noticed and what variables should be introduced into the criterion function for the organization's performance."[8] Although public organizations have less domain choice flexibility than private firms[9] since their domain is determined and limited by legal mandate, those mandates have always permitted broad discretion as to whether, when, and how to enforce the law.

From 1960 to 1980 the Federal Communications Commission's environment changed from Type I to Type IV. The complexity of the environment increased as the number of relevant actors expanded and conflict among those actors intensified. The routineness of its relations with these environmental actors broke down and new types of relationships had to be developed. Actors and events became increasingly interconnected undermining the Commission's ability to pursue a "divide and conquer" strategy. Established policies were challenged as unsatisfactory and/or legally impermissible and demands for policy change escalated. The response of the Commission fell into three separate phases: an initial phase of attempted domain preservation; a second phase of domain expansion, and the current phase of domain contraction. All three phases were characterized by attempts to manipulate the agency's environment and restore lost equilibrium. The first two phases were inarguably failures; the third phase, typified by deregulation, may be more successful but also may jeopardize the agency's survival.

THE FCC'S 1960 ENVIRONMENT: PLACID-RANDOM

The FCC's general environment in the early 1960s appeared to be relatively stable although some important changes were occurring that should have alerted it to future problems. The most stable aspect of the general environment was the legal component and especially the FCC's authorizing statute and mandate to regulate, the Communications Act of 1934.[10] The least stable aspect was in the area of technological conditions where sweeping changes in cable television and other areas of telecommunications were recognized by astute observers but largely ignored by the FCC.

The Communications Act was written when television existed only on an experimental basis, cable television was nonexistent, communications satellites were unthinkable, and the power of the mass media referred to how many kilocycles the local radio station used in broadcasting. Despite the massive changes that had occurred in communications technology, Congress had not substantially revised the 1934 Act by 1960 and still has not to this day. The Act is a masterpiece of vague, and some would argue nonexistent, standards to guide administrative conduct. The FCC was given the power to allocate frequencies and to regulate broadcast licensees and the telecommunications industry. The standard it was to apply in all of its actions was "the public convenience, interest or necessity." The impact of this vagueness on FCC regulatory outcomes had been twofold: it had given the Commission tremendous discretion to determine the overall contours of communications policy, but the lack of specific statutory standards had also made it vulnerable to regulatee pressure and ultimately to regulatee capture. The lack of clear standards combined with the constant interaction between the Commission and the broadcast industry had resulted in regulatory policy based on the assumption that the interest of the broadcasters and the public interest were identical.[11] The second major impact of the broad delegation had been indecisiveness, an inability on the part of the FCC to deal with and decide controversial issues,[12] preferring instead to ignore them or to delay consideration of them as long as possible.

Nowhere was the FCC's indecisiveness and identification with the broadcast industry more clearly illustrated than in its initial handling of cable television: it did not attempt to keep pace with technological developments in cable but instead relied on the broadcast industry's assessment of the "proper" role of cable television.[13] Initially broadcasters viewed cable as a useful ancillary to their services and consequently neither they nor the FCC believed there was any need for a clear and decisive policy toward the new technology. In 1959, when some small western television stations complained vigorously about the economic impact of cable on their stations, the National Association of Broadcasters (NAB) failed to support them. The result was an FCC decision that it lacked jurisdiction over cable television and a refusal to get involved in its development. Despite pressure from small television stations, Congress also refused to amend the Communications Act to include specific regulatory power over cable.[14]

If the general standards provided by the Communications Act were extremely vague, there were also specific provisions within the Act that were contradictory. For example, Section 326 explicitly barred the FCC from exercising the powers of censorship over licensees: "No regulation or condition shall be promulgated or fixed by the commission which shall interfere with the right of free speech by means of radio communication." On the other hand Section 315 contained the equal time requirement for political broadcasts and in 1959 had been amended to include the Fairness Doctrine, requiring broadcasters to "afford reasonable opportunity for the discussion of conflicting views on issues of public importance." Additionally, the federal obscenity statute prohibited anyone from uttering "obscene, indecent or profane language" by means of radio communication.[15] The explicit contraditions that barred the FCC from interfering with a broadcaster's free speech but also required it to insure that they carried certain types of programs and not others, created a difficult regulatory situation which could have resulted in constant conflict between the agency and the broadcast licensees. By 1960 the FCC had developed policies that avoided such conflicts but still protected its authority. Although licensees were required to keep detailed program logs so the Commission could determine if the licensee had satisfied obligations under the Fairness Doctrine, past performance was actually ignored and license renewals were routinely granted. Furthermore, although licensees were required to specify intended future programming, they were never compelled to adhere to those promises and most licensees routinely disregarded them.[16] "A renewal application has never been denied solely because of a failure to meet community needs, excess commercials, lack of public service announcements, inadequate news, public affairs or other nonentertainment material."[17]

If the FCC's general environment was relatively stable in 1960; its specific environment was equally so. At that time the FCC presented one of the clearest examples of a subgovernment at the federal level. Although the FCC had two discrete clientele groups, broadcasters and the telecommunications industry (AT&T), they were not competitors, and the Commission was able to deal with them on a "separate but equal" basis. The broadcast industry was represented collectively by the National Association of Broadcasters, the lobbies maintained by the three major networks, and the Federal Communications Bar Association whose members make their livelihood by representing individual broadcasters in FCC proceedings. The closeness and compatibility of the relationship between the FCC and the broadcasters was guaranteed by constant contact, social lobbying, gifts, and a pronounced regulator-regulatee cycle: from 1945-1971, twenty-one of the thirty-three commissioners (64%) who left office went to work for the communications industry.[18] The relationship with the Bar association was even closer with law firms frequently providing direct assistance to the FCC staff to help them "speed up" FCC processes.[19] The result was an atmosphere of shared interests and a common perspective on the proper solution to any problems that might confront the FCC. To protect this closed environment from outside intruders, the FCC had taken a strict and narrow view on who would have standing to intervene in licensing proceedings and limited participation to those who could show economic injury or electrical interference.

Within Congress the relevant actors were primarily limited to the Communications Subcommittees of the House and Senate Commerce Committees. These subcommittees had always been sympathetic to the problems of the broadcast industry partly because at one point in time both chairmen (Oren Harris and Warren Magnuson) held stock in broadcasting concerns, but more consistently because of the special power that the broadcast industry has over the political survival of members of Congress. Survival requires reelection and that requires recognition by their constituents. Broadcasters have the ability to provide members of Congress with ongoing media coverage and publicity, not only in news broadcasts but also by supplying free time, as a public service, for reports filmed or taped by members of Congress—a service currently utilized by 70 percent of the Senate and 60 percent of the House.[20] This meant ready access for broadcasters to members of Congress, a generally sympathetic response to their problems, and a willingness to intervene in FCC proceedings on their behalf when necessary. Like the FCC, the subcommittees and members of Congress were not receiving any substantial pressure from groups powerful enough to counteract broadcast interests.

Presidential intervention into the broadcast regulation triangle was sporadic and frequently unsuccessful. As an independent regulatory commission the FCC is largely immune from direct presidential intervention. The appointment of "vast wasteland" Newton Minow as chairman of the FCC did slightly disconcert the broadcast industry, but his two years on the Commission failed to alter its identification with the broadcast industry. John Kennedy's attempt to reorganize the FCC and give the chairman more power was defeated in the House of Representatives, and his unsuccessful attempt to get Minow to pressure the electronic news media for more favorable news coverage terminated his active involvement with the Commission.

The courts, and particularly the Court of Appeals in Washington, D.C., which has jurisdiction over all appeals of FCC decisions in broadcast licensing matters, are an important part of the agency's environment. In the early sixties, however, the courts were likely to exercise judicial restraint and not intervene in agency decisions as long as proper procedures had been followed. Consequently, they presented little threat to the stable environment that had developed in the broadcast regulatory arena.

The general and specific environments in which the FCC existed in 1960 were calm and relatively closed. Within this environment the Commission had established an equilibrium primarily by structuring its outputs, policies, rules, and licensing decisions, so that they did not antagonize any of the relevant actors. Although the Commission might have been viewed as a weak and ineffectual agency by "outsiders," to organizational participants it was satisfactorily accomplishing its goals. Deregulation would, at that point in time, have been neither desirable nor acceptable.

THE FCC'S ENVIRONMENT: THE 1970S

By 1980 the FCC was suffering from a severe case of future shock which was quite understandable, given the rapid changes that had occurred in its general and specific environments. Both had become increasingly turbulent, complex, and unbalanced. Technological change had occurred in many areas that directly affected the FCC. Perhaps no area affected and threatened the FCC more than the burgeoning growth of cable television. From a small, localized industry whose revenues totalled only $35 million in 1961, cable TV had grown to a $2 billion a year industry.[21] The technical capabilities of cable called into question the basic reason for the FCC's existence: "Cable television with its multiple channel capability, solved the problem of spectrum scarcity—the rationale and rationalization for nearly all of the FCC's basic regulatory policy and indeed the Communications Act itself."[22]

Citizen band radio had grown from a method of communication used primarily by hobbyists, isolated farmers, and truck drivers, to a means of communication used by at least 20 million people.[23] Low power television, satellite broadcasting, and sweeping changes in the telecommunications field had all outstripped the FCC's capabilities to regulate and undermined the logic of such regulation.

The one constant in the FCC's environment remained the Communications Act. By 1981 it had still not been substantively revised and if its vague standards had offered little guidance in 1960, they appeared to have even less relevance in the late 1970s. The extent of the Commission's jurisdiction over cable television remained unclear, as did its proper role in regulating program content. There were important additions to the FCC's statutory environment during this period. In 1967 Congress passed the Public Broadcasting Act which may well have surpassed the Communications Act in vagueness. The act was to encourage the "growth and development of noncommercial educational radio and television."[24] However, the FCC was denied any enforcement role over the newly established Corporation for Public Broadcasting (CPB), except, of course, that public broadcast stations had to be licensed by the FCC and were subject to the same regulations, or lack thereof, as commercial stations. Since CPB channeled funds into program production, there was also a nebulous area concerning the enforcement and applicability of the Fairness Doctrine in public broadcasting. The period under examination also resulted in major expansions of federal concern in the area of civil rights for minorities and women. Title VII of the Civil Rights Act of 1964 prohibited discrimination based on race, sex, or national origin in employment practices by any employer with twenty-five or more employees. Although not aimed specifically at the FCC, this act also had a considerable impact on the Commission's operations.

The other major statutory change occurred with the addition of the Freedom of Information, Privacy, and Government in the Sunshine Act to the Federal Administrative Procedure Act. Of the three, the Sunshine Act had the most serious impact on FCC procedures. Passed in 1976, the Sunshine Act applied to all multiheaded agencies, including the FCC. It required that all meetings of such agencies must be open to the public unless by majority vote the members determine that to do so would not be in the public interest. The Act also declared it to be "the policy of the United States that the public is entitled to the fullest practicable information regarding the decisionmaking processes of the Federal Government."[25] Although the wording appeared innocuous, it was to cause serious adaptation problems for the FCC.

Meanwhile, major changes were occurring in the social, political, and economic environment. One of the most commonly noted phenomena of this period was the rise in visibility and activism of "public interest" groups. Although there is considerable controversy as to what the term includes, an appropriate definition of a public interest group would seem to be, "an organizational entity that purports to represent very broad, diffuse, noncommercial interests which traditionally have received little explicit or direct representation in the processes by which agencies, courts, legislatures make public policy."[26]

This definition encompasses consumer groups, environmental groups, taxpayers' associations, concerned citizens groups, and groups representing the poor, minorities and women. Although many such groups had been in existence for decades, the late 1960s and 1970s saw an enhancement of their activity and power. The reasons for this development are many but the social, economic, and political environment during this time period was particularly hospitable to their development and power. Broad-based public approval, social and political turmoil, the emergence of effective, dedicated leadership, and the availability of funding from public foundation and computerized mass solicitations all contributed to their rise to prominence.[27] By the late 1970s additional changes had occurred in the political and economic environment which were reflected in the growing number of individuals in both the public and private sectors who questioned the desirability and efficacy of government regulation of the economy.

The changes in the FCC's general environment were reflected in its specific environment. The increased economic power of cable television was accompanied by increased interest group organization, activism, and power. The National Cable Television Association (NCTA), founded in 1952 with an initial membership of nineteen, had grown by 1980 to 1700 members distributed throughout the United States. NCTA's power base was considerably larger than membership size indicated. Most cable systems were locally franchised and cable owners had shown considerable sophistication in establishing a local power base and using that base to enhance their power at the national level. When a cable owner went into a community to obtain a franchise, the first step he usually took was to organize a board composed of twenty to thirty of the community's leading citizens, all of whom were likely to have immediate access to their representatives in Washington, D.C.[28] NCTA and the regional cable organizations also utilized the traditional methods of ensuring access and counterbalancing the broadcaster's influence: honoraria and campaign contributions. For example, in 1978 when communications deregulation bills were being considered in both houses of Congress, Ernest Hollings, Chairman of the Senate Communications Subcommittee reported receiving honoraria from the South Carolina Cable Television Association, the National Cable Television Association and the Southern Cable Television Association. His counterpart in the House, Lionel Van Deerlin, who is also a former broadcast journalist, received honoraria from NCTA, Florida Cable Television Association, Southern Cable TV Association and the Kentucky Cable Television Association.[29]

The level of conflict between the cable operators and traditional broadcasters intensified throughout this period as both sides pressured the FCC for action favorable to their interests. The station owners, the networks, the NAB, and new trade organizations, such as the Association of Maximum Service Telecasters and the Council of UHF Broadcasters, fought to prevent the expansion of cable. The cable television policy arena also broadened to encompass other interests and other groups including the FCC's single most powerful client, AT&T. Like the broadcasters, AT&T had initially underestimated the significance and potential of cable. By 1965, however, the rapid growth of cable had attracted its attention. The most efficient way to string cable was to attach it to already constructed telephone poles. Bell Telephone's response to that was that however efficient such a procedure might be it was not going to be cheap. Barred by federal court decree from entering the cable TV industry itself, Bell began to construct cable systems to "lease" to cable operators. Other telephone operators not constrained by court order began to enter the business directly. The cable operators protested and the FCC was confronted with another enduring conflict situation. As the potential of cable as a two way communications medium developed, AT&T became increasingly concerned about the threat posed to its local monopoly and more insistent that the FCC act to protect it.[30] Finally, cable brought into the FCC's environment copyright owners of programs being used by cable. The Motion Picture Association was the largest of such groups, and although it favored cable development, it wanted to protect its members by ensuring that they received copyright fees.

Simultaneous with this proliferation of involved groups in cable, came the explosion of public interest groups into FCC hearing rooms, meetings, and offices. A *partial* listing of such groups that attempted to influence the FCC during this period would include:

Accuracy in Media (AIM)

Action for Children's Television (ACT)

Black Efforts for Soul on Television (BEST)

Citizens Communication Center (CCC)

Media Access Project (MAP)

National Association for Better Broadcasting

National Black Media Coalition

National Citizens Committee for Broadcasting (NCCB)

National Citizens Communication Lobby

National Latino Media Coalition

National Organization of Women (NOW)

National Parents-Teachers Association

Office of Communication, United Church of Christ

Stern Community Law Firm

These groups challenged almost every traditional FCC policy in the area of broadcast licensing and on every challenge they came into direct conflict with the broadcasters and their representatives. Like the cable associations they also took their case to Congress, becoming active participants in nomination processes and in committee hearings. They even established their own version of a regulator-regulatee cycle. Former FCC commissioner Nicholas Johnson became head of the National Citizens Committee for Broadcasting; former FCC general counsel Henry Geller became chairman of the Citizens Communications Center and former staff members of CCC, NCCB and the Stern Community Law firm were hired by the Federal Communications Commission.[31]

The increased conflict among interest groups also affected the relationship between Congress and the FCC. Congress could have helped resolve some of the FCC's environmental adaptation problems by passing legislation clarifying the Commission's jurisdiction over cable and providing clear standards for FCC action in both cable and program content regulation. As was indicated, it failed to do so. In 1977 the House Communications Subcommittee did initiate a two-year effort to rewrite the Communications Act. After twenty months a bill was introduced which would have substantially deregulated the communications industry and also would have abolished the FCC. But the same pressures that were making the FCC's existence so difficult were turned on Congress. Broadcasters wanted to be deregulated, but they did not want cable deregulated; cable wanted to be deregulated, but it did not want AT&T deregulated; newspapers wanted the restrictions on media crossownership lifted, and the public interest groups did not want anybody deregulated.[32] Congress however had an option which the FCC did not have—inaction—and in December 1979 all provisions relating to radio, television, and cable were deleted from the Communications Act rewrite.

The changed interest-group configuration disrupted the normal relationship between Congress and the FCC. The House Communications Subcommittee became increasingly critical of the FCC's handling of cable and in 1976 issued a report stating that "the FCC has continually refused to confront the basic issues presented by cable television," suggesting that it end its "protectionist policies" toward broadcasters.[33] The subcommittee also pressured the FCC to take a more "aggressive" role in reviewing the fairness of documentaries following the CBS presentation of "Selling of the Pentagon."[34] The number of Congressional committees that became interested in the FCC proliferated. From 1970-1977 over thirty subcommittees reviewed specific aspects of FCC policy.[35] The results of such reviews were almost unanimously critical of FCC policy.

The Presidency also became more actively concerned and involved with communications policy and at one point in 1971 completely usurped the FCC's policy-making role in cable television. The most consistent intervention occurred during the Nixon and Ford administrations. In 1970 the Office of Telecommunications Policy was created within the Executive Office of the President. Headed by Clay Whitehead, the OTP "became an active agency in day to day regulatory matters that had already been assigned . . . to the FCC."[36] Generally displeased with the quality of media news coverage, the Nixon administration also directly pressured the networks to change their practices. In both 1970 and 1971, the administration submitted legislation to Congress that would have altered FCC powers. The 1970 bill would have extended license terms to five years, but would have made licensees responsible for counterbalancing the networks ideological biases.[37] The 1971 proposal, which would have completely deregulated radio, was in direct response to NAB pressure and displeasure with the increased power of public interest groups. The most intrusive action involved cable television. On August 5, 1971, the FCC sent a Letter of Intent to Congress notifying it of the FCC's intention to formulate rules for cable television. The actual rulemaking process took place in the White House. Whitehead invited broadcasting, cable, and program production industry representatives to participate in negotiations held in his office. They worked out a consensus agreement that became the FCC's 1972 cable rules.[38] The entire procedure was of questionable legality since it completely ignored the procedural requirements of the Federal Administrative Procedure Act (APA). The FCC accepted the agreement and "in effect abandoned its role as formulator of policy."[39]

An equally important type of presidential input was the general climate that Nixon, Ford, and Carter attempted to create regarding undesirable government regulation of economic activity. Both Nixon and Ford supported legislation to deregulate major sections of the communications industry. Carter endorsed deregulation of the telecommunications but did not extend his endorsement to broadcasting. Carter's most important influence on the FCC may well have been his appointment of Charles Ferris as chairman. Ferris appeared to have no clearly developed policy preferences when he was appointed to the Commission. He had no experience in communications, no connections with the industry, and had wanted to be deputy attorney general but had settled for the FCC. "He was an unknown quantity,"[40] and he played a critical role in reshaping FCC policy.

Throughout this period the courts also played a crucial role in FCC's environment. The Court of Appeals effectively thwarted the FCC's attempt to restrict participation of public interest groups in its proceedings, thus ensuring constant conflict in licensing decisions.[41] It invalidated the FCC's attempt to establish two-step renewal procedures that would have protected licensees from all challenges.[42] It struck down FCC cross-ownership rules which allowed most pre-existing newspaper-media combinations to continue although that decision was overturned by the Supreme Court.[43] It required the Commission to hold hearings on program format changes when a significant sector of the listening community opposed and presented substantial evidence that the format was both unique and financially viable.[44] It compelled the FCC to apply the Fairness Doctrine to advertising for large-engine cars and high-test gasoline.[45] It struck down the FCC's subscription television rules; indicated that extensive ex parte contacts in rulemaking were illegal;[46] and invalidated FCC rules requiring cable operators to have 20-channel capacity.[47] The combined impact of these decisions prevented the FCC from limiting the expansion of its environment and insured that all competing interests would become permanent actors in that environment.

The FCC's environment had been transformed into a Type IV turbulent environment and the FCC was compelled to search constantly for methods that would enable it to establish equilibrium. This required the Commission to develop policies that would either reduce the level of conflicting demands put upon it or balance out the demands. The FCC's search for such policies was lengthy, inconsistent, and largely unsuccessful.

FCC RESPONSES TO ENVIRONMENTAL CHANGE

Phase I: Domain Preservation 1960-66

The FCC's initial response to these environmental changes was a concerted attempt to restore the status quo before 1960. Its response to pressure from public interest groups was to exclude them from meaningful participation in the Commission's policy process. This was accomplished by two different methods: refraining from formulating binding legislative rules concerning criteria for licenses and renewals, and denying the groups standing to intervene in licensing cases on the grounds that they had asserted no invasion of a legally protected interest. Instead of formulating rules, the Commission relied heavily on a case-by-case approach supported by "Policy Statements." The APA specifies procedure that requires notice and comment in legislative rulemaking, thus guaranteeing public interest groups an opportunity to provide substantive input. Once promulgated, legislative rules would be legally binding on both the Commission and licensees, which would further expand the ability of public intervenors to challenge Commission decisions. Policy statements, however, are classified as "informal" actions beyond the scope of the APA. There are no statutory guidelines restricting the formulation process and they do not have the same legal enforceability as legislative rules. They can be drawn up by the Commission by whatever process it deems appropriate and they may be adhered to or ignored at the Commission's discretion. Policy statements are an excellent way to foreclose public interest group participation in general FCC policy-making. Barring them from participation in individual license renewal cases effectively removed them as an element of contention in the FCC's environment.

Cable television was more problematic. Conventional broadcasters were beginning to perceive it as a threatening influence in the early sixties. Given the compatibility of the broadcasters and the FCC at that time, it was inevitable that they would turn to the Commission for protection and that the cable operators would be drawn into the FCC's environment. From an organizational perspective, the FCC's attempt to exclude them was a predictable response. The interests of cable and conventional broadcasters were mutually antagonistic. Any concessions the FCC might grant to cable television would be contested by the broadcasters. Only if the FCC completely side-stepped the problems cable was creating and refused jurisdiction, could it avoid the conflict and maintain a peaceful environment. For a relatively brief period of time this was what the FCC attempted.

In 1960 cable television was small business, locally-owned and operated, primarily located in the fringe areas of American society. The only broadcasters that were negatively affected by its operation tended to be small, remote television stations that had little power within the NAB or with the FCC. As cable expanded, it attracted the attention and money of large investors such as Chase Manhattan, Morgan Guaranty Trust, and Mutual of New York. The influx of new money facilitated the expansion of cable into new, heavily populated markets and placed them in direct competition with large broadcasters and the networks.[48] An attempt by the FCC to encourage the NAB and NCTA to work out a compromise legislative proposal for cable regulation failed in 1964 when the NAB rejected the compromise and the FCC abandoned the attempt.

The external conflict surrounding the FCC was reflected in the internal operations of the Commission. In 1962 Kenneth Cox became chief of the Broadcast Bureau, and proceeded to pressure the Commission to take a more protective attitude towards the broadcasters in cable license decisions.[49] His efforts were successful and the FCC refused to permit Carter Mountain Transmission, a microwave carrier, to expand microwave service to a cable operator in Riverton, Wyoming, on the grounds that it would have an adverse economic impact on the local television station. The FCC's authority was upheld by the court in *Carter Mountain Transmission v. FCC*.[50] The Commission then imposed a freeze on all cable authorizations unless the operator promised to carry all local television stations without duplication from other markets.

To insure that its future involvement in cable would be even more limited, the FCC attempted to persuade the states to take over regulation of cable systems. The states, for various reasons were equally unwilling to move into this new regulatory area and only Connecticut passed legislation asserting authority. Unfortunately for the FCC, the Connecticut legislation was viewed unfavorably by the NCTA and it vigorously opposed further state regulation. The ultimate result of that opposition was to push cable back onto the FCC's policy agenda.[51]

Conflict over the "proper" role of cable was also increasing within the broadcast industry. The networks had begun purchasing cable systems and moderating their opposition to cable expansion. The NAB split into three factions: smaller station owners, large station owners and station owners who had purchased cable systems. Each of the factions formed their own associations which attempted to pressure the FCC to regulate cable and protect the interests of their members.

The FCC's efforts to maintain its domain and restrict expansion of its environment failed. The Court of Appeals decision in *Office of Communications, United Church of Christ v. FCC* in 1966[52] compelled it to recognize public interest groups and allow them to intervene in license renewal cases. The attempt to neutralize the conflict over cable by limiting the Commission's power and foisting the problem on the states had also failed. It had satisfied none of the relevant interest groups and had actually increased the conflict among them. Equilibrium had not been established and the Commission was being pressured from all sides to change its policy. Although there was no agreement among the relevant interest groups as to what the new policy should be, all agreed that the FCC had to act decisively. The pressure for action intensified when Senator John Pastore, chairman of the Senate Communications Subcommittee and House chairman Oren Harris joined the chorus of those calling for Commission action. By 1965 the FCC recognized the futility of its attempt at domain preservation and reluctantly abandoned it.

Phase II: Domain Expansion

As the pressure from public interest groups increased, the FCC sought to accommodate their demands through limited domain expansion primarily by symbolic actions aimed at reassuring the groups that their opinions were weighed in Commission deliberations. More infrequently the Commission made substantive decisions that at least partially accommodated the demands made by these groups. Unfortunately, from the Commission's perspective, neither symbolic reassurance nor partial accommodation satisfied the public interest groups and they continued to pressure the Commission to make decisions that were strongly resented and opposed by the broadcasters. The Commission attempted to favor the broadcasters by either explicitly changing its policies or not enforcing them. The public interest groups responded by challenging the FCC in court. The courts generally refused to allow the Commission to withdraw from the conflict and compelled it to include public intervenors in the broadcast policy arena.

The FCC's most publicized and possibly least successful foray into symbolic politics was its decision to hold a series of *en banc* meetings with representatives of public interest groups. The purpose of these meetings from the FCC's perspective was "to construct a dialogue" with the groups.[53] The group representatives, however, were more interested in substantive action from an agency that they viewed as historically unresponsive to their needs, than in polite conversation. The first of the meetings was held in 1973 with representatives of the Latino Media Caucus. They requested that the Commission establish a task force to develop methods to ensure more equitable treatment of minorities in programming and employment practices in broadcasting. The Commission took no subsequent action on the proposal and the Latino coalition, evidently disenchanted with the FCC's lack of response, did not participate in any further Commission "come, let us reason together," meetings.

The FCC *en banc* meetings with women and black groups were considerably more volatile and uncomfortable for Commission members than the Latino meeting had been. In both meetings the Commission was denounced for its past and present practices and insensitivity toward minority groups. The substantive proposals put forward by both groups were treated similarly to those of Latino's—filed and forgotten. Despite the apparent lack of success of these meetings, the FCC continued to hold them, and group representatives, except for NOW and the Latino caucus, continued to appear.

During this period the FCC also held regional meetings throughout the United States and encouraged members of the public to express their concerns and grievances with both the broadcast industry and the FCC. The Commission was inundated with complaints from a wide variety of groups and individuals in all of these meetings. If the Commission had thought these meetings would placate the disgruntled by allowing them to express their grievances, it was wrong. The actual result may have been to increase frustration with the FCC[54] when the participants discovered that it either would not or could not take action to satisfy them. The meetings had two other results: they encouraged the groups to rely on legal and judicial methods to pressure the Commission, and they increased the Commission's sympathy with the broadcasters who had to deal with these individuals and groups on a regular basis.[55]

Other Commission efforts at symbolic reassurance during this period also failed to satisfy the public interest groups. In the area of equal employment opportunity, the FCC was the first regulatory agency to incorporate Title VII of the Civil Rights Act of 1964 into its own rules. Beginning in 1970, all licensees with five or more employees were required to file EEO-AA reports with the Commission. Public interest groups contended the FCC failed to enforce the rules and that most of the improvement in minority employment reported by broadcasters was the result of statistical manipulation by the stations and the Commission.[56] In 1971 the Commission considered creating an Office of Public Counsel but in the face of opposition from the broadcasters did not do so. Instead, in 1974 after the Court of Appeals remanded the prime time access rule partly because of the insufficient efforts to solicit public input, it created a Consumer Assistance Office to act as an information distribution and referral system for groups and individuals with no financial interest in broadcasting.[57] The Office was given no substantive powers and its major achievement has been the publication of *Actions Alert*, a summary of pending rulemaking procedures which is distributed to interested groups and individuals. In 1974 the Commission also made program logs available for public examination and agreed to provide indigent groups involved in adjudicatory proceedings with free copies of transcripts.

Action for Children's Television (ACT), a group composed of parents and other individuals dissatisfied with the quality and quantity of children's programming, succeeded in compelling the FCC to take the problem under active consideration, but they too were dissatisfied with the largely symbolic response they received. The Commission did create a Children's Television Bureau after being urged to do so by Torbert McDonald, chairman of the House Communications Subcommittee, but by 1976 it was staffed by only one employee.[58] It also instituted a lengthy inquiry into children's television which culminated in the issuance of a Policy Statement in 1974. Although the Policy Statement included the FCC's interpretation of what the "public interest" might require as far as advertising, timing, and quantity in the area of children's programming were concerned, it mandated no new changes and opted instead for industry self-regulation. ACT was far from satisfied and immediately appealed the Policy Statement to the Court of Appeals. The Court upheld the FCC but ACT refused to withdraw from the arena. In 1978 it petitioned the FCC to reopen the inquiry to determine how well industry self-regulation was working. The FCC reopened the inquiry on July 31, 1978.

In 1970 at the urging of another interest group, the National Association of Independent Television Producers and Distributors (NAITPD), the FCC agreed to limit network control over television programming and adopted the prime time access rule (PTAR I). PTAR I involved the Commission in another area of controversy to which it responded in its typical fashion—one step forward, one step back. The original rule prohibited network affiliates from presenting more than three hours of network programming during the four hours of evening prime time (7-11 PM EST) with exceptions for special programs such as public affairs and children's programs. The rule was greeted with complaints and petitions for reconsideration were filed. The FCC reconsidered and amended the rule to exempt Sundays and the first half-hour of prime time. NAITPD immediately sought judicial review of the amended rule. The Court held the FCC acted too precipitously in making the revision and remanded it to the Commission for further consideration.[59] The response to the Commission's request for further comments clearly illustrates how crowded and contentious its environment had become:

Comments were filed by 17 "public groups," all but one of which supported the original rule. . . . The Department of Justice, NAITPD, ABC, Westinghouse, some program suppliers and others also urged return to the original rule. The White House Office of Telecommunications Policy, six major film companies, CBS, the Screen Actors Guild and others urged repeal of the rule entirely. NBC supported the PTAR II compromise.[60]

In this instance, the FCC sided with the public groups and reinstituted PTAR I. The controversy did not subside and criticisms of the rule's impact continued to be made to the Commission.

Pressure from Congress as well as public interest groups encouraged the Commission to make another extremely controversial decision. For some time various groups had been complaining about the amount and explicitness of sex and violence on television. In 1974 the House Appropriations Committee ordered the FCC to submit a report to the Committee on what it was doing concerning this problem. Exactly what Congress expected the FCC to do without violating the legislative and constitutional ban on censorship was unclear and FCC chairman Wiley doubted that any *formal* action would be permissible. Consequently, he initiated negotiations with network executives to persuade them to do willingly what he suspected the FCC could not do legally. His persuasion however was always backed up by threat: "The bottom line . . . remained . . . —Do something to curb 'offensive' material or we the FCC, will be forced to take action."[61] The networks did something; they agreed to amend the NAB Television Code and establish the "family hour." From the FCC's perspective this was an excellent solution. It should have placated both the interest groups and

Congress and it had required no formal action by the Commission. However, writers and producers of programs that were bumped from the family hour were less pleased and once again the FCC's behavior was challenged in court. The District Court in California was particularly displeased with the FCC's blatant attempt to side-step legally required procedures in favor of closed door negotiations.[62]

Other FCC efforts to expand its domain and incorporate the demands of public interest groups were equally unsuccessful and resulted in increased demands and dissatisfaction from all participants. In no area was the conflict more severe or prolonged than in the area of FCC application and interpretation of the Fairness Doctrine. Strongly resented by broadcasters as a restriction on their freedom of speech and press, the Fairness Doctrine provided the public interest groups with a legal basis for challenging broadcasters' policies and compelling the FCC to act. In 1966 the FCC ruled in response to a complaint filed by John Banzhaf that stations which carried cigarette advertising must provide "a significant amount" of time broadcasting anti-cigarette material. The ruling stressed that it was applicable only to cigarette advertising and although it was opposed by the broadcasters, it was upheld by the Court.[63] The affirmation of the constitutionality of the Fairness Doctrine by the Supreme Court in 1969[64] increased its utility to public interest groups as a basis for pressuring the FCC.

Despite the FCC's emphasis on the limitations of the cigarette ruling, the broadcasters' worst fears materialized when the Friends of the Earth filed a Fairness Doctrine complaint with the Commission protesting the refusal of a New York City station, WNBC, to air viewpoints opposing paid advertisements for high-powered cars and high-test gasoline. The FCC's refusal to take action against WNBC was appealed to the Courts. The Court of Appeals was dissatisfied with the FCC's inconsistency in interpreting its own Fairness Doctrine and remanded the case to the Commission.[65] The FCC attempted to withdraw from this contentious area of regulation by issuing a reformulation of the Fairness Doctrine in 1974:

We do not believe that the cigarette cases should serve as precedent . . . that the usual product commercial can realistically be said to inform the public on any side of a controversial issue of public importance. . . . In the future we will apply the Fairness Doctrine only to those commercials which are devoted in an obvious and meaningful way to the discussion of public issues.[66]

This attempted withdrawal from conflict was far from successful. Although the 1974 policy statement was thoroughly approved by broadcasters, the response of public interest groups was negative and they bombarded the FCC with petitions for reconsideration.

The Fairness Doctrine was also used in other areas by a wide variety of public interest groups, and almost inevitably the FCC's decisions were challenged in court by the losing party. Anti-Vietnam War groups used it in an attempt to compel station owners to sell them time for spot commercials against the war. The FCC rejected their argument and was ultimately upheld in the Supreme Court.[67] Accuracy In Media argued that NBC had violated it in airing a program critical of private pension systems. The FCC ordered NBC to discharge its fairness obligation. The Court of Appeals overturned the FCC's decision.[68] The American Security Council Education Foundation challenged the "biased" nature of CBS news coverage of national security issues and demanded the FCC order CBS to provide opportunity for conflicting views. The FCC refused to do so and was challenged (unsuccessfully) in court.[69]

Unable to get satisfactory rules and general policy responses from the Commission, the public interest groups turned to intervention in license renewal proceedings as a supplementary method of increasing their influence over broadcast policy. Their right to intervene and be heard had been guaranteed by the Court and they had been encouraged by the FCC's denial of the renewal application of WHDH television in 1969. The groups attempted to turn license renewal proceedings into meaningful reviews of a licensee's performance. The FCC's response was unenthusiastic and it resisted the intervenors as much as it legally could, consistently refraining from applying its established criteria in renewal cases. Despite this, the public interest groups evidently hoped that they could compel the FCC and licensees to abide by its own criteria. In 1969 a citizens group in Texarkana filed a petition to deny renewal of KTAL-TV's license. The station agreed to negotiate with the group and the result was a thirteen-point policy statement in which the station agreed to modify its programming and employment practices. The FCC implicitly accepted the agreement as a condition in the license renewal. The implications of this action were quickly realized by broadcasters and the Commission and it attempted to draw back from this dangerous precedent. In 1970 it issued a Policy Statement establishing a two-step renewal process. In step one a licensee's past performance would be examined and if it had "substantially" served the local community's interests and needs, the license would be automatically renewed. Only if it were determined that the licensee had failed to do so would a comparative hearing be scheduled. The Policy Statement was immediately challenged by the Citizens Communication Center, and the Court of Appeals held it to be in violation of the Communications Act.[70] The FCC and NAB turned to Congress but were unsuccessful in persuading it to enact the Policy Statement.

The citizens groups continued to file petitions to deny and to pressure the broadcasters to sign negotiated agreements which the FCC was expected to enforce, and for a brief period the FCC appeared to accept this new responsibility. From 1972-1974 the Commission promulgated a series of rules which seemed to indicate that it was attempting to accommodate the citizens group's demands. The rules required license applicants to conduct two specific surveys, one of community leaders and the other of the general public, to ascertain community problems. Although broadcasters complained about the added burden, the requirement was little more than symbolic politics since the Commission failed to specify what, if anything, they were required to do with survey results. The Commission also adopted rules requiring that all renewal applications where licensee performance had dropped below specific and rather arbitrary performance standards would be subject to automatic full Commission review. Whatever promise these rules conveyed was also not delivered, since they were ignored by the Commission.[71] In 1974 the chairman of the Commission instructed the Broadcast Bureau to prepare and send warning letters to those licensees who were deviating from their programming promises. Finally, the Commission issued the "Broadcast Procedure Manual" explaining what public intervenors could do and how best to go about doing it.

In no area of regulation did the Commission demonstrate greater reluctance at responding to citizen demands than in program format changes by radio licensees. In 1972, Zenith Corporation, the licensee of WEFM, a classical music station in Chicago, had contracted to sell the station to GCC Communications. GCC's application for a license transfer specified that the station would be switching to a format of contemporary music. When a citizens' group objected and petitioned the FCC to deny the application or at least conduct a hearing, the FCC denied their petition. Once again the Court of Appeals overruled the FCC and required it to hold a hearing whenever a "significant sector" of the community protested and alleged that the format to be abandoned was both unique and financially viable.[72] The FCC did not approve of the court's decision and in this particular issue strongly resisted attempts to compel it to broaden its jurisdiction.

A final example of the FCC's attempt to expand its domain to respond to environmental pressures further illustrates the futility of this approach as a strategy to establish equilibrium in a turbulent environment. The FCC had long had a policy favoring diversity of ownership in the broadcast media, but like most other FCC policies, this one had not been strictly interpreted or enforced. By 1970, however, the Commission was being pressured from several different interests to make the diversification of ownership policy more explicit and enforceable. The Justice Department and the White House were concerned; the Senate Judiciary Subcommittee on Antitrust was concerned and the citizens groups were concerned. Once again the Commission responded in its typical compromising manner aimed at pleasing everyone but ultimately satisfied no one and was challenged in the courts. In 1970, the Commission adopted rules limiting the number of AM-FM and television stations that a single entity could own, and in 1975 adopted rules limiting crossownership by newspaper-broadcast media corporations. Always attentive to its prime clientele, the FCC "grandfathered" in most pre-existing combinations, requiring devestiture only where a single corporate entity controlled the only daily newspaper and the only broadcast station. No matter how satisfactory that may have been to broadcasters, it pleased neither the Justice Department nor the public interest groups and once again an FCC decision was challenged in court. Although its decision was overruled by the Court of Appeals, the FCC was ultimately upheld in the Supreme Court.[73]

Simultaneously with the FCC's attempt to expand its domain to incorporate public interest groups and political pressure groups, the war over cable television regulation inexorably escalated. The futility of the Commission's attempt to limit cable's growth and the threat cable posed to broadcasters and the FCC-broadcaster alliance became increasingly apparent in the late 1960s. Pressure on the Commission to modify its stance was both external and internal. Response to the freeze on cable was overwhelming. Twenty-six broadcast organizations, eight cable groups, and eight other interest groups, including the Grange and National Farmers Organization, submitted written reactions to the Commission. The networks wanted stricter curbs on program use by cable; the broadcasters wanted cables to pay copyright fees; antenna manufacturers wanted stricter limits on the expansion of cable. Both subcommittees in Congress wanted the FCC to improve its regulation but gave no legislative guidance as to how that should be done. In spite of the freeze, cable continued to expand and more large corporations entered the industry.

Internally, conflict reflecting the external pressure was developing at both the staff and Commission level. A cable task force created by the Commission had quickly developed a pro-cable orientation and urged the Commission to foster cable's growth. The task force which became a formal bureau in 1970 had responsibility for processing cable applications, preparing the cable TV agenda, and providing most of the information on which the Commission based its decisions. The task force's handling of cable applications essentially nullified the Commission's efforts to prevent its growth since it granted almost all requests made by cable operators.[74] Cable's strongest supporter on the Commission in the late 60s was Lee Loevinger who believed that Commission policies were unduly restrictive of cable expansion. The Broadcast Bureau was equally adamant in its support of and identification with the broadcast industry and their staunchest supporter on the Commission was Kenneth Cox, ex-chief of the Broadcast Bureau.

Until 1968 no one was certain that the Commission actually had jurisdiction over cable and if it did, what the extent or purpose of that jurisdiction was. Officially, Congress had given no explicit guidance; unofficially the feeling was that the Commission did have authority and no new legislation was needed. The Supreme Court affirmed the Commission's regulatory authority over cable to the extent that it was "reasonably ancillary" to its statutory responsibility to regulate over-the-air broadcasting.[75] That same year the Court also held that cable operators were not required to pay copyright fees.[76]

With its power thus affirmed the Commission issued new and even more restrictive rules on cable operations. In formulating the new rules, the Commission again displayed its willingness to avoid the rulemaking procedures required by the Administrative Procedure Act and the assured conflicts that would result from the required public notice and comment procedures. The rules were labelled as "interim" rules which could be immediately implemented with no debate.[77] The rules required cable operators to secure retransmission consent for each program from the originating station. The 1969 rules were added requiring cable operators to originate their own programming in addition to importing signals. In 1970 rules were promulgated prohibiting ownership of cable companies by telephone companies, the networks, and local television station owners.

Pressure for a more comprehensive regulatory approach to cable continued to build. Within the Commission, the Cable Task Force was urging action; externally the cable associations, the broadcasters, and the program producers were all dissatisfied with the current state of affairs. With the issuance of the August 5, 1971 Letter of Intent the Commission indicated its willingness to broaden its role in cable television into a comprehensive scheme of regulation. However, as indicated earlier, the Commission's role as policy formulator was preempted by the White House, apparently at the insistence of the broadcast industry which viewed the proposed rules as too favorable to cable. Once the consensus agreement had been accepted by all the participants in the OTP-Whitehead Conference, the FCC had no alternative but to accept it—unless Congress were willing to intervene in its behalf. Congress, however, was not willing to act at that time and the consensus agreement became the FCC's 1972 rules on cable television.

Although it might have seemed that the consensus agreement had resolved the conflict over cable regulation and allowed the Commission to establish balance among the competing interests, appearances were deceiving. After a suitable time for reflection, almost no one was satisfied with the consensus rules. UHF operators had never liked the agreement since they had received no protection or advantages from it.[78] The program producers and the Motion Picture Association still had not been granted copyright fees from the cable companies; the cable industry felt the rules were overly restrictive and began to pressure the FCC to change the rules before they went into effect. The FCC cable staff agreed with them. Eventually, the White House under Gerald Ford, the House Subcommittee on Communications and the courts also disavowed major portions of the regulatory scheme established by the consensus agreement.

The FCC expanded its domain in one other important area during this period, once again in response to pressure from broadcasters. In 1969 the Commission issued rules relating to subscription television and pay cable. The initial rules imposed no limitations on the types of programming that pay cable could carry. The broadcasters immediately petitioned the FCC for reconsideration and the FCC responded with its "anti-siphoning" rules which prohibited pay cable and subscription TV from carrying advertising, any movies between four and ten years old; from devoting more than ninety percent of their cablecast hours to sports and movies; and sharply restricted their ability to carry live sports events. The rules placated broadcasters but angered theatre owners, cable and subscription owners, and the Justice Department, all of whom petitioned for reconsideration. After two years of considering the petitions the FCC denied them but did institute an inquiry into the rules. Finally, in 1975 the commission issued revised rules which were little different from the 1970 version and were equally protective of conventional broadcasters.

At the same time that the FCC was surrounded by constant conflict among persistent and powerful interest groups, it was also being inundated with applications for citizen band radios. CB, however, concerned no powerful groups, corporations and institutions and as a result the FCC was left relatively free to determine how CB licensing should be handled. Since no one opposed CB and millions of Americans favored it and were using it, the FCC made no attempt to control or restrict CB development.[79] From the perspective of an organization that was already overloaded, there was no incentive to devote scarce organizational time and resources to an issue that could be avoided. De(or non)regulation was the most practicable strategy for the Commission and the one that it pursued in this area. Complete deregulation in CB was accomplished in 1976 when the Commission suspended all fees and made the granting of a CB license automatic.

Phase III: Domain Contraction—Deregulation

The FCC had attempted to respond to the increasing complexity of its environment by a variety of actions aimed at placating the numerous and hostile actors that it was unable to ignore. None of these attempts at domain expansion had been successful and the level of conflict surrounding the agency continued to increase. The FCC had discovered, as several other federal agencies had, that public interest groups are not easily placated. They tend to take clear and uncompromising positions on what constitutes acceptable regulatory action. From their perspective, agencies never act soon enough or strongly enough to protect what they believe to be the public interest, and they are unlikely to be satisfied with symbolic gestures. In the area of communications policy they were on a collision course with the broadcast industry and the FCC was in the middle. Similarly, the conflict between cable and conventional broadcasters also appeared to be unresolvable unless conventional broadcasters were allowed to take over competing cable companies, but both Congress and the Justice Department would have objected to that.

The FCC's domain expansion had not succeeded in reestablishing a stable and placid environment. From the agency's perspective, the failure required a search for new strategies. One of the most apparent and appealing was to jettison those portions of its authority and activities that were most subject to conflict which the FCC proceeded to do on several fronts simultaneously. Some forms of deregulation were relatively noncontroversial. In 1976 the Commission dropped requirements that radio broadcast licensees submit technical information and operating logs; held that radio stations were not required to originate local programming; and developed a new short-form renewal application that eliminated several previously required informational categories. The Commission also expressed its displeasure over the increasing number and scope of citizen group-licensee agreements, and in refusing to accept one such agreement (KTTV) the Commission announced that there was no obligation for licensees to negotiate. In December 1975 the Commission issued a policy statement announcing that it would sanction no agreement in which a licensee delegated programming responsibility to another group.

Typically, the Commission relied on policy statements to announce some of its most controversial withdrawals from involvement in regulating broadcast programming practices. In 1976 it issued a Policy Statement rejecting the Court of Appeals decision in *Citizens Committee to Save WEFM v. FCC*.[80] The statement asserted that competition was effective in producing format diversity and that regulation under *WEFM* would deter innovative programming and improperly invaded First Amendment interests. In 1977 the Commission issued a policy statement refusing to establish quantitative standards for news, local, and public affairs programming to be used as criteria in license renewal cases: "We have no illusions that quantitative standards would be other than an encroachment on the broad discretion licensees now have to broadcast the programs they believe best serve their audiences. We do not believe such a result is justified."[81] The lack of such criteria would also make challenges to renewals far more difficult to prove.

At the same time, the Commission was pressing for legislation that would modify the Fairness Doctrine. Since the Fairness Doctrine is part of the Communications Act, the Commission's ability to limit enforcement of it is restricted and subject to judicial challenge. Several public interest groups had filed petitions for reconsideration of the 1974 Fairness Report disagreeing with the exemption for product advertising and suggesting various methods to ensure that licensees satisfied their fairness obligations. The Commission denied all the petitions, reiterated its commitment to the 1974 report and its view that in this, as in all other matters, the licensee's discretion must be preserved. Predictably the denials were challenged and the Court of Appeals remanded two of the proposals put forth in the petitions to the Commission for further consideration.[82] One of the proposals, suggested by Henry Geller, former general counsel of the FCC, would have required licensees to adopt a "ten-issue" approach to meeting fairness obligations. This proposal was ultimately incorporated into the radio deregulation rules of 1981.

The radio deregulation rules culminated the Commission's attempt to placate broadcasters and to limit the ability of public interest groups to challenge licensees. The rules eliminated the time requirements for non-entertainment programming, the ascertainment of community needs requirement, the commercial advertising limits guidelines, and the requirements to keep detailed program logs. The licensee would be required to keep in its public file an issues-program list containing at least five to ten issues of importance to the community (Geller's proposal), and an explanation of how those issues were selected and presented. The licensee would be allowed to use "any reasonable means" to ascertain community needs. The overall intent of the deregulation was to "allow marketplace forces" to substitute for specific regulatory guidelines.[83]

In cable television the FCC pursued the same strategy of withdrawal from conflict with considerable informal pressure from Congress and the Presidency. In 1975 the Senate Judiciary Subcommittee on Antitrust and Monopoly held hearings on the anticompetitive impact of FCC and broadcasters' activities on cable television. In February 1976 the Justice Department filed suit challenging the FCC's rules restricting the programs that could be carried by cable, alleging that the rules had an anticompetitive effect. The House Communications Subcommittee released an even more critical report of FCC handling of cable, charging it with pursuing a "protectionist policy" toward broadcasters, deliberately stifling the development of cable, and arguing that the FCC lacked authority to regulate local franchising procedures.[84] The major official guidance Congress provided during this period was the passage of the Copyright Act of 1976 which required all licensed cable operators to pay royalty fees which would be distributed to copyright holders. The Ford Administration added to the pressure by submitting a regulatory reform proposal calling for the deregulation of cable television.

The courts added their own pressure to the FCC in 1977 by striking down its rules on pay cable and subscription television programming. The Court of Appeals held in *Home Box Office, Inc. v. FCC*[85] that the rules served no important or substantive governmental interest, that they exceeded Commission jurisdiction and that they were "grossly overbroad." *Home Box Office* also addressed the permissibility of ex parte contacts in rulemaking. As the Court pointed out, not only had several "participants contacted individual commissioners during the rulemaking procedures, but the Commission had solicited opinions from various individuals outside the formal procedure." When the Court ordered the FCC to submit a list of ex parte communications, the report submitted by the Commission was sixty pages long. Among those who had made such contacts were representatives for

ABC, members of Congress, broadcast and cable lobbyists, National Association of Broadcasters staff members, and Henry Geller, who had filed the amicus brief challenging such communications. The Court of Appeals was very dissatisfied with this procedure which it felt violated both section 553 of the Administrative Procedure Act, which requires agencies to maintain and respond to the public record compiled in the rulemaking process, and the government in the Sunshine Act. The court ruled that such ex parte contacts were impermissible in rulemaking and remanded the record to the FCC with instructions "to hold, with the aid of a specially appointed hearing examiner, an evidentiary hearing to determine the nature and source of all ex parte pleas" made to the Commission during the rulemaking proceeding. In 1979 the Supreme Court invalidated FCC rules requiring CATV operators to have twenty-channel capacity on their cables as a violation of the Communications Act that broadcasters were not common carriers.[86]

The FCC had begun (on its own) to deregulate cable television. The 1972 rules were never stringently enforced and most of them were rescinded before their effective date. The technical requirements were delayed on the grounds that there was "insufficient proof of harm to broadcasters."[87] The requirements for local government and public access channels were regularly waived and undermined. The leapfrogging rules which limited cable's ability to choose which stations they chose to import were also relaxed at the urging of the cable bureau and cable operators.[88]

On reconsideration of the 1972 rules, at the suggestion of cable operators, the Commission allowed cable to carry network programs which were not cleared for broadcast by the local network affiliate. The rule requiring expansion of cable capacity was suspended. In May 1976 the Commission deleted requirements that cable systems in major markets must have capacity for one non-broadcast channel for each channel used for broadcast programming; exempted systems with less than 3500 subscribers from all requirements; and extended the deadline for meeting the twenty-channel requirement.[89]

In November 1976, backlogged with 7400 cable applications, the FCC proposed new rules for its cable certification procedures.[90] The result was the adoption of rules that freed cable operators and local franchisers from holding public hearings, and from limits on franchise duration, timetables for construction, and complaint procedures. The rules did retain limitations on franchise fees that local governments could charge. Little substance was left to the 1972 consensus agreement-FCC rules and in July 1980 the "last of the regulations the cable industry considered restrictive" were lifted—the distant signal and syndicated exclusivity rules.[91]

If these deregulation efforts are successful they will allow greater discretion to broadcasters, limit the Commission's involvement in the controversial area of program content, make it more difficult for public interest groups to challenge a licensee's performance, and ultimately reduce the level and amount of conflict with which the FCC has to contend. Similarly cable deregulation should remove the cable operators as a contentious force from the FCC's environment. There are two major problems with this attempted domain contraction. First, groups that feel adversely affected by deregulation have not accepted the Commission's attempted abdication of authority. Public interest groups are particularly displeased with broadcast deregulation and have taken their case both to court and Congress. Similarly both the National Association of Broadcasters and Malrite Broadcasting Corporation have challenged cable deregulation in the courts. Whatever the outcome of the cable case, it is highly unlikely that the broadcasters will cease their attempts to pressure the FCC for reconsideration of its decision.

The second major problem with broadcast deregulation is that it is of dubious legality. Even FCC chairman Ferris who supported the deregulation felt that it would require legislative sanction and Senator Robert Packwood, chairman of the Senate Commerce Committee agreed with him: "I remain convinced that ultimately statutory deregulation will be necessary and desirable, because the FCC's decision to deregulate is sure to be litigated."[92] The Media Access Project has appealed the deregulation contending that it violates the public interest standard of the Communications Act.

The clearest indication of the Court of Appeals' attitude toward voluntary deregulation, generally and specifically, was given in 1979 in *WNCN Listeners Guild v. FCC*.[93] The case involved another program format abandonment and the FCC's 1976 Policy Statement's attempted abdication from responsibility in this area. The Court viewed the FCC's response to WEFM as particularly unsatisfactory, especially the Commission's repeated references to the WEFM decision as the "policy" of the Court. "We should have thought that WEFM represents not a *policy*, but rather the *law* of the land as enacted by Congress and interpreted by the Court of Appeals and as it is to be administered by the Commission." The decision also expressed grave doubts about the permissibility of deregulation and the substitution of market forces: "In WEFM the court . . . was speaking solely in the context of the current regulatory scheme laid down by Congress. . . . Congress . . . can hardly be thought to have had so limited a concept of the aims of regulation." On appeal, however, the Supreme Court upheld the FCC's position that diversity of format could best be preserved by allowing market forces to determine which formats could generate sufficient listener interest and support.[94] Although that decision did not guarantee that all FCC deregulation efforts would be upheld, the possibility that at least some of them would withstand legal challenges was considerably increased.

CONCLUSION

In the twenty-year period under consideration, both the general and the specific environments of the Federal Communications Commission changed dramatically. The stable, low conflict, scarcely populated environment within which the Commission had established equilibrium changed to a volatile, high conflict, densely populated one. The changes which increased the demands on the agency and subjected it to unremitting cross-pressures also penetrated its boundaries. Personnel changes at both the Commission and staff level reflected the environmental changes and the increased conflict within the organization.

The Commission pursued three different strategies of domain modification to re-establish and maintain equilibrium. The initial strategy was domain preservation aimed at excluding competing groups from the agency's environment by refusing to assert authority over substantive areas of regulation which involved high levels of conflict. This strategy failed when the courts refused to allow the Commission to exclude public interest groups from its decision-making processes and when the single most powerful group in the FCC's environment, the broadcast industry, persisted in demanding that the agency protect it from cable operators.

The second strategy of domain expansion also proved unsatisfactory. Still motivated primarily by a desire to protect broadcasters, the FCC attempted to broaden its jurisdiction to include the public interest groups and the cable industry. Its attempts at accommodating the public groups were mostly symbolic gestures which displeased the broadcasters, dissatisfied the public intervenors, and were frequently rejected by the courts. Its expansion of regulatory authority over cable was also counter-productive. Again the Commission's major goal was protection of broadcasters and the cable industry whose economic and political power had steadily increased and who refused to accept the imposed restrictions. It turned to Congress, the Presidency, and the courts and involved them in the FCC's environment. Instead of alleviating the conflicts surrounding the Commission this strategy intensified them.

The most recent strategy of the Commission has been domain contraction through deregulation. Although it could be nullified by the courts, this strategy has considerable potential for stabilizing the Commission's environment and allowing it to re-establish equilibrium. If accepted by the courts, deregulation will significantly reduce the ability of public interest groups to pressure the Commission, remove the cable industry as a source of contention, and also limit the broadcasters' ability to compel the Commission to protect them from cable competition. Even if the courts were to reject deregulation, the Commission may still be able to deflect the controversy away from itself and into the congressional policy arena. Given the dominant attitudes within Congress at this time it is likely that the FCC's deregulation policies will be supported and granted legislative authorization.

Domain contraction, particularly the severe reduction of an agency's power, is a potentially dangerous strategy for any organization to pursue since it may ultimately raise questions about the need for the agency's continued existence. Since the members of most organizations have a vested interest in the continued survival of the organization, they will normally and rationally oppose such a strategy. This was not the case with the FCC and the strategy of deregulation was promoted by both Commission and staff members. Support at the Commission level is not difficult to understand. The majority of Commissioners are "short termers" who do not identify strongly with the agency and may not be particularly concerned about its long term survival. Support at the staff level is equally rational in this particular instance. No matter how much the FCC curtails its involvement in program content regulation or in cable television, its existence in one form or another is guaranteed for the foreseeable future. As long as over-the-air broadcasting exists, there will be a need for a "traffic cop" to prevent electrical interference. Similarly, in other areas where the FCC exercises jurisdiction—telephone, telegraph, satellite broadcasting—technical oversight will also be necessary. Deregulation can be supported because it does not severely threaten the agency's existence and because it may restore environmental equilibrium.

NOTES

1. Barry Mitnick, *The Political Economy of Regulation* (New York: Columbia University Press, 1980), pp. 418-19.

2. Edwin Krasnow and Lawrence Longley, *The Politics of Broadcast Regulation*, 2d ed. (New York: St. Martin's Press, 1978), p. 2.

3. Mitnick, *The Political Economy of Regulation*, p. 21.

4. Daniel Katz and Robert Kahn, *The Social Psychology of Industry* (New York: Wiley, 1966), pp. 15-20.

5. Frederick Mosher, "Some Notes on Reorganization in Government Agencies," in Frederick S. Lane, *Managing State and Local Government* (New York: St. Martin's Press, 1980), p. 129.

6. Robert Miles, *Macro Organizational Behavior* (Santa Monica, Calif.: Goodyear, 1980), pp. 189-96.

7. Shirley Terreberry, "The Evaluation of Organization Environments," *Administrative Science Quarterly* 12 (1968): 590-613.

8. William McWhinney, "Organization Form, Decision Modalities and the Environment," *Human Relations* 21 (1968): 272.

9. Gary Wamsley and Mayer Zeld, *The Political Economy of Organizations* (Boston: Lexington Books, 1973), p. 58.

10. 47 U.S.C.A. § 1.

11. For a general discussion of the impact of vague standards on regulatory agency behavior, see Marver Bernstein, *Regulating Business by Independent Commissions* (Princeton, N.J.: Princeton University Press, 1955), pp. 263-67.

12. Louis Jaffe, "The Illusion of the Ideal Administration," *Harvard Law Review* 86 (1973): 1183.

13. Richard Berner, *Constraints on the Regulatory Process: A Case Study of Regulation of Cable Television* (Cambridge, Mass.: Ballinger, 1976), p. 15.

14. Don R. LeDuc, *Cable Television and the FCC: A Crisis in Media Control* (Philadelphia: Temple University Press, 1973), pp. 95-113.

15. 18 U.S.C. 1464.

16. Barry Cole and Mal Oettinger, *Reluctant Regulators: The FCC and the Broadcast Audiences* (Reading, Mass.: Addison-Wesley, 1978), p. 134.

17. Sydney Head, *Broadcasting in America: A Survey of Television and Radio* (Boston: Houghton Mifflin, 1976), p. 425.

18. Cole and Oettinger, *Reluctant Regulators*, p. 8.

19. Cole and Oettinger, *Reluctant Regulators*, p. 33.

20. Krasnow and Longley, *The Politics of Broadcast Regulation*, p. 70.

21. *Broadcasting* (January 5, 1981): 75.

22. Glen O. Robinson, "The Federal Communications Commission: An Essay on Regulatory Watchdogs," *Virginia Law Review* 64 (1978): 245.

23. Krasnow and Longley, *The Politics of Broadcast Regulation*, p. 162.

24. 47 U.S.C. § 396.

25. 5 U.S.C. § 5526.

26. Peter Schuck, "Public Interest Groups and the Policy Process," *Public Administration Review* (March/April 1977): 133.

27. James Q. Wilson, *The Politics of Regulation* (New York: Basic Books, 1980, p. 385.

28. Bill Keller, "Long Faced with Federal Regulation . . . Broadcasters Turned to Lobbying," *Congressional Quarterly* (August 2, 1980): 2181.

29. "Financial Disclosure in Congress," *Congressional Quarterly* (September 1, 1979): 1855.

30. Bruce Owen and Ronald Brautigam, *The Regulation Game: Strategic Use of the Administrative Process* (Cambridge, Mass.: Ballinger, 1978), p. 136.

31. Krasnow and Longley, *The Politics of Broadcast Regulation*, p. 81.

32. Ann Cooper, "House Panel Considers Major Overhaul of 1934 Communications Act," *Congressional Quarterly* (June 14, 1977): 1114.

33. Owen and Brautigam, *The Regulation Game*, p. 157.

34. Krasnow and Longley, *The Politics of Broadcast Regulation*, p. 83.

35. Ibid., p. 86.

36. Head, *Broadcasting in America*, p. 420.

37. Ibid., p. 421.

38. Berner, *Constraints on the Regulatory Process*, pp. 42-47.

39. From the dissenting opinion of Commissioner Nicholas Johnson, quoted in Berner, *Constraints on the Regulatory Process*, p. 48.

40. "The Laissez Faire Legacy of Charlie Ferris," *Broadcasting* (January 19, 1981): 37-38.

41. Office of Communications, United Church of Christ v. FCC, 358 F.2d 994 (D.C. Cir. 1966).

42. Citizens Communications Center v. FCC, 447 F.2d 1201 (D.C. Cir 1971).

43. FCC v. National Citizens Committee for Broadcasting, 436 U.S. 775 (1978).

44. Citizens Committee to Save WEFM v. FCC, 506 F.2d 246 (D.C. Cir. 1977).

45. Friends of the Earth v. FCC, 449 F.2d 1164 (D.C. Cir. 1971).

46. Home Box Office v. FCC, 567 F.2d 9 (D.C. Cir. 1977).

47. FCC v. Midwest Video, 446 U.S. 689 (1979).

48. LeDuc, *Cable Television and the FCC*, p. 118.

49. Berner, *Constraints on the Regulatory Process*, p. 13.

50. Carter Mountain Transmission v. FCC, 321 F.2d 359 (D.C. Cir. 1960).

51. LeDuc, *Cable Television and the FCC*, p. 127.

52. 359 F.2d 994 (D.C. Cir. 1966).

53. Former FCC Chairman Dean Burch, quoted in Cole and Oettinger, *Reluctant Regulators*, p. 98.

54. Cole and Oettinger, *Reluctant Regulators*, p. 115.

55. Ibid., p. 101.

56. Ibid., p. 170.

57. Ibid., p. 76.

58. Krasnow and Longley, *The Politics of Broadcast Regulation*, p. 86.

59. NAITPD v. FCC, 502 F.2d 249 (D.C. Cir. 1971).

60. *Prime Time Access Rule*, 50 FCC 2d 829 (1979).

61. Writers Guild of America, West, Inc. v. FCC, 423 F Supp 1075 (S.D. Cal. 1976).

62. 423 F Supp 1064 (1976).

63. Banzhaf v. FCC, 405 F.2d 1082 (D.C. Cir. 1968).

64. Red Lion Broadcasting Co. v. FCC, 395 U.S. 367 (1969).

65. Friends of the Earth v. FCC, 449 F.2d 1164 (D.C. Cir. 1971).

66. *Handling of Public Issues*, 48 FCC 2d 26 (1974).

67. CBS Inc. v. Democratic National Committee, 412 U.S. 94 (1973).

68. NBC v. FCC, 516 F.2d 110 (D.C. Cir. 1974).

69. American Security Council Education Foundation v. FCC, 607 F.2d 438 (D.C. Cir. 1979).

70. Citizens Communication Center v. FCC, 447 F.2d 1201 (D.C. Cir. 1971).

71. Head, *Broadcasting in America*, p. 424.

72. Citizens Committee to Save WEFM v. FCC, 506 F.2d 245 (D.C. Cir. 1974).

73. FCC v. National Citizens Committee 436 U.S. 775 (1978).

74. Berner, *Constraints on the Regulatory Process*, pp. 64-66.

75. U.S. v. Southwestern Cable, 392 U.S. 157 (1968).

76. Fortnightly Corp. v. United Artists, 392 U.S. 396 (1968).

77. LeDuc, *Cable Television and the FCC*, p. 175.

78. Berner, *Constraints on the Regulatory Process*, p. 53.

79. Krasnow, and Longley, *The Politics of Broadcast Regulation*, p. 173.

80. 506 F.2d 246 (1974).

81. Quoted in Douglas Ginsberg, *Regulation of Broadcasting: Law and Policy Towards Radio, Television and Cable Communications* (St. Paul, Minn.: West, 1979), p. 145.

82. National Citizens Committee for Broadcasting v. FCC, 567 F.2d 1095 (D.C. Cir. 1977).

83. *Broadcasting* (January 19, 1981): 32.

84. "FCC Regulation of Cable Television," *Congressional Quarterly* (February 14, 1976): 336.

85. Home Box Office, Inc. v. FCC, 567 F.2d 9 (D.C. Cir. 1977).

86. FCC v. Midwest Video, 446 U.S. 689 (1979).

87. Owen and Brautigam, *The Regulation Game*, p. 140.
88. Berner, *Constraints on the Regulatory Process*, p. 77.
89. Ginsburg, *Regulation of Broadcasting*, p. 350.
90. Ibid., p. 412.
91. *Broadcasting* (January 5, 1981): 34.
92. *Broadcasting* (January 19, 1981): 32.
93. WNCN Listeners Guild v. FCC, 610 F.2d 838 (D.C. Cir. 1979).
94. FCC v. WNCN Listeners Guild, 455 U.S. 914 (1981).

4

The Politics of Rewriting
the Federal Communications Act

INTRODUCTION

THE Communications Act of 1934 is as comfortable as an old shoe to broadcasters. *Broadcasting* magazine has called it "the indispensable Linus blanket of the industry."[1] The Act, much of which actually dates to 1927, has formed the basis for radio regulation since radio's early days. Television was born under the Act's provisions and has grown to have the pervasive impact it has today.

Though it has endured, the Act has failed to keep pace with technological changes unforeseen in 1927, just as the United States Constitution could not possibly have anticipated the changes in American society. Because the Act has failed to keep pace with technology, there have been sporadic attempts at piecemeal amendment.[2] Despite those attempts, however, the underpinnings of the Act went largely untouched through the mid-1970s. Federal regulators, broadcasters, public interest groups and—most important—members of Congress lived with known rules that, if modified at all, would be done so incrementally. Sweeping change was not on anyone's agenda.

Barry Cole, a consultant to Congress and the Federal Communications Commission, said it well when he noted that "most broadcasters are satisfied with the status quo and haven't asked for that many changes in the law. What's been more important to the broadcast lobby has been blocking legislation it doesn't like, and it's very effective at that."[3]

Because of the pattern of incremental change, or no change at all, a lot of knowledgeable people were taken by surprise in August 1976 when Congressman Lionel Van Deerlin, a California Democrat, proposed a "basement to penthouse rewrite" of the Communications Act.[4] As chairman of the House Communications Subcommittee, Van Deerlin—a former radio and television news editor—achieved some notice with his statement. But it was difficult for most people in the broadcast realm to take Van Deerlin seriously. There had been no clue that anything like a rewrite was in the offing, not even in the broadcast trade press, whose vigilance is legendary.[5]

Two astute observers of broadcast politics have noted that Congressional control of broadcast policy by statute has been of "relative unimportance," adding that from 1970 through 1977 Congress enacted only one significant amendment to the Communications Act.[6] So, what was Van Deerlin doing, anyway?

At the time of his rewrite announcement, Van Deerlin had chaired the subcommittee for just four months. His predecessor, Massachusetts Democrat Torbert Macdonald, had not tried anything so ambitious during nearly a decade as Subcommittee chairman. In the Senate, Communications Subcommittee chairman John Pastore, a Rhode Island Democrat, had not entertained the notion of a rewrite for twenty years. After all, the 1934 Act was familiar. Why make waves when ripples were all anybody had tried to make in the past? Or, as Van Deerlin kept hearing, "If it ain't broke, don't fix it." Whatever could have possessed the House Communications Subcommittee to undertake such a massive, politically risky initiative?

The answer is important to the history of communications policy. If the rewrite attempt had fizzled immediately, as so many observers predicted it would, it might not even have been a footnote in textbooks. But the initiative did not turn out to be futile. The rewrite effort stayed very much alive for three years and spawned less sweeping but significant legislation in the House and Senate. Furthermore, the rewrite effort led to a painful but useful re-examination of basic legislative and regulatory tenets.[7]

The causes of any major legislative initiative are complex. Superficial accounts of the rewrite published in newspapers, magazines, and elsewhere since 1976 have contained scattered speculation about the origin of Van Deerlin's "surprise" rewrite.[8] We must go beyond speculation and address the main question: What forces combined to give birth to the highly unusual rewrite attempt? This chapter will assess the role of each of the six main sectors in broadcast policy-making—Congress, the Federal Communications Commission (FCC), the White House, the courts, private industry groups, and private groups purporting to act in the public interest.[9]

One cannot start a few months, or even a few years, before the 1976 announcement in order to arrive at a thorough understanding. History, particularly the history of broadcast policy, is often useful to review as a harbinger of later events. History held one obvious lesson for Van Deerlin, a lesson he decided to ignore—that getting sweeping broadcast legislation through all the hurdles in Congress has never been easy.

A BRIEF HISTORY OF BROADCAST POLICY—MAKING

The first radio law was adopted by Congress in 1910. Called the Wireless Ship Act, its provisions were limited to the use of radio as a life-saving device at sea. The law was just a page long; but then, that was a simpler time. True broadcasting was at least a decade away. In 1912, anticipating new uses for radio, Congress approved the Radio Act, which in seven pages spelled out public policy and standards of operation for the medium.[10]

Broadcasting for the public seems to have had its origin around 1920 in the home of Frank Conrad, an engineer for the Westinghouse Company, which was a major manufacturer of electrical equipment during and after World War I. Conrad obtained a license for a transmitter he built in his home and began to broadcast signals from there. He learned that people in the area were picking up the signals on their amateur receiving sets. Soon Conrad started to play victrola records over the air and as word spread about the miraculous music, the demand for receiving sets increased.

Westinghouse executives saw commercial possibilities in manufacturing sets for home use. They decided to construct a large transmitter in East Pittsburgh to stimulate sales of home receivers. Thus, station KDKA was born in 1920. The Pittsburgh experience was so successful that imitators quickly followed. Transmitters in New York City began broadcasting in 1921 and, in the last half of that year, thirty-two new stations received licenses followed by another 254 in the first half of 1922.

Herbert Hoover, later president of the United States, was secretary of commerce as broadcasting began to boom. At first, the Commerce Department allocated a single wavelength for broadcasting. When it became obvious that one would not be enough, another was added, mainly for weather forecasts and crop reports. But the 1912 Radio Act was unable to handle such growth. Privately operated radio stations interfered with each other's programming but the Commerce Department could do little and continued to issue transmitter licenses.

With little guidance from Congress, Hoover called a conference of fifteen delegates in Washington, D.C., in order to get legal and technical advice. They recommended increased regulation by the federal government and in 1923 the House of Representatives approved a bill that included the delegates' recommendations, but the bill died in a Senate committee. A year later, Hoover called a second conference. The delegates reiterated the need for Congressional action, but Congress could not agree on a radio bill.

Stations were unable to survive the chaos. During a four-month stretch in 1923, about 150 stations shut down. Interference from neighboring stations was one problem; another was financing broadcasts. The larger electrical manufacturers were underwriting their stations from profits on the sale of receiving sets. But this was a limited expedient for them, and useless to station owners who were not electrical manufacturers.

Hoover convened a third radio conference in 1924, and a fourth in 1925. The fourth time it worked. The 400 delegates voted to limit the number of stations, even if it meant driving some off the air. Under heavy pressure to act, Congress finally approved the Radio Act of 1927 which President Calvin Coolidge quickly signed. Everybody in broadcasting seemed to be relieved by the Congressional action and there were few complaints about government encroachment on free enterprise.

The Act established the premise that radio is a public domain in which the use of transmitters must be in the best interests of the public. Licenses would be renewed every three years based on the judgment of the Federal Radio Commission (FRC). Despite its high-sounding mission, the five-member bipartisan agency got off to a slow start. President Coolidge nominated the commissioners with dispatch, but Congress approved only three of them before adjournment. Two of those three died before the end of 1928. The new agency had to share space with Hoover's staff in the Commerce Department because Congress did not allocate funds to the Radio Commission for offices or a staff. Amidst its tribulations, however, the agency tackled some of the problems it was established to address. Christopher Sterling and John Kittross wrote in their history of broadcasting that "the commission established important technical, procedural and legal precedents which still stand today. . . . In its seven years, the FRC cleared away the worst of the growth period's interference, established detailed regulations and standards, and made them stick in a series of important court cases."[11]

The Federal Radio Commission was short-lived despite its accomplishments under adverse conditions. Congress never gave it long-term authority, preferring to renew its life from year to year. The agency had to share its authority with the more established Commerce Department and Interstate Commerce Commission. Proposals surfaced to consolidate federal regulation of broadcasting into one agency. Congress finally acted at the behest of Franklin Roosevelt when he assumed the presidency in 1933. The committee which Roosevelt appointed recommended the establishment of a new agency—the Federal Communications Commission.

Broadcasters in 1933 were not as enthralled with the idea of government regulation as they had been six years earlier. The National Association of Broadcasters openly opposed a broadened federal role, but Congress approved the recommendations of the president's task force and the Communications Act of 1934 took effect July 1 of that year. The new law incorporated most of the provisions of the 1927 Act and established the FCC, with seven members appointed by the president for staggered seven-year terms.

Just as Congress was reluctant to enter the realm of broadcasting in the 1920s and 1930s, it pretty much ignored the topic legislatively in the decades to follow. Between 1934 and the mid-1970s, the underpinnings of the law remained unchanged, despite vast technological changes. Many observers such as Van Deerlin had realized that the law had been outpaced by events and inventions, but not even the most severe critics of the 1934 Act had called for a "basement to penthouse rewrite."

If thinkers in the broadcast world had conceived of a rewrite, however, they might have kept the idea to themselves; it surely would have been derided as politically impractical. The perceived power of the broadcast industry, especially the National Association of Broadcasters, was great, and it was the conventional policy within the industry to oppose change. Besides, without any pressure from outsiders to disturb the status quo, Congress had no reason to revamp the 1934 Act. The issues were not compelling and they would have fallen flat back in the home constituencies.[12]

THE GESTATION OF THE REWRITE

So when 1975 began, there was no reason for anyone to believe that a rewrite of the Communications Act was on the horizon. The Senate Communications Subcommittee traditionally took the lead on broadcast issues, but in an interview with *Broadcasting* at the start of the year, Subcommittee counsel Nicholas Zapple said the priorities would be funding for the public broadcasting system, and general oversight of the FCC.[13] Chairman John Pastore favored oversight rather than legislation to bring about change. Until he retired voluntarily in 1976, Pastore had had a stranglehold on broadcasting matters in Congress for two decades. His power was enhanced by his simultaneous chairmanship of the Senate Appropriations Subcommittee with jurisdiction over the FCC budget. Without Pastore's blessing, little could be done.

In the House, Congressman Harley Staggers, a West Virginia Democrat, chaired the Committee on Interstate and Foreign Commerce, the parent of the Communications Subcommittee. Until forced to do so in February 1975 by rebellious colleagues, Staggers had allowed the Subcommittee almost no staff. Without staff to help conceive and carry out the plan, a rewrite would have been unthinkable. At the start of 1975, one of the few Subcommittee staff members was Harry Shooshan III, who had just moved over from the personal office of the chairman, Torbert Macdonald. The Subcommittee also had responsibility for energy matters, and Shooshan said broadcasting would have to take a back seat to the more pressing energy dilemma.[14]

Within just a few weeks, though, things had changed. The House revamped many of its committees and procedures. One of the committees most heavily altered was Interstate and Foreign Commerce. Communications was split from energy, and a new subcommittee with jurisdiction over communications only emerged. Macdonald won the chairmanship of the new subcommittee on an eighteen to ten vote. Ironically, Van Deerlin—who was to announce the rewrite just eighteen months later—chose to leave the Communications Subcommittee to become chairman of a new subcommittee on consumer protection and finance.[15]

Staggers lost his vise grip on the professional staff. Congress was undergoing a change from committee government to subcommittee government. In 1974, the House subcommittee with jurisdiction over broadcasting had one professional staff member and one secretary. Their salaries, paid from the full committee's budget, totaled $44,000. The 1975 budget request for the new subcommittee—with narrower responsibilities—proposed four professionals and two secretaries. The House eventually granted the subcommittee $223,000.[16]

Expansion of the staff did not automatically mean there would be a rewrite of the Communications Act, of course. But the expansion was a necessary condition, even if not a sufficient one. "I don't see how the subcommittee got along before that, with just one professional staff member," Van Deerlin said later.[17] Joseph Fogarty, a member of the Federal Communications Commission after a stint as counsel to the Senate Communications Subcommittee, said he watched "with amazement" as the House staff grew. "Once the staff reaches a certain level, that staff has to do something," Fogarty said.[18]

Broadcasting's editors knew that the expanded staff almost certainly meant more Congressional activity. The editors were not pleased with that prospect, especially given the background of some of the new staff members. In an editorial the magazine said the Subcommittee was "operating with a bloated budget and growing staff, which includes such unpromising members as a protégé of Nicholas Johnson (a former FCC commissioner perceived as anti-industry) and an FCC economist who said revenue from children's programming would not decline if the government cut back commercial content."[19]

Anyone who thought about it would have realized that the House of Representatives was going to take a more active role in broadcasting matters than ever before. Macdonald chose the Communications Subcommittee chairmanship over the more politically attractive energy and power panel because he knew a great deal could be accomplished under the new structure. The Subcommittee's budget justification, drafted in early 1975, said:

The jurisdiction of the subcommittee on communications includes interstate and foreign communications, including all communications by satellite, broadcast, radio, common carrier, interstate communication by wire and such jurisdiction over communications and media as is in the jurisdiction of the full committee. Now that responsibility for energy matters has been shifted to another subcommittee, the subcommittee on communications intends to assume much greater responsibilities than it has in any previous Congress. The subcommittee has already begun a series of overview hearings which will lead to an expanded oversight role, including, for the first time, oversight of the [White House] Office of Telecommunications Policy and other related telecommunications offices.[20]

Nowhere in that ambitious agenda was a rewrite of the 1934 Act mentioned. Shooshan, the Subcommittee's thirty-year-old counsel, had a vague notion at the start of 1975 that sooner or later the law would need reexamination from top to bottom. But it was not until the spring of 1976 that

Shooshan would decide a rewirte could be done all at once, rather than piecemeal.[21]

Meanwhile, Macdonald, apparently at Shooshan's urging, began hinting in mid-1975 that it might be time to stop putting out fires and address the cause of the fires instead. His remarks were barely noticed. *Broadcasting* made a passing reference in the last paragraph of a news story about a bill sponsored by Macdonald to overhaul the structure of the FCC. After discussing the bill, the magazine said Macdonald "indicated that the time is ripe for a re-examination of the entire Communications Act, enacted in 1934. He said the act 'is the product of a time when telecommunications technology was in a relatively primitive stage."[22]

In late 1975 it became clear that the House subcommittee would not have time to do some of the specific things it had set out to do, much less think about an overhaul of the basic law. But two events occurred near the end of the year that would have profound implications in 1976. First, Macdonald and Shooshan agreed that between the Congressional sessions the Subcommittee should perform a study of the cable television industry. Second, Macdonald, whose health had been poor for some time, learned that his condition was worse than he had realized.

The cable television study helped bring home to key Subcommittee staff members that much of the Communications Act was hopelessly out of date.[23] As a result, this phrase appeared in the Subcomittee's 1976 budget justification, drafted by Shooshan: "The subcommittee intends to undertake the redrafting of the Communications Act of 1934." The budget document said that the redraft would probably be a title by title effort, beginning with Title II which related to communications common carriers. Judging by the already mentioned surprise expressed when a sweeping rewrite was announced in August 1976, the phrase in the budget justification went unnoticed, or at least unheeded, by the broadcast industry.

The cable television study led to hearings beginning in May 1976.[24] By then, Macdonald's health had deteriorated so much that he had resigned from the Subcommittee chairmanship and he died soon after. Van Deerlin surrendered the chairmanship of the Consumer Protection and Finance Subcommittee to replace Macdonald. Without question, Van Deerlin's assumption of the new post was another necessary, if not sufficient, condition for a rewrite. Macdonald had been much too ill to tackle anything so massive even if he had been inclined to try.[25]

But the importance of Van Deerlin's ascension went beyond the state of his physical vigor. Because of his professional experience as a broadcaster, his grasp of the issues was perhaps greater than that of any other member of the House. His interest in shaking up the premises by which broadcasting was regulated was intense. Yet almost nobody saw Van Deerlin's switch to the Communications Subcommittee as a harbinger of sweeping change. *Broadcasting* reported that "Van Deerlin said last week his taking over the

chairmanship would not mean the opening of a whole new chapter in communications oversight and legislation."[26]

There were signs for the careful observer that despite Van Deerlin's
statement a "new chapter" was about to be written. Once again, hardly
anybody seemed to notice. One clear sign came on May 17, 1976, the first
day of the Subcommittee's cable television hearings. Van Deerlin did not
hint at a rewrite in his statement opening the hearings, but Louis Frey, Jr.,
of Florida, the Subcommittee's senior Republican, inserted a statement in
the official record in absentia. After noting the need to develop a "national
cable television policy," Frey said, "Of course, developing this policy will
be a tough job, and it may well be that in order to do so, we may have to
think in terms of re-examination of the entire Communications Act."[27]

Frey left the House in 1978 to run for governor of Florida; after losing in
the primary election, he returned to Washington, D.C., to practice law. In
an interview, Frey explained why he decided a comprehensive rewrite was
needed:

I saw an explosion of technology while serving on the House Science and
Technology Committee and also on the Communications Subcommittee, where we
were working with a law that was couched in the language of the 1800s. My
statement in the cable television hearings was my first public statement of something
that had been building in my mind for a long time. It went right by people at first—
the 1934 Act was a sacred cow, and people just didn't allow it to register.[28]

Frey's mention of the rewrite may have been the first—not even Van
Deerlin is sure.[29] But it certainly was not the last. In fact, later that same
day—May 17, 1976—the possibility arose in an interchange between Van
Deerlin and witness Clay Whitehead, who once directed the White House
Office of Telecommunications Policy. During his testimony, Whitehead
said Congress had to act because the 1934 law "is patently obsolete, and
increments to present complex rules in technological jargon is no way to
proceed on so fundamentally important an issue."[30]

Whitehead's testimony set off something in Van Deerlin, prompting the
Subcommittee chairman to pose the following question to Whitehead:

In suggesting that what we ought to be doing is revamping the Communications Act
itself rather than continuing to apply bandaids, you suggest a somewhat wider scope
than even I was laying out at the outset of the hearing. How seriously do you feel
that the Communications Act is limited by, as [former FCC chairman] Dean Burch
mentioned, not even containing the word "television"? Have we tried to follow a
regulatory pattern based on a totally inadequate view of the communications world
as it has developed since 1934?[31]

The cable television hearings ran an additional six days in May, five days
in July, and two days in August before Van Deerlin announced the basement-

to-penthouse rewrite. During those additional days, the concept of revamping the 1934 Act was alluded to a few more times. Probably the most
unequivocal reference came from Donald McGannon, chairman of Westinghouse Broadcasting Company. Testifying on August 5, McGannon
urged the Subcommittee to "embark on a thorough modernization of the
Communications Act of 1934 to meet the needs of these times. This statute,
the embodiment of our country's communications policy, has been in effect
for over forty years without major revision. . . . It simply is not adequate
to lead us into the twenty-first century."[32]

A few moments later, Van Deerlin commented to McGannon, "Trying to
modernize it and bring it into the new era will still leave us with, I suppose,
decisions which are to be bitterly contested as favoring one technique or
another." McGannon responded, "I am not suggesting that this is a noncontroversial suggestion."[33]

Van Deerlin's rewrite announcement came just several days after McGannon's testimony, but to conclude that what Frey, Whitehead, McGannon,
and other speakers said during the cable television hearings had caused the
rewrite announcement would be gross oversimplification. Many forces
were at work simultaneously. As Shooshan said in retrospect, "It's hard to
pinpoint a date that the rewrite began. . . . There are many fathers of the
rewrite."[34]

Alan Pearce, who was a Subcommittee staff member in 1976 and an
assistant to FCC chairman Burch before that, said during an interview that
there were "numerous catalysts" which came together in an opportune way
for the advocates of sweeping change: the creation of a new Subcommittee
in the House at the same time the companion Senate Subcommittee was in
decline due to the retirement of chairman Pastore and counsel Zapple; the
staffing of the House Subcommittee with bright, energetic professionals
who were devoted to a chairman willing to take risks; the technological
changes so obviously outstripping attempts to keep the 1934 Act up to date;
and thorny communications controversies that members of Congress did
not want to deal with piecemeal, or, if they could help it, at all.[35]

The future of cable television was certainly one of those thorny issues.
Another frequently mentioned was the Consumer Communications Reform
Act, more commonly known as the "Bell Bill." The legislation was
introduced in 1976 at the behest of American Telephone and Telegraph in
an attempt to write the phone company's traditional dominance into
statute. The proposed bill "favored a single integrated system free from
marketplace competition, finding that such competition resulted in inefficiencies and was 'contrary to the public interest.' "[36] "The Bell Bill was a
factor in the rewrite coming when it did," Frey said later. "It was such a bad
bill, and I thought, my God, if Bell is going to make such a grab, this will
make it easier to sell the idea of rewriting the entire 1934 Act."[37]

Timothy Wirth, a Subcommittee Democrat from Colorado, stressed the impact of the Bell Bill about a month after Van Deerlin announced the sweeping rewrite. Noting that Bell had found 175 House members to sponsor the measure, Wirth said, "It's either a damn good piece of legislation or somebody is exerting an awful lot of pressure."[38]

The Bell Bill never passed, despite the pressure. Part of the reason was Van Deerlin's rewrite announcement. In effect, Van Deerlin told his colleagues that there was no point voting on the Bell Bill as a separate measure when it would be reviewed as part of a sweeping examination of the 1934 Act. Bell lobbyists were not pleased, believing their bill should take precedence since it had been introduced well before Van Deerlin ever mentioned the word "rewrite."[39]

THE REWRITE IS BORN

Nobody involved in the events leading up to the rewrite can agree on how much weight to assign the various influences, although there is general agreement on what influences to include in the catalogue. What is certain is that during the first week of August 1976, Van Deerlin talked publicly about revamping the Communications Act all at once, rather than title by title in separate proceedings. The announcement was informal, even tentative, and so the primary forum became the lead news story in the August 9 issue of *Broadcasting*. The story said that the cable television hearings "may be just a prelude to an even more ambitious project now in the mind of subcommittee chairman Lionel Van Deerlin—to revise the entire Communications Act." In the story, Van Deerlin used the phrase "basement-to-penthouse" revamping, and added that it would not be easy. "It's a laudatory goal, but that's not to say it can be achieved," said Van Deerlin. "Maybe it would be 1984 before we finished."[40]

The idea was now in the public domain. Today supporters and detractors of the rewrite strategy talk of it as revolutionary, but in August 1976 it was having trouble gaining attention. In an editorial, *Broadcasting* hardly took the effort seriously: "If the Congress really buckles down to a revamping job, it may expect to be deafened by a cacophony of conflicting cries for legislative recognition of this service's desires and that service's problems." Commenting on Van Deerlin's reference to 1984 as a target date, the editorial said, "Perhaps he was thinking of the seven years it took to rewrite the Radio Act of 1927 into the Communications Act of 1934, back when communications were simple."[41]

Planning for the rewrite was feverish inside the House Subcommittee, but was generally ignored until the Subcommittee made it formal in an October 11, 1976, news release headlined "'Basement to Attic' Revamping of Communications Act Ordered by House Subcommittee on Communications." Van Deerlin and Frey were quoted as saying that "we need to go back and take a look at the whole basis of regulation, and see where Congress could improve things by starting anew."

That many people had failed to take the effort seriously until the official news release, was confirmed in a *Broadcasting* editorial the next week. It said

No longer is there any doubt that the House Communications Subcommittee intends to begin in the next Congress the enormous job of rewriting the Communications Act. The subcommittee chairman, Lionel Van Deerlin, and its ranking minority member, Lou Frey, have issued a joint invitation for comments and even drafts of a bill. It is an invitation that must be taken seriously.[42]

By the end of 1976, the rewrite had attracted more interest. A speech by Subcommittee counsel Shooshan drew a sellout crowd at the Federal Communications Bar Association. The increased interest, however, did not signify support. Shooshan said he kept hearing rumors that broadcasters were planning to sabotage the rewrite once its specifics became known. "If everybody spent more time making input and less time going around Washington complaining about who's making input, we'd all be better off," Shooshan told his audience.[43]

The general public never shared the intense interest shown by communications lawyers and broadcast industry lobbyists in Washington. That is partly because the general public received little information about the debate. ABC, CBS, and NBC almost totally ignored the story on their national newscasts. The *Washington Post*, the *New York Times*, and a few other general circulation newspapers with reporters covering the Federal Communications Commission part-time carried occasional pieces about the debate. But those stories were often buried in the business section, or placed in other back pages of the newspaper. Most members of Congress stayed away from the issue—partly because of its complexity, and partly because of their perception that most voters were happy with the status quo. After all, their televisions entertained them and their telephone service was almost always reliable.

THE AFTERMATH

The rewrite had little backing outside the House Communications Subcommittee. It was an effort generated almost solely by a few members of Congress and their staff, timed to take advantage of inexorable outside forces, such as the growth of cable television and the seemingly unchecked power of AT&T. But despite its lack of a constituency, the rewrite effort did not die immediately, as so many observers predicted it would.

After a winter of study, the Subcommittee in April 1977 released about nine hundred pages of "options papers" that outlined new directions for communications policy. In one section, Shooshan wrote:

Despite the widely acknowledged impact of broadcasting on our society, Congress has rarely addressed itself to broadcast policy in a comprehensive fashion, choosing instead to deal with limited areas such as license renewal, political broadcasting or television violence. As a result, broadcast policy has evolved with more guidance from the FCC and the courts than from Congress. Recent court decisions and reversals by the FCC of its own long-standing precedents call into question the wisdom of this evolutionary approach.[44]

After release of the options papers, the Subcommittee heard plenty of reaction, some of it during panel discussions convened by Van Deerlin in July and August 1977. Not surprisingly, almost every special interest group found much to complain about; the status quo was so much more comfortable. But Van Deerlin, Frey, and the Subcommittee staff never lost sight of their goal. In June 1978, they unveiled the rewrite bill, which was given the number H.R.13015.

Although the rewrite was no longer theoretical, passage was anything but assured. Van Deerlin knew from the beginning that no matter what the field, sweeping changes tend to run aground in Congress. Historian Erik Barnouw, an eminent scholar of broadcasting, said he did not plan to study the rewrite bill carefully because he was "sure it wouldn't go through in any form resembling the way it is now. The commercial broadcasters will attack the notion of the fees to support public broadcasting and the media access people will attack everything else. They'll probably both succeed in chipping away at it."[45]

The Communications Subcommittee held hearings in Washington, D.C., and other cities during the last half of 1978, but did not push for immediate passage through the legislative maze. Van Deerlin was prepared to take his time; besides, from a practical standpoint, no rewrite bill had been introduced in the Senate Communications Subcommittee now chaired by Ernest Hollings, a South Carolina Democrat. Without Senate action, no rewrite could become law. The Senate probably would have moved in the same direction as Van Deerlin if it had not been for voters in Indiana. After Pastore announced his retirement, his logical successor as Subcommittee chairman was Vance Hartke, an Indiana Democrat, who had indicated he favored the rewrite approach.[46] But Hartke lost his 1976 bid for re-election in Indiana. Hollings, who got the chairmanship instead, was not an advocate of Van Deerlin's approach.[47]

H.R.13015 found support for some of its sections and opposition for others. The majority of FCC commissioners were more negative than positive.[48] Henry Geller, the chief communications advisor to President Jimmy Carter, was more positive than negative.[49] By the end of 1978, Van Deerlin was saying that the odds had shifted from almost no chance of success to some chance. He promised to introduce a new version in early 1979 "with revisions that we hope will help to build a consensus of support for it."[50]

Before Van Deerlin introduced that new bill, there were stirrings in the Senate. The House rewrite effort was clearly the catalyst for more limited but still substantial legislative efforts. Hollings introduced S.611, which he termed a bill "to modify" the Communications Act of 1934. The same day, Arizona Republican Barry Goldwater, the ranking minority member of the Senate Communications Subcommittee, introduced S.622. The Goldwater bill was similar to Hollings's in most ways, but differed significantly in several sections.[51]

Two weeks later, on March 29,1979, Van Deerlin introduced his "son-of-rewrite," H.R.3333. If he thought the interest groups would forge a consensus based on the new language, he was wrong. By the end of May, he was complaining bitterly about negative lobbyists: "If the song needed a title it would have to be 'Please Fence Me In.' And each refrain is the same, too. It goes 'All I Want Is a Fair Advantage.' "[52]

In July, Van Deerlin convened the Subcommittee to begin perfecting the language of the bill, in the hope of bringing it to a Subcommittee vote before the end of 1979. After one day of mark-up, however, he realized that the sweeping rewrite approach was in grave trouble, even within his own Subcommittee. Van Deerlin halted further mark-up sessions, and in a letter told Subcommittee members that changes in the Communications Act would proceed on a piecemeal basis.[53]

In December 1979, the House Subcommittee began work on another bill, H.R.6121. But it set out to change only the telecommunications sections of the Communications Act. No broadcasting provisions were included. The basement-to-penthouse rewrite was dead. Van Deerlin continued to hope that a rewrite could be accomplished in a number of bills and throughout 1980 he did his best from his post as Subcommittee chairman to act as cheerleader.

But in November 1980, the cheers were quieted. The voters in Van Deerlin's home of San Diego defeated him at the polls. The defeat was an intriguing political story, but it probably had little to do with the Communications Act rewrite. The defeat was partly due to a Republican landslide which helped Van Deerlin's opponent, and also related to Van Deerlin's overconfidence about the security of the House seat he had held for so long. The polls did not show him in trouble, so he did not campaign nearly as vigorously as he might have.[54]

When Congress reorganized in early 1981, the jurisdiction of the House Communications Subcommittee was broadened to take in a variety of non-communications topics. That meant a dilution of emphasis on changing the Communications Act. The new chairman, Colorado Democrat Timothy Wirth, held a briefing shortly after assuming the post in which the word "rewrite" never was mentioned.[55]

SOME TENTATIVE CONCLUSIONS

Each of the six sectors involved in broadcast policy-making played a role in the birth of the rewrite and in its death.

Congress took the lead in the birth of the rewrite and Van Deerlin and

Frey were trying to lead public opinion rather than react to a groundswell of public opinion, but other parts of Congress were resistant, including the key actors in the Senate and many members of Van Deerlin's own Subcommittee. Few members of Congress saw any sense of urgency. After all, tens of millions of Americans watched television every day without complaint, telephones worked better than in almost any other country in the world, and so on. As one Senate staff member said, "It's not like the Clean Air Act, where you know you have dirty air and people are going to die from it."[56]

The FCC did little to support the rewrite. The commissioners publicly opposed some important sections, perhaps fearing loss of the regulatory flexibility they possessed under the 1934 Act. Spurred by the legislative threat, the agency began to take actions that undercut Van Deerlin's calls for reform—deregulation of radio, the use of lotteries to award broadcast licenses, discussion of a spectrum fee imposed on licensees.[57]

Meanwhile, the White House watched from the sidelines. Henry Geller, an assistant secretary of commerce who was perceived as President Carter's chief spokesman on communications issues, found much to like in the rewrite bill, but he was just one voice. Carter as a candidate had talked from time to time about the need to review the 1934 Act, but Carter as president never jumped into the debate himself, reducing Geller's effectiveness.

The courts had some small role in the origin of the rewrite because numerous decisions overturning FCC actions indicated that the law—at least the law as interpreted by the agency—was failing to keep up with the times.

Interest groups in the private sector had little to do with initiating the rewrite, but plenty to do with killing it. Van Deerlin knew he would antagonize the television networks and the National Association of Broadcasters. As he said, "The rewrite gave old, prosperous industries a good elbow in the ribs."[58] He was fully aware that broadcasters wield clout: "I suppose if there are two people in our home communities [congressmen] don't want to offend, it's first the newspaper publishers and second the broadcasters. When we go home to our district, we don't want to be ignored by reporters or by broadcasters. It's our lifeblood. And therefore we tend to listen to these fellows."[59]

All the interests that eventually combined to kill Van Deerlin's specific rewrite bill did not really kill the spirit of the rewrite, however. The fallout from the attempt at a basement-to-penthouse rewrite has not stopped. Respected observers of the broadcast realm agree with observations made by Van Deerlin after he gave up on changing the 1934 Act with one piece of legislation:

The rewrite is more than a bill—thousands of those are introduced in each Congress. To borrow a phrase from business, the rewrite is "something new." But unlike the latest detergent, it's a true original. It represents the first national debate on communications policy in this country. . . . As a long-time observer and participant, I tell you this—things will never be the same again.[60]

NOTES

1. "Square One," *Broadcasting* (July 24, 1978): 114.

2. For a recounting of those attempts, some successful and some not, see the legislative history of broadcast regulation in the "options papers" prepared by the staff of the Subcommittee on Communications, House of Representatives Committee on Interstate and Foreign Commerce. The document is dated May 1977 and designated Committee Print 95-13.

3. Barbara Matusow, "When Push Comes to Shove," *Channels of Communications* (August-September 1981): 39.

4. "Rewrite of Communication Act Serious Subject on Hill," *Broadcasting* (August 9, 1976): 19.

5. Barry Cole and Mal Oettinger, "Covering the Politics of Broadcasting," *Columbia Journalism Review* (November-December 1977): 58-63.

6. Erwin G. Krasnow and Lawrence D. Longley, *The Politics of Broadcast Regulation*, 2d ed. (New York: St. Martin's Press, 1978), pp. 73, 79.

7. This conclusion is my own, but it is backed by many persons who have been participants in the controversy to rewrite the 1934 Act. Krasnow, Longley, and Herbert A. Terry make the same point in the case study of the rewrite included in the third edition of *The Politics of Broadcast Regulation*.

8. As an example of such informed speculation, see Theodore B. Merrill, Jr., "A Slick, Thoughtful Overhaul of the Communications Industry," *Business Week* (July 10, 1978): 86.

9. The six-sector division is borrowed from Krasnow and Longley, *The Politics of Broadcast Regulation*, p. 27.

10. The history of broadcasting is drawn from dozens of books, articles, and monographs. A special debt is owed, however, to the following works: Melvin L. DeFleur and Sandra Ball-Rokeach, *Theories of Mass Communication*, 3d ed. (New York: Longman, 1977); Frank J. Kahn, ed., *Documents of American Broadcasting* (New York: Appleton-Century-Crofts, 1972); Ernest Martin, Jr., *FRC Program Regulation, 1927-34*, Freedom of Information Center Report 218 (Columbia, Mo.: School of Journalism, University of Missouri, April 1969); Christopher H. Sterling and John M. Kittross, *Stay Tuned: A Concise History of Broadcasting* (Belmont, Calif.: Wadsworth, 1978).

11. Sterling and Kittross, *Stay Tuned*, p. 131.

12. For similar views, see, for example, Paul W. MacAvoy, ed., *Deregulation of Cable Television* (Washington, D.C.: American Enterprise Institute for Public Policy Research, 1977) and *Congressional Quarterly Almanac 1977*, "House Panel Considers Major Overhaul of 1934 Communications Act," pp. 563-66.

13. "First Things First," *Broadcasting* (January 20, 1975): 3.

14. Ibid.

15. "Staggers Down One More Peg as Shake-up of Commerce Ends," *Broadcasting* (February 3, 1975): 26.

16. "Bigger Bucks," *Broadcasting* (March 10, 1975): 10.

17. Personal interviews with Lionel Van Deerlin, Washington, D.C.,April 6, 1979, and February 3, 1981.

18. Personal interview with Joseph Fogarty, Washington, D.C., March 20, 1979.

19. "Changing Order," *Broadcasting* (June 16, 1975): 68.

20. From the budget justification in the Subcommittee office, Rayburn Building, Washington, D.C.

21. Personal interview with Harry Shooshan III, Washington, D.C., April 16, 1979.

22. "Macdonald Wants a Tether on FCC, Some Fat Trimming," *Broadcasting* (June 23, 1975): 31-32.

23. U.S. Congress, Committee on Interstate and Foreign Commerce, Subcommittee on Communications, *Staff Report on Cable Television: Promise versus Regulatory Performance*, 94th Congress, 2d sess., 1976.

24. U.S. Congress, Committee on Interstate and Foreign Commerce, Subcommittee on Communications, *Cable Television Regulation Oversight*, 2 vols., 94th Congress, 2d sess., 1976, Serial 94-137, 138.

25. This was verified in a personal interview with Peter Knight, Washington, D.C., March 14, 1979. Knight was Macdonald's administrative assistant before the congressman's death.

26. "Van Deerlin Moves In as Macdonald Steps Down," *Broadcasting* (April 12, 1976): 21-22.

27. See volume 1 of *Cable Television Regulation Oversight*, p. 2.

28. Personal interview with Louis Frey, Jr., Washington, D.C., March 19, 1979.

29. Van Deerlin, personal interview, April 6, 1979.

30. See volume 1 of *Cable Television Regulation Oversight*, p. 18.

31. Ibid., p. 19.

32. See volume 2 of *Cable Television Regulation Oversight*, p. 1182.

33. Ibid., p. 1184.

34. Shooshan, personal interview, April 16, 1979.

35. Telephone interview with Alan Pearce, March 6, 1979.

36. Angele A. Gilroy, *Proposals for Revision of the Communications Act of 1934*, Congressional Research Service Issue Brief IB81150 (Washington, D.C.: Library of Congress, October 1981), p. 1.

37. Frey, personal interview, March 19, 1979.

38. Wirth said this in a speech given to the North American Telephone Association on September 17, 1976.

39. Richard E. Cohen, "Communications May Never Be the Same When Congress Gets Done," *National Journal* (February 5, 1977): 211-13.

40. "Rewrite of Communication Act Serious Subject on Hill," *Broadcasting* (August 9, 1976): 19.

41. "Seven-Year Itch," *Broadcasting* (August 16, 1979): 66.

42. "Main Event," *Broadcasting* (October 18, 1976): 74.

43. "What Happens to Broadcasting if Regulatory Act Is Rewritten?" *Broadcasting* (December 20, 1976): 25-26.

44. Options papers, as cited in note 2.

45. Don Shirley, "The TV Column," *Washington Post*, June 13, 1978.

46. "Rewrite of Communication Act Serious Subject on Hill," *Broadcasting* (August 9, 1976): 19.

47. "Seed of Rewrite May Be Sprouting on Senate Side," *Broadcasting* (October 16, 1978): 22.

48. "FCC Consensus Is Against Key Elements of H.R. 13015," *Broadcasting* (July 24, 1978): 80.

49. "Geller Wants Full Authority over Allocation of Spectrum Space," *Broadcasting* (July 24, 1978): 84.

50. This is quoted from the draft of an article Van Deerlin wrote for publication in the *New York Post*.

51. For Hollings's statement, see *Congressional Record*, March 12, 1979, pp. S-2501 to S-2510. Goldwater's statement is in the same day's *Record*, pp. S-2525 to S-2530.

52. "Rewrite on Reef?" *Television Digest* (May 28, 1979): 1.

53. "Rewrite Written Off," *Broadcasting* (July 16, 1979): 24.

54. This interpretation of Van Deerlin's defeat is mine. It is based on personal interviews, including one with Van Deerlin, February 3, 1981.

55. I attended the briefing, held in the Rayburn Building, Washington, D.C.

56. *Congressional Quarterly Almanac 1977*, "House Panel Considers Major Overhaul of 1934 Communications Act," p. 563.

57. For a discussion of this, see a speech given by Van Deerlin to the International Radio and Television Society on September 13, 1979.

58. Van Deerlin speech to the International Radio and Television Society.

59. Matusow, "When Push Comes to Shove," p. 34.

60. Van Deerlin's speech to the International Radio and Television Society.

5

MICHAEL J. STOIL

The Executive Branch and International Telecommunications Policy: The Case of WARC '79

THE appropriate role of interest groups in democratic policy-making is an emotionally charged issue. Reformers as far back as the early years of this century have maintained that policies can be created by a neutral, dispassionate bureaucracy, guided by legislative direction and armed with hard facts and rational judgment.[1] When policies fail, critics who do not necessarily accept this premise nevertheless often blame the bureaucracy as if this ideal standard were reality: why didn't the bureaucrats foresee the consequences of this decision or that action? An opposing view is illustrated by those who see the bureaucracy as merely another battleground for the conflicting interest groups of democratic, pluralist society.[2] In this perspective, the primary function of government agencies is to provide access to the policy-making process for their client interest groups.

Most of the world's nations strive to maintain a policy-making process for international communications which approximates the "rational bureaucratic" ideal described above. International communications is usually viewed as analogous to national defense in that it falls within the "natural" exclusive jurisdiction of the public sector. International communications policy is therefore usually authored by a select group of technocrats within the national ministry of communications or its equivalent. The policy-making process itself tends to be closed to public scrutiny, and attempts at intervention by representatives of the private sector are viewed as somewhat shady at best, and totally corrupt at worst.

The United States is almost unique among major nations in its explicit rejection of the "rational bureaucratic" model for international communications policy-making. No federal agency is empowered to establish a permanent set of national interests or objectives to be pursued in the field.[3] Instead, the tendency in the United States is to oppose government initiative in international telecommunications policy as inherently antithetical to

American principles, except where national security or a similar goal is at risk. Barry Goldwater, current chairman of the Senate communications subcommittee, expressed this view succinctly in early 1981 when he complained of the activism of the Federal Communications Commission:

The FCC's participation in the planning of international communications facilities has been of concern to me for several years. What initially was an attempt to resolve disagreements over authorization of the TAT-7 submarine cable has become a permanent process involving the FCC in discussions and decisions properly left to those private corporations responsible for providing the capital to construct the facilities, and the provision of service over those facilities.[4]

It is important to recognize that Senator Goldwater did not object to the quality or content of the FCC's intervention in international communication facilities planning. On the contrary, the senator was arguing that any government action beyond the extension of "good offices" to adjudicating disputes between private interests is unwarranted.

Given the prevalence of Senator Goldwater's attitude, it might be expected that the Federal government role in the formulation of international communications policy generally approximates David Truman's model of bureaucracy as a conduit for "client" interests. This expectation is partially fulfilled. The major government role is indeed the collection and reconciliation of the autonomous demands of communication suppliers and users, and public interest groups. As a result, U.S. "national" policy in international communications often takes the form of a shopping list of negotiated objectives advocated by competing interest groups.

Nevertheless, the image of the bureaucracy as a passive conduit for private sector interests is unrealistically limited. First, federal agencies themselves are among the largest U.S. suppliers and users of international telecommunication services. The armed forces, the Voice of America, and the National Oceanic and Atmospheric Administration (NOAA), among other agencies, depend on the availability of highly specialized international telecommunication services to perform their basic missions. Since none of these agencies has a mandate to formulate international telecommunications policy, they approach the policy-making process on equal footing with private sector users and suppliers of such services. In effect, they add their individual demands to the policy positions advocated by private sector interest groups.

Second, as noted by Francis E. Rourke, bureaucrats are often the only source of expertise in relatively obscure policy fields.[5] Some forms of international communications fall into this classification; who, for example, will argue with a twenty-year veteran of the NASA space program insisting that his agency needs an additional allocation of radio frequency spectrum in the bands around 11.5 Ghz to meet the needs of the Space Shuttle's communication systems? A special problem is invoked when Defense Department personnel argue that specific bandwidths are necessary for national security but refuse to explain further on the grounds that the specific projected uses of the radio frequencies are military secrets.

Above all, the methods adopted by the bureaucracy to provide access to the decision-making process constitute the single most important activist role of the federal government in international telecommunications policy. Again, citing Rourke:

One of the historic functions of bureaucracy in American society has been to provide a means of effective expression in policy deliberations for . . . groups that are inarticulate, poorly organized, or for some other reason unable to speak for themselves. With administrative help, these stepchildren of the political system may acquire a political equality with other groups that they could never hope to attain through the ordinary process of politics alone.[6]

The converse of Rourke's statement is that methods for enlisting private sector participation in policy-making may be weighted heavily in favor of the status quo, so that interest groups with inherent influence acquire still more influence. The decisive factor is the structure of the process established by the agency or agencies responsible for collecting and reconciling private sector contributions to policy formulation.

The following observations on policy formulation in preparation for U.S. participation in the 1979 World Administrative Radio Conference (WARC '79) focus on the issue of who becomes involved in international communications policy-making and with what impact. This, in turn, provides insight into how the means developed by the bureaucracy to manage interest group involvement in policy-making shapes the policy formulation process and, indirectly, the policy outcomes of the process.

WARC '79 AS A CASE STUDY IN U.S. POLICY-MAKING

Most international telecommunications policy is formulated within the framework of the Radio Regulations of the International Telecommunications Union (ITU), the fifty-year-old organization charged with promoting efficient transnational communications. The Radio Regulations provide the basis for every use of the radio spectrum, from the operating frequencies of microwave ovens to the orbit assignment of the latest INTELSAT V communications satellite. The World Administrative Radio Conference convened by the ITU in Geneva, Switzerland, in September 1979 was the first full review and revision of the Radio Regulations since the 1950s. Over 1600 delegates from 142 countries attended, making WARC '79 one of the largest international conferences ever held. WARC '79 has also been one of the most thoroughly-studied conferences in recent history. Private scholars, corporate researchers, U.S. delegates, and trade journals have devoted considerable effort to WARC *post mortems,* and the FCC, the State Department, and the congressional Office of Technology Assessment have each produced extensive analyses of U.S. participation in the conference and the impact of the conference decisions on U.S. telecommunications. The openness of U.S. preparations for WARC '79, combined with this wealth of analysis, contributes to the value of the 1979 World Administrative Radio Conference as a case study in U.S. international telecommunications policy formulation.

A second reason for selecting WARC '79 as a case study is its importance to the entirety of U.S. telecommunications and to the future of U.S. participation in the ITU. The WARC Final Acts are expected to guide global development and use of telecommunications into the next century. Adverse actions by the conference could potentially have prevented expansion of AM radio broadcasting in the U.S., delayed development of critical electronic warfare equipment, reduced the effectiveness of the Voice of America, scuttled U.S. proposals for direct broadcasting satellites—in short, placed millions of dollars and years of effort in telecommunications investment at risk. Interest in WARC among suppliers and users of telecommunication services and equipment was understandably high, and participation in U.S. preconference activities was unusually extensive. Such participation was apparently influenced by fear that the Third World nations would use their numerical superiority and the one-nation/one-vote principle of the ITU to dominate the conference. Some commentators warned that radical lesser-developed countries would use the concept of the New World Information Order to rally support against benefits enjoyed by the technically-advanced countries in the existing Radio Regulations. Such concerns, voiced as early as 1974 by FCC Commissioner Robert Lee,[7] gave the U.S. preparatory activities a note of urgency not often found in other discussions of radio spectrum frequency assignments and operational standards.

COMPETITION AMONG THE AGENCIES: DIVVYING UP THE "ACTION"

Bureaucratic authority in Washington is defined in terms of "who's got the Action?"; in other words, which agency is assigned responsibility for the final outcome of the policy-making process. Determining which agency was to effectively have "the Action" was one of the first steps to be addressed in U.S. preparations for WARC '79. It also proved to be one of the most difficult.

Officially, all international communication matters are foreign relations issues and therefore fall under the jurisdiction of the U.S. Department of State. The Office of International Communications Policy (OICP) under the Assistant Secretary of State for Economic and Business Affairs was assigned the formal responsibility for WARC '79 preparations until the president selected an ambassador to assume full responsibility for U.S. participation in the conference. Despite the presence of a handful of extremely well-qualified specialists, it was recognized that the small OICP has neither the budget nor the personnel resources required to actually coordinate U.S. activities for a conference as complex as WARC. Further, the State Department is handicapped in a communications policy-making role by its lack of responsibility for implementation of communications policy. For these reasons, the State Department delegated the major effort of managing interest group involvement in WARC policy-making to other agencies.

WARC preparations began during the Nixon administration's quest for White House control over policy-making,[8] and it was probably inevitable that the White House Office of Telecommunications Policy (OTP) would be extensively involved in WARC preparations. Indeed, OTP was the first federal agency to take the initiative in organizing preparations for U.S. participation in the conference. Since OTP had implementation authority for all ITU decisions affecting federal agencies, it was viewed as the appropriate agency for coordinating federal government proposals for U.S. positions on WARC issues. The abolition of OTP and the transfer of its functions to the National Telecommunications and Information Administration (NTIA) of the U.S. Department of Commerce by President Jimmy Carter did not change this. Under the authority of Executive Order No. 12046, which provides NTIA with ambiguous authority in international communications, the former OTP staff members continued to supervise the collection of federal agency positions on WARC issues from their new offices at NTIA.

The appropriate role for the Federal Communications Commission (FCC) in managing interest group inputs presented the serious problem in divvying up "the Action" for WARC. The State Department and the OTP/NTIA staff viewed the FCC as suitably employed in coordinating private sector participation in U.S. preparations for WARC. A significant group of FCC personnel did not share this view. Commissioner Lee and other FCC officials expected their agency to be responsible for coordinating *all* U.S. proposals for WARC, under general policy guidance from the State Department. They maintained that the FCC and NTIA should share responsibility for managing Federal agency inputs through close collaboration between FCC staff and their NTIA counterparts. As illustrated in Figure 5-1, these differences represented a fundamental disagreement over whether OTP/NTIA enjoyed equal responsibility with the FCC for WARC preparations, or was merely an important source of input into the FCC's policy-making for the conference.[9]

A further potential source of tension between NTIA and the FCC was the identity of the ambassador who would chair the U.S. delegation to Geneva. The FCC staff generally assumed that precedent would be followed and an

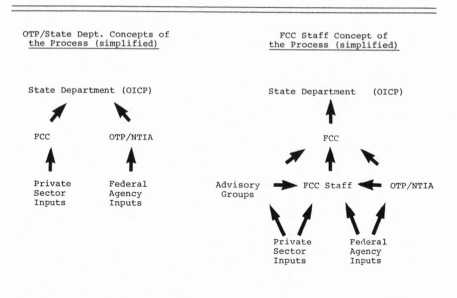

Figure 5-1. Alternative Concepts to the WARC Policy-Making Process

FCC commissioner appointed to chair the delegation. The OTP/NTIA staff preferred one of "their" people to be named. For nearly four years, the U.S. preparations for WARC '79 remained headless while the issue of delegation leadership was stalled. In late 1977, President Carter broke the deadlock by choosing law professor and former FCC Commissioner Glenn Robinson as ambassador-designate, and appointing two officials from each of the three "lead" agencies—the FCC, the State Department, and OTP/NTIA—to serve as vice chairmen. Robinson, who had resigned from the FCC only one year earlier, never completely satisfied the expectations of members of the NTIA staff, who continued to see him as the FCC's candidate and carped about his leadership style. In effect, despite Robinson's attempt at neutrality in interagency disputes, the government members of the U.S. delegation remain divided between pro-Robinson and mildly anti-Robinson cliques, evidently based primarily on their agency affiliation.[10]

The appointment of Ambassador Robinson and the formation of a 20-man "core" delegation chosen from a half-dozen federal agencies in April 1978 did not completely eliminate the tension between the FCC and NTIA. Ambassador Robinson was reluctant to reduce his academic duties and generally accepted the State Department view that the FCC should limit its preconference activities to coordinating private sector inputs into the U.S. positions for WARC. As a result, conflicts between private sector demands,

championed by the FCC, and federal agency demands for spectrum assignment, actively advocated by the NTIA staff, frequently occurred. On more
than one occasion. Ambassador Robinson was flown into Washington for
late night meetings with senior officials of the FCC and NTIA to iron out a
compromise between the private and public sector interests.

Another by-product of the division of responsibility for U.S. preparations
for WARC among several agencies was the relative ease with which the
normal policy-making process was bypassed by determined, influential
interest groups. The Defense Department, for example, succeeded in winning arguments about its own radio frequency needs by withholding vital
supporting data under the cloak of "secret national security requirements."
It was alleged by some disgruntled participants in the policy-making process
that the Defense Department spokesmen themselves had little or no idea
why certain spectrum assignments were required, and used the ploy of
describing the requirements as "classified" merely to hide their own
ignorance.

Perhaps the most spectacular example of successful lobbying outside the
established policy channels occurred when the demand of the Board of
International Broadcasting of the U.S. Information Agency (USIA) for
greatly increased frequency allocation for the Voice of America was rejected
by both NTIA and the FCC. Officials in both agencies and in the State
Department accurately predicted that attempts by the U.S. to obtain more
of the spectrum for Voice of America would be rejected at Geneva as a
blatant attempt by a Great Power to grab more of the scarce high frequency
(HF) radio bands for propaganda dissemination. After failing to win
support for their demands among the agencies responsible for WARC
preparations, officials of the Board of International Broadcasting secured
the aid of Zbigniew Brzezinski, President Carter's national security advisor,
and had their demands inserted into U.S. proposals to WARC over the
heads of Ambassador Robinson and his associates. This circumvention of
the normal policy-making procedure was made possible by the combination
of an interest-based approach to policy advocacy which legitimized the
Board of International Broadcasting's insistence on the incorporation of its
proposals into the U.S. positions for WARC, regardless of their impact on
other U.S. proposals, and Ambassador Robinson's lack of a power base
with which to counter the influence of the President's national security
advisor.[11]

Incidents like the Board's end run were fortunately rare during the final
year of U.S. policy formulation for WARC '79. In general, although the
division of "the Action" among three agencies remained a potential source
of friction within the U.S. delegation to Geneva, the personnel of the
agencies succeeded in developing an effective working relationship. As
noted in Table 5-1, personnel from the State Department, the FCC, and
NTIA eventually constituted nearly half of the delegation membership; a

Table 5-1. Composition of U.S. Delegation to WARC '79 by
Organizational Affiliation

Organizational Affiliation	Number of Delegates	Percent of Delegation
FCC	17	26.5
NTIA and other Commerce Dept.	8	12.0
Department of State	6	9.0
Department of Defense	6	9.0
NASA*	4	6.0
International Communications Agency**	2	3.0
Department of Transportation	2	3.0
National Science Foundation	1	1.5
White House office of Science and Technology Policy	1	1.5
TOTAL FEDERAL GOVERNMENT	48	71.5
Private Corporations:		
COMSAT	3	4.5
AT&T	1	1.5
Hughes Aircraft	1	1.5
Motorola	1	1.5
Rockwell International	1	1.5
Satellite Business Systems	1	1.5
Western Union	1	1.5
Industry Associations	3	4.5
All other (e.g., public interest groups, academics, etc.)	7	10.5
TOTAL PRIVATE SECTOR	19	22.5
TOTAL DELEGATION	67	100.0

*includes private consultants
**includes Board of International Broadcasting

serious rift would have severely hampered the delegation's performance. Instead, Ambassador Robinson was impressed with the dedication of NTIA personnel at Geneva in defense of U.S. positions at WARC, notwithstanding the reservations which NTIA personnel privately expressed about some of the U.S. issue stands and about the make-up of the delegation leadership.[12]

FORMULATING U.S. POSITIONS: THE REWARDS OF PERSISTENCE

The nature and extent of private sector involvement in U.S. preparations for WARC '79 has been a controversial topic among those reviewing U.S. performance at Geneva. Most participants in the process believe that private sector participation was as open as possible and stands out as one of the most successful aspects of the policy-making process. Significant minority views, however, claim that private sector participation was skewed either in favor of industry or in favor of self-designated public interest representatives, depending on whom is making the complaint. A congressional Office of Technology Assessment (OTA) survey of over 150 veterans of preconference planning and preparations is useful in placing these opposing views into appropriate perspective.[13]

Table 5-2 provides an overview of the controversy. A majority of the government respondents to the OTA survey described the federal government's efforts to involve the private sector in WARC preparations as highly effective. Only one government respondent in ten described the efforts as "minimally effective." In contrast, barely a fourth of the private sector respondents were enthusiastic about efforts to broaden participation in WARC preparations, and almost a third of the private sector respondents described such efforts as "minimally effective" or ineffective.

One possible explanation for the discrepancy is the means used by the three lead federal agencies to inform the private sector of the function and schedule of the preconference, policy-formulation activities. According to the OTA survey, the three most important sources of information on WARC preparations in the U.S. were:

- the FCC Notices of Inquiry, published in the *Federal Register*, constituting official invitations to all interested parties to send comments to the FCC on WARC issues and to draft potential U.S. proposals for the conference,

- meetings of government-sponsored advisory bodies such as the FCC Industry Advisory Committee and the U.S. International Radio Consultative Committee (USCCIR), and

- informal consultation with government officials.

Access to all three of these sources presumes that the "interested parties" in the private sector are in the practice of perusing the *Federal Register* or maintaining frequent contact with Washington officials and agencies. Relatively large corporations, such as those who ultimately sent representatives on the U.S. delegation to WARC '79, enjoyed a decided advantage in staying informed of the government's effort to involve the private sector in WARC policy-making because they maintain Washington offices on a full-time basis. Such firms, according to one member of the delegation, "practically slept with the agencies." In contrast, public interest organizations, industry associations, and small firms lacking the resources to maintain constant Washington liaisons often did not learn of WARC-related activities until it was too late for them to participate. The means chosen by the government to inform the "interested" parties in the private sector clearly reinforced the advantages of an existing "old boys' network" during the WARC preparations. This is reflected in part by the relatively large number of private sector participants in the OTA survey who expressed dis-

Table 5–2. OTA Survey Respondents' Evaluation of Overall Effectiveness of
U.S. Efforts to Involve the Private Sector in WARC Preparations
(N = 103)

	Highly* Effective	Effective	Minimally Effective	Ineffective
Government Respondents	55%	35%	10%	--
Private Sector Respondents	26%	42%	30%	2%
Total Respondents	41%	39%	19%	1%

*combines two response categories indicating some degree of superior performance

satisfaction with the federal government's efforts to disseminate information about the U.S. preparations for WARC, as illustrated in Table 5-3.

Although the officials responsible for encouraging private sector participation in U.S. policy-making for WARC acknowledged that reliance on the
use of the *Federal Register* and informal agency-industry contacts delayed
the involvement of "small" players in WARC preparations, many of them
deny that this had a detrimental effect on the pluralist nature of the WARC
policy-making process. A recurrent theme among federal communications
officials is that those industries which maintain the resources and telecommunications expertise to make substantive contributions to the WARC
policy formulation process "know how the game is played" and were therefore involved early in the preparatory process. As one senior Carter
appointee at NTIA explained, "We feel that the information is out there and
you're big boys: go out and get it."[14]

According to this view, members of the private sector who complain that
they learned too late about the U.S. preparations to be fully prepared with
their own proposals for WARC lacked the expertise to make significant
contributions to policy-making or even to understand the issues facing the
U.S. at Geneva. Such views are held to be especially applicable to such
public interest groups as Consumers' Union whose participation was
actively sought by the government; it is frequently said that "public
interest" involvement was unnecessary and ineffective because the "public
interest" representatives did not understand the relationship between
potential changes in the international Radio Regulations and the development of telecommunications in the U.S.[15]

This view is somewhat supported by the qualitative differences between
proposals for U.S. positions submitted to the FCC and NTIA by major
corporations, and those submitted by other domestic interest groups. Such

Table 5–3. OTA Survey Respondents' Evaluation of Government Effort to Disseminate Timely, Accurate, and Detailed Information on WARC Preparations

	Highly* Effective	Effective	Minimally Effective	Ineffective
Government Respondents	40%	45%	15%	--
Private Sector Respondents	22%	39%	37%	2%
Total Respondents (N=101)	32%	41%	26%	1%

*combines two response categories indicating some degree of superior performance

entities as ComSat and AT&T approached the FCC with well-defined concepts of exactly what they wanted to see in the WARC Final Acts. Pouring hundreds of hours of effort into researching and writing proposals for specific changes in the Radio Regulations or in the Table of Frequency Allocations, these firms took great care in justifying their positions from both economic and engineering perspectives. Their representatives at FCC and NTIA deliberations were well-prepared to fight for their proposals and, as a result, generally succeeded in having them included among the final U.S. positions for presentation at Geneva.

The smaller players in the telecommunications field and the public interest groups in general lacked the means and the sophistication to duplicate this level of preparation. Their proposals were often unsupported by engineering data and tended to demand "more" spectrum to be allocated to a specific communications activity wthout specifying how much of what part of the spectrum should be used. One example of this approach was provided by an educational association's proposal that the U.S. support provision of radio frequency and satellite transponders for the purpose of direct communication between teachers in the developed countries and classrooms in the Third World. The association never attempted to document a demand for this type of service, failed to provide any cost data, and never explained why the teachers couldn't simply use telephone, amateur radio, or any other form of cheaper alternative to communication via satellite.

A problem related to the disparity in the sophistication of interest group preparations was the inability of the leadership of groups outside the telecommunications industry to sustain an interest in WARC. One vice president of a major telecommunications trade association, for example, reported that he faced quarterly battles with the ever-changing board of directors over funding for his WARC-related activities. Virtually each of his appearances before the directors required an hour-long lecture on what the WARC Final Acts could mean to the association membership and why his apparently excessive foreign travel was important for liaison on WARC issues with overseas members of the industry. Other interest groups, such as the Girl Scouts of America, dropped out of the process as WARC policy-making became a series of long FCC inquiries, hearings, and negotiations. Participation in the process was simply not cost effective to groups which lacked a major financial interest in the WARC results. In effect, much of the private sector struggle over U.S. positions to be proposed to the conference took the form of a battle of attrition, which rewarded those interests which accepted the costs of merely remaining involved in the process during the three years of sustained preconference activity.

It should be noted that a similar phenomenon occurred among federal agencies with potential interest in the outcome of WARC '79. Harold Kimball, chief of communications and frequency management at NASA, insisted upon his agency's involvement in every phase of WARC preparations. He hired outside contractors to provide support services for NASA's preparatory efforts and traveled as extensively as possible to coordinate his agency's positions with those of the European Space Agency (ESA) and other foreign counterparts. NASA was rewarded with several slots on the U.S. delegation to Geneva and significant support for the NASA proposals from the FCC, NTIA, and the State Department. In contrast, the Agency for International Development (AID) and the Department of Justice—neither of which maintains an office equivalent to Kimball's devoted specifically to telecommunications—quickly lost interest in WARC '79 preparations. As a result, they failed to allocate resources for their staff's participation in the final stages of the policy-making process and were unrepresented on the U.S. delegation.

SIDESHOW: THE PUBLIC ADVISORY COMMITTEE

By mid-April 1978, U.S. preparations for WARC '79 were far advanced. The U.S. delegation had a chairman and a "core" membership of twenty federal officials. More important, the FCC and NTIA were in the final stages of collating and reconciling the various proposals to be placed before WARC that had been advocated by the representatives of the private sector and the federal agencies. Submission of the completed Final Reports defining the U.S. proposals was less than eight months away.

Despite this progress, the State Department was facing two unexpected difficulties in its nominal leadership of the policy-making process. First, members of Congress were placing pressure on the Department and Ambassador Robinson to take a more active role in the preparations. During 1977, the House communications subcommittee had elicited assurances from

Deputy Assistant Secretary of State Joel Biller that his agency was able to draw on expertise outside of the FCC and OTP in shaping international telecommunications policy;[16] as far as WARC '79 was concerned, it had failed to do so. In addition, there were grumblings among some participants in the policy-making process—including such major corporations as Western Union—that they were being effectively frozen out of the key decisions. Their complaints were beginning to attract attention within Congress. In addition, Ambassador Robinson's personal commitment to broad, pluralistic participation in telecommunications policy-making was being frustrated by the impact of attrition on the policy-making process; by the time of his formal appointment, relatively few interest groups outside of the telecommunications industry and the federal agencies remained active in either the FCC hearings or the NTIA activities.

The State Department's response to this situation was the creation of a 38-member Public Advisory Committee comprised of nineteen members from industry and nineteen members from "the general public." The public members, in fact, were drawn from interest groups which the Department believed might have an interest in telecommunications; the principal exceptions to this rule being a handful of astronomers and communications professors selected on the basis of their personal reputation. In selecting the Public Advisory Committee membership, special consideration was given to the inclusion of women and blacks, both from industry and from the public interest groups. As a result of this policy, several individuals—including Sharon Nelson, an attorney with Consumers' Union, and Howard White, a senior vice president of ITT World Communications—were actively recruited onto the Committee despite their previous lack of involvement with WARC issues. Thus, the Public Advisory Committee combined the goals of bringing disaffected interest groups back into the U.S. preparations for WARC '79 and recruiting "minority" involvement in a policy-making process which had been dominated by white males.

The ostensible purpose of the State Department's Public Advisory Committee was to advise the State Department and Ambassador Robinson on all WARC matters and to develop positions and negotiating strategies for the Conference.[17] In fact, the committee could do neither. First convened in midsummer 1978, the committee was organized too late in the process to have any effective voice in the proposals to be submitted to WARC by the U.S. delegation. The committee's membership was divided between technical specialists who thoroughly understood only a very narrow range of WARC issue areas and nontechnical personnel who lacked the expertise to critique the broad range of proposals emerging from the FCC and NTIA preconference activities; most of the committee's time was therefore spent listening, to briefings about what had already been decided elsewhere. Moreover, since the committee membership was recruited on the basis of their ability to reflect societal interests rather than on the basis of being trusted advisors, the members did not receive any information on fall-back positions and strategies to be adopted by the U.S. delegation to Geneva; there was too much danger that a leak by one of the committee members prior to the conference might sabotage the negotiating process. Thus, for all intents and purposes, the committee lacked any real function from the moment it was convened, except to provide evidence that the State Department had tried to involve the public in WARC policy-making and, secondarily, to provide a recruiting ground for potential private sector members of the U.S. delegation to WARC '79.

The Public Advisory Committee illustrates a problem in attempting to democratize the policy-making process in the highly technical field of telecommunications. The Committee fulfilled the ideological objective of "involving" a broad range of public interests in the process through representation of a wide variety of interest groups. Beyond that objective, however, the committee had nothing to do. It is interesting to speculate whether it would have been possible to bestow an effective advisory function on the committee if it had been organized two or three years earlier. Had this occurred, however, it is likely that the committee membership would have suffered the same problem of attrition that appeared in other WARC-related activities. There is little support for a repetition of this type of advisory committee in future U.S. international telecommunications policy-making.[18]

INTEREST GROUPS AND U.S. PERFORMANCE AT GENEVA

As noted in Table 5-4, most informed U.S. observers believe that WARC '79 was basically a successful conference for the United States. Dr. Stephen Lukasik, chief scientist of the FCC, finds particular satisfaction in the fact that the majority of U.S. proposals for "little ticket items" at Geneva— allocations for such esoterica as radioastronomy and amateur radio which were not championed by major organized interests—were adopted by the Conference.[19] In addition, most of the U.S. positions initially advocated by civilian organizations with international ties were also adopted. These include ComSat's advocacy of broadcasting satellite service frequency sharing with U.S. domestic microwave services, and NASA's various proposals for its various space research and earth resources operations. In contrast, the U.S. delegation at Geneva received significant setbacks in championing the proposals of the Department of Defense for increased protection of military radar and mobile satellite services, and the proposals for more than 40 percent increase in HF broadcasting allocation forced upon the U.S. delegation by the Board of International Broadcasting and the President's national security advisor. In effect, those groups which successfully circumvented the policy-making process in the U.S. through "sanctification" of their proposals in the name of national security were

Table 5-4. OTA Survey Respondents' Evaluation of the Impact of WARC '79 on the National Interest and Their Own Organization's Operation

	Conference Results Were Favorable to National Interest	Conference Results Neither Favorable Nor Unfavorable	Conference Results Unfavorable to National Interest
Delegates to WARC '79	79%	10%	12%
Other Respondents	41%	45%	14%
Total Respondents	53%	33%	14%

	Conference Results Were Favorable to Organization's Operations	Conference Results Neither Favorable Nor Unfavorable to Organization	Conference Results Unfavorable to Organization's Operations
Delegates to WARC '79	75%	15%	10%
Other Government Responses	42%	53%	5%
Other Private Sector	41%	30%	29%
Total Respondents	58%	27%	15%

seriously disadvantaged at Geneva, where U.S. national security interests were hardly of paramount concern to the foreign delegations.

One oddity in the U.S. participation at WARC was that very few of the U.S. delegates could actually speak in conference sessions on behalf of their country's positions. A State Department interpretation of a recent federal regulation prohibited delegates employed in the private sector from making any statements on the U.S. proposals, for fear that they would use the opportunity to advance their employer's welfare at the expense of U.S. interests in general. Although the prohibition was lifted by last-minute legislation, the private sector members of the delegation came to Geneva unprepared to take an active role in U.S. negotiations.

The U.S. delegation was further handicapped by the nature of the pre-conference preparatory process. The delegates were committed to strenuously defending all of the U.S. proposals. Any trade-offs to achieve WARC acceptance of one proposal at the expense of another were perceived as an arbitrary "sell-out" of one domestic interest group's hard-fought position in favor of another interest group's equally hard-fought position. Without a coherent policy with which to measure the relative importance of the several hundred proposals submitted by the U.S. to WARC '79, there was no objective means of determining which spectrum allocations could or should be sacrificed in the name of U.S. national interest.

A related problem was the inability of the U.S. delegation to offer anything other than trade-offs in frequency allocations to obtain what it wanted from the conference. As noted earlier, U.S. preparations for WARC focused on domestic interest groups and federal agencies which wanted specific proposals to be made by the U.S. delegation. Groups which did not have demands or issue positions, but which could have offered technical or financial aid to developing countries in exchange for Third World concessions were involved neither in the preconference policy-making process nor in U.S. participation at Geneva. As a result, the U.S. delegation could only verbally support the demands of the developing world for aid in the development of telecommunications capabilities. The isolation of spectrum issues from technical assistance issues within the U.S. hindered U.S. negotiating ability at Geneva.[20]

Much of the success of the conference from the U.S. viewpoint must, in the end, be credited to the U.S. delegates as individuals or as representatives of agencies and interest groups, rather than to the efforts of the delegation as a whole. Ann Aldrich, an attorney recruited as one of the "minority" public interest members of the delegation, provides an excellent example of this. Despite her lack of previous interest in telecommunications, she ably served the U.S. on the WARC committee responsible for drafting the new Radio Regulations where her expertise as a multilingual specialist in legal terminology proved decisive. Similarly, the NASA delegates overcame feared opposition to the LANDSAT remote sensing satellite programs through personal lobbying and the use of a multilingual slide presentation on LANDSAT prepared for WARC by their agency. Through their efforts, all fifty U.S. proposals on LANDSAT were accepted by the conference.[21]

CONCLUSION: A HYBRID MODEL OF POLICY-MAKING

The State Department, as stated earlier, clings to the role of being a disinterested coordinator of the policy-making process in international communications. Although this concept of its role meets the opposition to government activism in policy-making voiced by Senator Goldwater, it places the department in the peculiar position of being responsible for the policy-making process but not the content of the policy. The drawback to this situation is illustrated in the following exchange between Congressman Louis Frey and Deputy Assistant Secretary of State Joel Biller during the 1977 congressional hearings on international communications services:

Mr. Frey: We have no communications policy and we are trying to figure out why not and who is to blame. Is the Secretary [of State] basically to blame?

Mr. Biller: The Secretary is responsible for conduct of foreign affairs. International telecommunications is a part of that.

Mr. Frey: The Secretary of State is responsible for the international telecommunications policies. If we don't like the way they are going, he is the fellow?

Mr. Biller: The ultimate responsibility is with the Secretary. There is a much wider input than the terms of Executive Order 11556 indicate from the [White House] Office of Telecommunications Policy [since transformed into NTIA], from the FCC, in terms of the kind of input that make up policy. . . .

Mr. Frey: If you are responsible you ought to have the wherewithal to do the job. If you don't have the wherewithal to do the job, this is one of the issues you should ask us about. . . . That is part of the problem in this area. Everybody is responsible but nobody really is.[22]

As Biller noted, international telecommunications policy is unlike other foreign policy in which a limited number of federal agencies provide the details for a general policy initiated by Congress and the President. As the policy-making process for WARC '79 illustrates, the details of international communications policy are first provided by interested groups in the public and private sectors and are reconciled through a process in which the State Department plays a very limited role. Frey's summary of the situation is a particularly apt one: the policy-making process diffuses responsibility for the content of international communications policy to the extent that no one entity is truly responsible for more than a small piece of the whole. A "big picture" is absent.

It is important to note that all U.S. foreign policy is not formulated as in the WARC case. Basically, foreign policy divides into crisis and non-crisis, "high" policy (national security, international politics, broad economic issues) and "low" policy (cultural affairs and specific economic issues). In most cases, it is presumed that the executive branch, particularly the White House, the State Department, and the national security agencies, should have the dominant say in "high" policy and crisis policy. There is little, if any, domestic input; Henry Kissinger once said that he had no idea of the U.S. interests that sought a destabilization of Chile in 1970 and, if he had known, he would have ignored them.

U.S. international telecommunications policy fits into none of these convenient pigeonholes. It is "low" policy in the sense that it deals with fairly arcane subjects outside the usual realm of State Department expertise; it is "high" policy in the sense that its impact in the 1980s provides big pay-offs for a large number of powerful domestic actors. It is therefore, in foreign policy terms, a highly atypical policy area.

This does not mean that there are *no* policy areas which appear similar to international telecommunications policy. Domestic telephony, domestic satellites, monetary policy, and—to a certain extent—domestic energy policy appear to exhibit similar traits. In each case, the stakes are high for a number of powerful private sector players *and* for a number of weak "public interest group" players. The subject matter in each case is highly technical and requires mastery of a specialized policy-making process in order to achieve influence. The government tries, and usually fails, to recruit some sort of voice for the "national interest," but in the end the big boys usually get what they want because they have the expertise and resources to dominate the process.

The lack of an overall government-determined U.S. policy on international communications does not mean that all interests involved in the policy-making process compete on an equal basis. WARC '79 illustrates that only a relatively small number of federal agencies and private sector entities have the will, interest, and resources to sustain a high level of activity in the policy-making process. Groups which lack one or more of these traits are disadvantaged, in part because they are outside of the informal relationships among the community of Washington-based international telecommunication specialists which play a major role in shaping the policies. The attempt to make policy-making more representative for WARC '79, through the formation of a Public Advisory Committee, cannot be considered a success.

In summary, international telecommunications policy in the U.S. is neither the product of a neutral, dispassionate bureaucracy nor the result of conflict between interest groups on a "neutral" battleground provided by the agencies. Federal agencies requiring telecommunication services for fulfillment of their statutory missions cannot be idle spectators in a policy-making process whose outcome will directly affect their operations. The FCC, the State Department, and NTIA have attempted to retain their own neutrality as the lead agencies of the policy-making process, but they have not succeeded. Some federal agencies, notably the Department of Defense and NASA, clearly benefit from the "neutral" policy-making processes devised by these lead agencies as do some private sector groups; other governmental and corporate entities, including many of the largest communication firms and industry associations, do not share these benefits. Nevertheless, the most-often mentioned alternative to the present approach would be to cast some federal agency in the role of national ombudsman for international communications policy—a form of bureaucratic monarchy repugnant to the American tradition of policy formulation.

NOTES

1. This is basically the core thesis in Max Weber's concept of the virtues of bureaucratic administration. See, for example, H. H. Gerth and C. W. Mills, *From Max Weber* (New York: Oxford Press, 1946).

2. See especially David B. Truman, *The Governmental Process* (New York: Alfred A. Knopf, 1951).

3. Walter R. Hinchman, "Telecommunications Law for the Eighties" (Address delivered at meeting of the Federal Bar Association, Washington, D.C., May 12, 1981).

4. Remarks before the Senate Subcommittee on Communications, February 18, 1981, as reported in *Telecommunications Reports* 47:8, 21.

5. Francis E. Rourke, *Bureaucracy, Politics, and Public Policy*, 2d ed. (Boston: Little, Brown, 1976), pp. 14-16.

6. Rourke, *Bureaucracy, Politics, and Public Policy*, p. 3.

7. Remarks of Commissioner Lee before the International Radio and Television Society, Inc., Americana Hotel, New York City, November 13, 1974.

8. See, for example, Richard P. Nathan, *The Plot that Failed: Nixon and the Administrative Presidency* (New York: John Wiley & Sons, 1975).

9. Interviews obtained by the author in preparing his contributions to U.S. Office of Technology Assessment, *Radiofrequency Use and Management* (Washington, D.C.: U.S. Congress, January 1982). These figures represent a distillation of the individual comments made by State Department, NTIA, and FCC personnel, rather than formal models of the process.

10. Ibid.

11. Ibid.

12. Interview with Ambassador Robinson, Charlottesville, Va., January 1981.

13. The full survey results are contained in *Radiofrequency Use*, Office of Technology Assessment, Appendix A.

14. Interview with Henry Geller, former Assistant Secretary of Commerce, Washington, D.C., January 1981.

15. This was a recurrent comment in the interviews obtained in preparation for the OTA study.

16. Hearings before the House Subcommittee on Communications on "The Need for an Improved and Expanded System of International Telecommunications," Serial No. 95-96 (March 22, 1977): 336-37.

17. "Report of the Chairman of the U.S. Delegation to the World Administrative

Radio Conference of the International Telecommunications Union," TD Serial No. 116 (Washington, D.C.: Department of State, undated), p. 6.

18. Interviews obtained in preparation for the OTA study.

19. Stephen J. Lukasik, "The 1979 WARC—Its Results and Subsequent FCC Actions," unpublished manuscript, December 1980.

20. See, for example, David E. Honig, "Lessons for the 1999 WARC," *Journal of Communications* 30:2 (Spring 1980): 48-58.

21. Office of Technology Assessment, *Radiofrequency Use*, p. 120.

22. Hearings, see note 16 (March 22, 1977): 329-30.

6

JON S. CRANE

Issues of Public Interest Regulation in Supreme Court Decisions: 1927-1979

THE debate over exactly what constitutes public interest in broadcast regulation is as old as the regulation of broadcasting itself. With the inclusion of the principle of public interest in the Radio Act of 1927 and the Communications Act of 1934, this regulatory standard has been the source of the "greatest rancor that most FCC attempts to regulate . . . have encountered from representatives of the . . . industry."[1] This rancor is due, in part, to the fact that public interest remains a largely undefined construct, except on a case by case basis. A key factor in this issue, according to Erwin G. Krasnow and Lawrence D. Longley, is vagueness of the term "public interest" in the original mandate from Congress to the Federal Radio Commission (later the Federal Communications Commission).[2] A plastic standard may have been desirable fifty years ago given the developing technology of radio and the lack of precedent in regulating the infant industry of the 1920s and 1930s. However, criticism has been leveled over the years that continuing to operate under a vague standard eliminates the possibility of predicting the outcome of cases which go before the commission.[3]

Also, Krasnow and Longley have argued that a vague standard in broadcast regulation has deterred the development of any coherent public policy because the legislative branch is free to state, "That is now what *we* meant by the public interest,"[4] thus leaving public interest open to many interpretations. Scholarship in the area, the authors argue further, has done little to add any real knowledge to the application of public interest for the regulation of public policy.[5] Nowhere was an attempt made to define exactly what they meant by the concept. It was left up to the commission and the courts to define it by application over the years.

From its inception public interest was not considered a "monolithic con-

This research was supported, in part, by a grant from the National Association of Broadcasters.

cept,"[6] in other words, it should be a flexible standard to meet changing times and new developments in the industry. Louis G. Caldwell, writing in 1930, said that only an "indefinite and very elastic standard should be prescribed"[7] due to the developing nature of the technology. He noted further that the standard of public interest had about as little meaning as any phrase the writers of the Radio Act could have used and still have fulfilled the constitutional need to provide the administrative agency with some regulatory guideline.[8]

Historically, the meaning of public interest has been used for political purposes by the White House, the courts, the FCC itself, and the Congress, as well as broadcasters and their audiences. All have played significant roles in the "interpretation, implementation and modification"[9] of broadcast regulation.

Part of the problem for scholarship in this area is the sheer volume of written evidence which contains applications of public interest to broadcast issues. Millions of words have come from the Federal Communications Commission, the local, state, and federal courts, and the United States Supreme Court. To understand the various interpretations of public interest, evidence was examined over time to discover those broadcasting and regulation issues to which public interest has applied. This research examined the decisions in broadcasting handed down by the United States Supreme Court between 1930, the first broadcasting decision, and 1979. There have been only 29 decisions relating to broadcasting and the public interest throughout the history of regulation. The issues were identified to which the high court has applied public interest in its decision-making process. They were chosen because, first of all, the decisions are a complete, yet manageable body of evidence. Second, these decisions include the issues and debate of earlier FCC and/or lower court decisions. And, finally, as Judge H. L. Friendly, among others, has pointed out, the Court offers the opportunity to examine concepts of law because beyond a delineation of what it is doing and the uniform application of any new rule forced, it usually sticks to this application "for a considerable period."[10] The Federal Radio Commission noted in 1928 that public interest had to be defined by the United States Supreme Court and that it should be done by a gradual process of decisions on particular combinations of facts.[11]

Thus, this research considers the following questions: (1) What were the issues in broadcasting to which the Supreme Court has applied public interest? (2) What were the relative weights of those issues over time? (3) What other issue or issues were concomitantly related when the Court addressed one issue of public interest?

METHOD

The following list represents the twenty-nine broadcast cases in which public interest was employed. A broadcast case was defined as one in which the broadcast (or cable) activities, actual or proposed, by one of the parties in standing was at issue. To be included in the corpus of evidence, the case had to include the term, "public interest," or some synonym thereof. The context of all occurrences of the term "public interest," or its synonyms were identified by the use of research assistants. A pre-test determined that in 90 percent or better of the cases, the complete context of the phrase could be established by counting fifty words ahead of the occurrence and fifty words back from the occurrence. This was done for all twenty-nine decisions. Cases in which citations of the term "public interest" contained no comment about the "public interest" itself were discarded. The resulting body of constructs of public interest totaled 189.

The next task was to identify in these constructs, the issues to which the Court had applied public interest in its decision-making process. This was done by an examination of each of the constructs generated by the method above. Judgments on these issues were made using a form of contingency analysis discussed by Ole R. Holsti which argues that a criterion word, in this case, "public interest," can take meaning from a set of index words which are semantically related to it.[12] Thus, if one construct read, " . . . interference is not in the public interest . . . ," it was interpreted that "interference" is one issue of the public interest. From this, it can also be inferred that the larger issue of interference-free airwaves serves and promotes the public interest. The thirty issues of public interest that were identified from the 189 constructs are given in the following listing. The issues were analyzed by frequency of occurrence per year of a decision. These were treated as ordinal data because it was judged that the frequency could only be construed to be the relative amount of attention given to an issue. In other words, though the Court may have used a given index term fifteen times, for example, in 1945 and thirty times in 1963, it cannot be inferred that the issue was twice as important to the Court in 1963 as in 1945. The frequencies best represent the relative attention given by the Court in applications of the public interest in a single year.

TABLE OF CASES

Chronology of Supreme Court Broadcast Decisions Applying the Public Interest Standard

Federal Radio Commission v. General Electric Co., 281 U.S. 461 (1930)

Federal Radio Commission v. Nelson Bros. Bond & Mortgage, 289 U.S. 266 (1933)

Federal Communications Commission v. Pottsville Broadcasting Co., 309 U.S. 124 (1940)

Federal Communications Commission v. Sanders Bros. Radio Station, 309 U.S. 470 (1940)

Federal Communications Commission v. Columbia Broadcasting System of California, Inc., 311 U.S. 132 (1940)

Scripps-Howard Radio, Inc. v. Federal Communications Commission, 316 U.S. 4 (1942)

Columbia Broadcasting System, Inc. v. United States, 316 U.S. 407 (1942)

National Broadcasting Company v. United States, 319 U.S. 190
          (1943)
Federal Communications Commission v. National Broadcasting Co.,
          Inc. (KOA), 319 U.S. 239 (1943)
Radio Station WOW, Inc. v. Johnson, 326 U.S. 120 (1945)
Ashbacker Radio Corporation v. Federal Communications
          Commission, 326 U.S. 327 (1945)
Federal Communications Commission v. KOKO, Inc., 329 U.S. 223
          (1946)
United States v. Petrillo, 332 U.S. 1 (1947)
Federal Communications Commission v. WJR, The Good Will
          Station, 337 U.S. 265 (1949)
Regents of the University System of Georgia v. Carroll, 338
          U.S. 586 (1949)
Radio Corporation of America v. United States, 341 U.S. 412
          (1951)
Federal Communications Commission v. Allentown Broadcasting
          Corp., 349 U.S. 358 (1955)
United States v. Storer Broadcasting Co., 351 U.S. 192 (1956)
Farmers Educational and Cooperative Union of America, North
          Dakota Division v. WDAY, Inc., 360 U.S. 525 (1959)
Head v. New Mexico Board of Examiners in Optometry, 374 U.S.
          424 (1963)
Federal Communications Commission v. Schreiber, 381 U.S. 279
          (1965)
United States v. Southwestern Cable Co., 392 U.S. 157 (1968)
Red Lion Broadcasting Co. v. Federal Communications Commission,
          395 U.S. 367 (1969)
United States v. Midwest Video Corp., 406 U.S. 649 (1972)
Columbia Broadcasting System, Inc. v. Democratic National
          Committee, 412 U.S. 94 (1973)
National Cable Television Association, Inc. v. United States,
          415 U.S. 336 (1974)
Federal Communications Commission v. National Citizens
          Committee for Broadcasting, 98 S. Ct. 2996 (1978)
Federal Communications Commission v. Pacifica Foundation, 98
          S. Ct. 3026 (1978)

ISSUES OF PUBLIC INTEREST

Upper-case abbreviations proceeding each issue are used subsequently to
express that issue in the analysis.

ADV	Advertising
ANT	Antitrust policy; antitrust violation; unfair methods competition
APP	Application process; application; applicant; standards for application
BRD	Broadcaster or licensee; duties and obligations thereof; rights thereof; accountability of the broadcaster; performance of the broadcaster
BUS	Business interest of the broadcaster or licensee; financial interests
CATV	Cable television; cable television operators
CB	Chain broadcasting; networking; the networks
CMP	Competition (economic)
CPA	Competing applications
ECINJ	Economic injury; financial hardship
FA	First Amendment
FCC	Federal Communications Commission; power and authority thereof; duties and responsibilities thereof
FD	Fairness Doctrine; fairness in broadcasting; equal time; personal attack rule; equal access of views
FREQ	Efficient and effective use of a broadcast frequency
HEAR	Hearing before the Commission; requirements and rights thereof; the hearing process

```
INF      Interference (electrical)
LIC      Licensing process
MOD      Modification process; modification of a license
OBS      Obscenity
OWN      Multiple ownership; cross-ownership; diversification
         of ownership
PO       Private ownership of broadcast stations; property
         right's questions
PRG      Programming; content (other than advertising)
PVP      Private v. public rights and interests in broad-
         casting; public rights v. the interests of private
         enterprise
QUAL     Qualifications of a proposed or existing licensee;
         financial qualifications
SCAR     Scarcity doctrine; limited frequency and channel
         availability
SER      Service; public service; the most effective service
         to the viewing/listening public
STA      Standing before the Commission; grounds for standing
SUBJL    The broadcaster or operation as subject to local,
         state, and/or federal laws other than broadcast
         status
TECH     Technical aspects of broadcasting; the color
         television standard
VR       Rights of the viewer as an individual; the viewer
         as an individual or group (as opposed to "the
         public")
```

Second, a weighted mean was calculated for that court term in that year from the frequencies. This was done by dividing the frequencies by the total number of index terms identified (30). The weighted mean then became a standardized indication of the relative amount of attention an issue received in a given year. Thus, the larger the weighted mean, the greater the attention given by the Court to that issue.

Third, L. L. McQuitty's factor-approximation technique was employed to examine the relationship between two or more issues.[13] The technique starts with the generation of a square correlation matrix based on point-biserial correlations using the presence or absence of an issue in a single year (regardless of its weighted mean). Once generated, the matrix was examined for the largest single correlation between any two items (see Table 6-1 for the diagonal matrix). The next step was to identify items which were significantly correlated with one or the other items in the original pair. As each item was selected, it was removed from the matrix. This was done until all items significantly related to the original pair were identified and removed. The next step was to find the next largest correlation of remaining items and repeat the process until all significant pairs had been removed.

It was decided to set the *alpha* level at .10 for the acceptance of a coefficient rather than the traditional .05 level of confidence, because of the nature of the data (ordinal) which does not represent true proportional relationships between the items. What was of interest was the pattern of relationships and not the specific point-biserial coefficients themselves. It was felt that too strict a level of acceptance might fail to reveal these patterns given the relatively small number of issues under investigation.

Table 6-1. Correlation Matrix

	ADV	ANT	BUS	BRD	CATV	CB	CPA	CMP	ECINJ	FD	FA	FCC	FREQ	HEAR	INF	LIC	OBS	OWN	PRG	PVP	QUAL	SCAR	SER	STA	SUBJL	TECH	MOD	VR	APP	PO
ADV	1.0	.27	.03	.21	-.14	.25	-.16	-.19	.19	.44	.25	.07	-.14	-.19	-.11	.21	-.07	-.11	.50	.25	.06	.10	-.06	.25	.33	-.19	-.14	.10	.03	.44
ANT		1.0	.46	.27	-.17	.14	-.21	.40	.08	-.14	.49	.09	.21	.08	.44	-.03	.54	.32	.64	.14	.22	.27	.05	.14	.21	.08	.21	.27	-.18	-.14
BUS			1.0	.59	-.09	.30	.05	.17	.17	.03	.30	.20	-.09	.17	.36	.15	.25	.03	.50	.55	.08	.38	.32	.55	.18	-.05	.46	.17	.19	.36
BRD				1.0	.27	.32	.32	.12	.21	.21	.32	.35	-.34	-.11	.21	.04	.15	-.14	.42	.32	.08	.25	.35	.32	.27	-.38	.27	.25	.15	.21
CATV					1.0	.27	.14	.12	.27	-.18	-.21	.09	-.17	-.24	-.14	-.33	-.09	-.14	.03	-.21	-.05	-.01	.34	-.21	-.17	.08	-.17	-.01	-.38	-.14
CB						1.0	.14	-.24	0	-.16	.06	.11	.14	.14	.25	.32	-.11	-.16	.49	.37	.35	.15	.15	.37	.14	.28	.14	-.10	.30	-.16
CPA							1.0	0	-.29	.25	.05	.11	-.21	0	-.16	.32	-.11	-.16	-.05	-.25	.10	.15	.15	-.25	.14	0	.14	.15	.05	-.16
CMP								1.0	.47	.19	.57	.13	.08	.20	.58	.12	.39	.19	.12	.29	.23	.54	.47	.28	-.24	.20	.40	.30	.17	.58
ECINJ									1.0	.19	.28	.13	.08	.20	.57	-.12	-.13	-.19	.14	.57	0	.30	.47	.57	-.24	.20	.40	.30	-.05	.44
FD										1.0	.67	.07	-.14	-.19	-.11	.21	-.07	-.11	.14	.25	-.27	.45	.27	.25	-.14	-.19	-.14	.45	-.30	.25
FA											1.0	.11	.14	0	.25	.33	.45	.25	.49	.37	.10	.68	.40	.37	-.21	0	.14	.68	.05	.25
FCC												1.0	-.54	.13	.07	-.15	.05	.07	.15	.11	-.28	-.31	.28	.11	.09	.13	.09	.16	-.25	.07
FREQ													1.0	.08	.32	.27	-.09	-.14	.03	.14	.22	.27	.05	.14	-.17	.40	.21	-.01	.18	-.14
HEAR														1.0	.57	.12	-.13	.19	-.12	.29	.23	.06	0	.29	.08	.20	.73	.30	.40	.19
INF															1.0	.21	-.07	-.11	.14	.67	.40	.45	.27	.67	-.14	.19	.79	.10	.36	.44

	LIC	OBS	OWN	PRG	PVP	QUAL	SCAR	SER	STA	SUBJL	TECH	MOD	VR	APP	PO
LIC	1.0	.15	.21	.19	.33	.53	.48	.13	.33	-.03	.12	.27	.25	.59	.21
OBS		1.0	.69	.35	-.11	.28	.31	.18	-.11	-.09	-.13	-.09	.31	.25	-.07
OWN			1.0	.14	-.16	-.40	.10	-.06	-.16	-.14	.19	-.14	.46	.36	-.11
PRG				1.0	.21	.36	.43	.08	.21	.34	.12	.03	.20	.06	.14
PVP					1.0	.10	.47	.42	.41	-.21	0	.49	.15	.30	.67
QUAL						1.0	.38	-.16	-.10	-.05	.23	.22	.04	.70	.06
SCAR							1.0	.38	.42	-.31	.06	.27	.34	.17	.45
SER								1.0	.41	-.22	.23	.34	.38	-.08	.07
STA									1.0	-.21	0	.49	.15	.30	.67
SUBJL										1.0	-.24	.21	-.01	.18	-.14
TECH											1.0	.08	.06	-.05	-.19
MOD												1.0	.27	.46	.33
VR													1.0	.17	.10
APP														1.0	.03
PO															1.0

RESULTS

Relative Weights of the Issues

Table 6-2 indicates the relative attention given to an issue in a given year. An examination of this table revealed that the means vary from as small as .03 (one occurrence) to as large as 1.13 (34 occurrences) in any given year. Two distinct eras of activity emerge when relative weights are summed over the years. If a cut-off point of .17 (five occurrences) or larger as a factor of relatively high attention to any one issue is used, the two most active eras of the Court are determined to be between 1940 and 1946 and then again between 1968 and 1978. This decision to break the activity of the Court into two separate eras may seem arbitrary at first but it becomes clearer when the nature of the issues receiving attention is known.

The period between 1940 and 1946 appears to be an era when the Court gave most of its attention to questions of power, authority, and functions of the FCC in terms of the broadcaster and his interests. If weighted means of .17 or higher are collapsed across this period, the following pattern occurs:

FCC	1.95
LIC	1.70
BRD	1.13
CB	.70
APP	.60
SER	.27
ECINJ	.20
INF	.20
STA	.17

In the terms of the public interest, the three issues that received the greatest amount of attention from the Court were the power and authority of the Commission to regulate broadcasting (FCC), the duty and obligations of the licensee (BRD), and the licensing process itself (LIC). This pattern may be better understood in light of Marver H. Bernstein's discussion of the life cycle of regulatory commissions. After a period of "gestation,"[14] in which the idea of a regulatory statute arises from a distressed sector of industry due to problems of self-regulation, there results a statute enacted by the government to address an acute public problem (one need only remember the era of chaos in radio broadcasting during the early 1920s). After the creation of the statute and appropriate government regulatory agency, that agency, according to Bernstein, enters its "youthful" phase.[15] In this phase the agency tries to establish its powers vis-à-vis an already established industry full of special interests. In doing so, Bernstein noted that the agency soon discovers that it can accomplish little until the Supreme Court has passed on the validity and constitutionality of its powers and authority. . . . Litigation forms the framework for the regulatory process until the courts have issued an authoritative decision or series of decisions outlining the legal scope of regulatory powers.[16]

Thus it is quite natural, according to this reasoning, that both the commission and the broadcasters would attempt to explore the boundaries of each one's rights and obligations. The fact that issues of interference (INF), standing (STA), and the application process (APP), as well as service responsibility (SER), and economic injury (ECINJ) appeared, reinforces this line of reasoning. These issues can be interpreted as aspects of the FCC's authority in granting and maintaining licenses. This particular era of Court activity could best be termed an era in which the constitutional parameters of the commission's powers were being tested and defined by the Court.

To one who is familiar with the nature of the cases heard during the period, it should not be surprising to see the issue of chain broadcasting (CB) appearing before the Court as a major issue of public interest. Two important network cases were decided between 1942 and 1943.[17] However, it must be remembered that in both cases, *Columbia Broadcasting System* and *National Broadcasting Co.*, the issue was one of the obligation of the individual licensee being able to provide the best possible service to his listening audience. It was felt by the commission, and subsequently upheld by the Court, that certain relationships between the licensee and the networks prevented him from discharging his public interest responsibilities.

In contrast to this era, the next heaviest period of Court activity was between 1968 and 1978. In this period, the Court gave much of its attention to social questions of public interest. It should not be surprising when one remembers that from the mid-1960s through the 1970s, the social conscience of America changed in terms of anti-war activities and rights of individuals and groups within society. It was also the age of consumer consciousness and political activism.

Using the same method of collapsing weighted means across the period from 1968 to 1978, the following pattern emerged:

BRD	243
FA	1.30
FCC	1.30
FD	1.27
CATV	.57
VR	.27
PVP	.23

These data reveal that the public interest statute was applied to issues of the broadcaster's duties and obligations (BRD) in the area of the Fairness

Table 6-2. Relative Weighted Means of Index Terms Across Years
of Decisions

	1930	1933	1940	1942	1943	1945	1946	1947	1949	1950
ADV	-	-	-	-	-	-	-	-	-	-
ANT	-	-	-	-	.27	-	-	-	-	-
APP	.03	-	.17	.03	.43	.20	.10	-	-	.13
BRD	-	-	.27	.33	.33	.20	.07	.03	-	-
BUS	-	-	.03	.03	.33	.03	-	.03	-	-
CATV	-	-	-	-	-	-	-	-	-	-
CB	-	-	-	.20	.50	-	-	-	-	-
CPA	-	-	-	-	-	.07	.03	-	-	-
CMP	-	-	.10	-	.03	-	-	-	-	-
ECINJ	-	-	.03	0	.20	-	-	-	-	-
FA	-	-	-	-	.07	-	-	-	-	-
FCC	.03	.03	.33	.23	.90	.46	.10	.03	.03	-
FD	-	-	-	-	-	-	-	-	-	-
FREQ	-	.03	-	-	.10	-	-	-	-	.03
HEAR	.03	-	.03	-	.03	.13	-	-	-	-
INF	-	-	.03	-	.20	-	-	-	-	-
LIC	-	.03	.30	.17	.70	.53	.13	-	.03	.07
MOD	-	-	.03	-	.10	.07	-	-	-	-
OBS	-	-	-	-	-	-	-	-	-	-
OWN	-	-	-	-	-	-	-	-	-	-
PO	-	-	.03	-	-	-	-	-	-	-
PRG	-	-	-	-	.03	-	-	-	-	-
PVP	-	-	.07	.07	.07	-	-	-	-	-
QUAL	-	-	.03	-	.07	-	.07	-	-	.07
SCAR	-	-	.03	-	.03	-	-	-	-	.03
SER	-	.07	.10	.10	.27	.03	-	-	-	-
STA	-	-	.03	.10	.17	-	-	-	-	-
SUBJL	-	-	-	-	-	.20	-	-	-	-
TECH	-	.03	-	-	.07	-	-	-	-	-
VR	-	-	-	-	.03	.03	-	-	-	-

1951	1956	1959	1963	1965	1968	1969	1972	1973	1974	1978
-	-	-	.13	-	-	-	-	.43	-	-
-	-	.10	-	-	-	-	-	-	-	.10
-	.03	-	.03	-	-	-	-	-	-	.07
-	-	.10	.07	-	.07	.80	.27	1.18	.03	.23
-	-	.10	-	-	-	-	.03	.03	-	.07
-	-	-	-	-	.20	-	.37	-	.10	.04
-	-	-	.03	-	-	-	.03	-	-	-
-	-	-	-	-	-	.03	.03	-	-	-
.10	-	-	-	-	-	.03	-	-	-	.03
.03	-	-	-	-	.03	-	-	.03	-	-
-	-	-	-	-	-	.33	-	.80	-	.17
.10	.17	.03	.10	.03	.07	.47	.13	.50	.07	.33
-	-	-	-	-	-	.50	-	.77	-	-
-	-	-	-	-	-	-	-	-	-	-
-	.10	-	-	.03	-	-	-	-	-	-
-	-	-	-	-	-	-	-	-	-	-
-	.07	-	.07	-	-	.07	.07	.07	-	.43
-	-	-	-	-	-	-	-	-	-	-
-	-	-	-	-	-	-	-	-	-	.07
-	.10	-	-	-	-	-	-	-	-	.37
-	-	-	-	-	-	-	-	.13	-	-
-	-	.03	.03	-	-	-	.10	.10	-	-
-	-	-	-	-	-	-	-	.23	-	-
-	.03	-	.03	-	-	-	.03	-	-	.03
-	-	-	-	-	-	.13	.07	.13	-	.03
.03	-	-	-	-	.03	.03	.13	.03	.03	.20
-	-	-	-	-	-	-	-	.03	-	-
-	-	.07	.10	-	-	-	-	-	-	-
.13	.03	-	-	-	-	-	.03	-	-	-
-	.03	-	-	-	.13	.10	-	.27	-	.03

Doctrine (FD) as well as the FCC's role in ensuring the rights of all parties concerned when individual cases during this era are consulted. It was, of course, the era which saw *Red Lion*[18] and *The Democratic National Committee*[19] go before the Court with issues of fairness and free speech (FA). This could best be described as an era of social regulation as opposed to issues affecting the parameters of the commission's powers vis-à-vis the rights of broadcasters which dominated the earlier period. These issues also included attention to the rights of the viewers as individuals or groups (VR) and the conflict of those rights with the business interests of the licensee (PVP).

This was also an era which saw the growth and expansion of the cable television industry (CATV) and thus both the industry and the commission sought to find the parameters of responsibility and rights in this arena.

Relationship Between Issues

The examination of issues presented above can provide little more than a relative ranking of issues during periods of Court activity. Additional information comes from the factor-approximation method discussed previously in the methods section. By generating clusters of relationships, concomitant issues can be studied. In other words, when the Court gave its attention to one issue of public interest, what other issue or issues were related? The results of the factor-approximation are reported in Table 6-3. These factors, or clusters, may be interpreted as an unrotated factor matrix, so that it can be assumed that there is a high degree of intercorrelation between items of different factors. However, it must be remembered that what is of interest here is the *pattern* of relationships between issues of public interest.

Table 6-3 may be read in the following manner: the number in the first set of parentheses is the correlation coefficient and the number in the second set of parentheses is the number of the issue in that cluster to which the item is significantly correlated. Thus for Factor 1, the coefficient of 1.0 for PVP is the correlation between that item and STA (2), or item number 2.

An examination of the seven clusters reveal that Factor 1 suggests a dimension of business practices and interests of the licensee. Strongly related in this cluster are questions of conflicts in the private business interests of the broadcaster versus his public responsibilities (PVP). Additionally, the fact that issues of economic injury (ECINJ) and standing (STA) are related documents one of the major disputes in broadcast regulation which has been about the rights of the broadcaster. This conflict can be seen as related on two levels in Factor 1: broadcaster versus broadcaster in the case of economic injury, and broadcaster versus the commission and/or the public in the case of his private and public rights.

Factor 2 reveals that the Court has concomitantly considered the issues of interference (INF) along with modification procedures (MOD) which may either have caused the interference or rectified a situation in which interference was a problem. It is not surprising that issues of economic competition (CMP) are related to interference in that interference has been deemed to be detrimental to the economic interests of a station.[20] Issues of hearing (HEAR) have been addressed in the modification process where the welfare of other stations and the public interest have been at stake.

When the relationship between Factors 1 and 2 were examined in the original correlation matrix (see Table 6-1), it was noted that there is a high degree of intercorrelation between items of both factors. What this suggests is that Factors 1 and 2 may be different dimensions of the same issue which is the application of public interest to the business practices and interests of licensees.

Factor 3, at first glance, is an enigma. Issues of multiple ownership (OWN) are strongly related to issues of obscenity (OBS). There seems to be no way to account for this occurrence other than the fact that in 1978, two unrelated but important cases dealing with obscenity in broadcasting[21] and problems of diversification of ownership of media[22] were decided by the high court. Thus, these two issues, obscenity and ownership, should be considered as separate issues. It is logical, however, to see issues of antitrust (ANT) arise in relation to ownership (OWN) in this factor. Any discussion of concentration of media ownership must raise concomitant issues of monopolies.

Factor 4 appears to be a cluster of social issues of public interest. The rights of viewers (VR) are highly correlated with First Amendment issues (FA) as are issues of fairness and balance in programming (FD). Issues of scarcity (SCAR) are related because one argument, among others, for the enforcement of fairness in broadcasting is based on the potential of a monopoly of voices given the limited resources in frequency allocations.[23] And finally, since many First Amendment and fairness questions have to do with the content of broadcasting, it is reasonable to expect that programming (or content) issues are relevant (PRG).

Factor 5 reveals a relationship between issues of the licensing process (LIC) and the application process (APP) with related issues of the qualifications for a license (QUAL) and issues of competing applications (CPA). It will be remembered that, when broken down by the two eras of Court activity, these issues dominated the Court in the initial period between 1940 and 1946.

Factor 6 shows the relationship between issues concerning the duties and obligations of the broadcaster (BRD) and his business interests (BUS) including his relationship with the networks (CB). It would seem natural that these issues are related because of the nature of the broadcast operation itself. It is at once a private business and a public trust. Questions of the business interests of a broadcaster are related to issues arising around his

Table 6-3. McQuitty Factor Approximations

FACTOR 1				FACTOR 5		
1.	PVP	(1.0)	(2)	1.	LIC	(.59)	(2)
2.	STA	(1.0)	(1)	2.	APP	(.59)	(1)
3.	ECINJ	(.57)	(1,2)	3.	QUAL	(.53)	(1)
4.	PO	(.67)	(1,2)	4.	CPA	(.32)	(1)

FACTOR 1

1.	PVP	(1.0)	(2)
2.	STA	(1.0)	(1)
3.	ECINJ	(.57)	(1,2)
4.	PO	(.67)	(1,2)

FACTOR 2

1.	INF	(.79)	(2)
2.	MOD	(.79)	(1)
3.	CMP	(.58)	(1)
4.	HEAR	(.73)	(2)

FACTOR 3

1.	OBS	(.69)	(2)
2.	OWN	(.69)	(1)
3.	ANT	(.32)	(2)

FACTOR 4

1.	VR	(.68)	(2)
2.	FA	(.68)	(1)
3.	SCAR	(.68)	(2)
4.	FD	(.67)	(2)
5.	PRG	(.50)	(2)

FACTOR 5

1.	LIC	(.59)	(2)
2.	APP	(.59)	(1)
3.	QUAL	(.53)	(1)
4.	CPA	(.32)	(1)

FACTOR 6

1.	BRD	(.59)	(2)
2.	BUS	(.59)	(1)
3.	SER	(.32)	(1)
4.	CB	(.30)	(2)

FACTOR 7

1.	FCC	(-.54)	(2)
2.	FREQ	(-.54)	(1)
3.	TECH	(.40)	(2)

public trustee obligations. One of those issues of business practices has been the working affiliation of a broadcaster to a national network.

And finally, Factor 7 demonstrates a relationship between the power and authority of the commission in enforcing the broadcast statutes and thereby providing for the most efficient use of frequencies (FREQ). Related to these issues are questions of technical excellence (TECH). Like the issues which comprise Factor 5, this area seems to be one which the Court has dealt with separately in defining the boundaries of activity of the Federal Communications Commission. It will be remembered that Factor 5 primarily dealt with the licensing process. This factor suggests the activity of maintenance of a license by the efficient use of the frequency as monitored by the commission.

In summary, seven related clusters of public interest issues have been identified from the twenty-nine Supreme Court decisions examined in this investigation. These clusters reveal that among the thirty issues of public interest addressed by the Court, many are related, or are different dimensions of a larger issue. It has been to the identification of those larger areas of issues that this research has addressed itself.

DISCUSSION AND CONCLUSION

This research has demonstrated that public interest applications are complex.[24] This complexity is easily demonstrated in another work by the author in which each one of these issues is broken down into its component parts by a detailed examination of the decisions themselves.[25] The particulars of these issues revealed a consistency on the part of the Court, over time, in equating the public interest with the Common Good in its traditional definition. Whether the question has been one of a technical issue, or a social issue, the Supreme Court has consistently applied public interest to mean that the public must receive the advantages of broadcasting. In this present research, it is not as important to simply demonstrate the complexity of the issues as it is to point out which issues are related to which other issues in the Court's thinking and reasoning.

However, what has been shown here beyond complexity over time, are the issues themselves. Given the relative weights of issues and their relationships across the twenty-nine broadcast decisions, it can be seen that certain themes have occurred with enough frequency to identify them as major aspects of the public interest. Armed with this knowledge, any approach to a single issue of the public interest, must take into account concomitant issues.

These results also suggest that those who are seeking to find a relatively neat and precise definition of the public interest in broadcast regulation must not only take into account single issues but must also account for the other issues, implicit or stated, in that issue. As Frederick W. Ford has argued, those "who long for a definitive statement" as to what constitutes the public interest "are seeking to simplify something which is inherently complex."[26] There is evidence for this inherent complexity in the results reported here.

If this inherent complexity is to have meaning to present and future policy in broadcast regulation, the broadcasters, their audiences, the commission, Congress and Courts must not fall into the trap of single-issue thinking. Given the interest of any one of the parties in the broadcast environment, it would be too easy to equate a single interest on the part of one group with the public interest. A single interest may be self-serving whereas the public interest, as demonstrated in this research, involves a number of levels of related issues. Thus any attempt to reduce a question of public interest to a private interest can defeat effective public policy-making.

And finally, if scholarship is to move towards a greater understanding of public interest itself, these issues, and others which can be identified over the history of regulation, must be seen as part of the growth and development of the industry and the commission against the socio-political thought of the times and those individuals who played a part as well. Such knowledge would add significantly to the field's understanding of the illusive nature of the construct of public interest in broadcasting.

NOTES

1. "NOTE, Regulation of Program Content by the FCC," in Donald M. Gillmor and Jerome A. Barron, *Mass Communication Law: Cases and Comment,* 2d ed. (St. Paul, Minn.: West Publishing Co., 1974), p. 775.

2. Irwin Krasnow and Lawrence Longley, *The Politics of Broadcast Regulation* (New York: St. Martin's Press, 1973), p. 16.

3. H. J. Friendly, "The Federal Administrative Agencies," *Harvard Law Review* 75 (March 1962): 867.

4. Krasnow and Longely, *The Politics of Broadcast Regulation*, p. 16.

5. Ibid.

6. Douglas H. Ginsburg, *Regulation of Broadcasting: Law and Policy Towards Radio, Television and Cable Communication* (St. Paul, Minn.: West Publishing Co., 1979), p. 83.

7. Louis Caldwell, "Standards of Public Interest, Convenience, or Necessity as Used in the Radio Act of 1927," *Air Law Review* 1 (July 1930): 296.

8. Ibid.

9. Sydney W. Head, *Broadcasting in America: A Survey of Television and Radio*, 3d ed. (Boston: Houghton Mifflin, 1970), p. 319.

10. Friendly, "The Federal Administrative Agencies," p. 880.

11. *Federal Radio Commission Second Annual Report* 166 (1928).

12. Ole R. Holsti, "Introduction to Part II," in *The Analysis of Communication Content: Developments in Scientific Theories and Computer Techniques*, George Gerbner et al., eds. (New York: John Wiley and Sons, 1969), pp. 109-21.

13. L. L. McQuitty, "Elementary Factor Analysis," *Psychological Reports* 9 (1961): 71-78.

14. Marver H. Bernstein, *Regulating Business by Independent Commission* (Princeton, N.J.: Princeton University Press, 1955), p. 74.

15. Ibid., p. 79.

16. Ibid., p. 81.

17. See Columbia Broadcasting System, Inc. v. United States, 316 U.S. 407 (1942), and National Broadcasting Co. v. Federal Communications Commission, 319 U.S. 196 (1943).

18. Red Lion Broadcasting Co., Inc. v. Federal Communications Commission, 395 U.S. 367 (1969).

19. Columbia Broadcasting System, Inc. v. Democratic National Committee, 412 U.S. 94 (1973).

20. See Federal Communications Commission v. Sanders Bros. Radio Station, 309 U.S. 470 (1940) at 474; see also 319 U.S. at 247 and 269.

21. Federal Communications Commission v. Pacifica Foundation, 98 S.Ct. 3026 (1978).

22. Federal Communications Commission v. National Citizens Committee for Broadcasting, et al. 98 S.Ct 2096 (1978).

23. See 319 U.S. 218.

24. The limitations of this investigation are obvious. It is primarily descriptive in its approach and results. Secondly, it has used for purposes of analysis only those sections of Supreme Court decisions in which public interest has been specifically addressed. Other issues have not been included.

25. Jon S. Crane, *Supreme Court Interpretations of "Public Interest" in Broadcast Decisions: 1927-1979*, Ph.D. diss., University of Massachusetts, 1980.

26. Frederick W. Ford, "The Meaning of the 'Public Interest, Convenience, or Necessity,'" *Journal of Broadcasting* 5 (Summer, 1961): 213.

PART TWO

Communications Policy and Interest Group Activity

SARAH SLAVIN
AND M. STEPHEN PENDLETON

7

Feminism and the FCC

INTRODUCTION

THE numerous media reform organizations that surfaced in the late 1960s varied in size, prestige, focus, and effectiveness. By the mid-seventies, the women's liberation movement had become thoroughly involved in this area of pressure politics. The National Commission on the Observance of International Women's Year included in its final report to the president a chapter entitled "Mass Media: Friend or Foe?" which stated:

The media have enormous impact on the formation and reinforcement of behavior and attitudes. When women are constantly portrayed in stereotyped ways, these images affect their lives and their aspirations. Increasingly, women have become more concerned with their limiting portrayal and employment in the media.[1]

Organizations such as the American Association of University Women actively sought to improve the status of women in the media. They were joined by new organizations—nationally, by Media Women in Action among others, and locally, by the Media Group of the Los Angeles Women's Liberation Union, to name one. *Media Report to Women*, a high quality weekly newsletter published and edited by Donna Allen, served as a clearinghouse for the activities of these organizations, and offered information of common concern, including lists of license renewal dates for the broadcast media in individual states.

One of the earliest and most active of the women's liberation movement organizations was the National Organization for Women (NOW). This study focuses on NOW as one representative of the women's liberation movement's efforts to achieve media reform through the Federal Communications Commission (FCC). NOW was probably the most prestigious and visible mainstream organization involved. It was also chosen in order to develop a representative case study; the National Organization for Women was then, in the context of the women's liberation movement, a middle-ground organization with increasingly feminist aspirations. Thus, NOW presents the case of a reasonably representative organization with the beginnings of ideological grounding. NOW's activities demonstrate the application of an emerging feminist world view to the development and usage of strategy and tactics for media reform.

The pressure exerted by NOW, through the FCC, on the broadcast medium of television is the primary focus here. While television may not be the most dominant medium in the United States, it is the only national one.[2] Television also is a highly consolidated industry,[3] and hence relatively vulnerable to regulatory efforts. Although the broadcast networks' programming processes are not subject to direct regulation, television stations themselves are. Further, although the actual impact of television is debated, few deny that it has an extraordinary opportunity to frame or strip program content.[4] Additionally, a Screen Actors Guild survey of about ten thousand television viewers in 1975 revealed that 67.2 percent of the female respondents (83.6 percent of the sample) and 66.6 percent of the male respondents (15 percent of the sample) wanted to see women on television in positions of authority, and that 70 percent of the women and 61.8 percent of the men did not believe the images of women on television were truthful and believable.[5] Undoubtedly NOW considered factors such as these in giving the television industry the attention it did.

REGULATORY POLITICS

Murray Edelman has argued that relatively small groups of well organized regulatees can obtain tangible, material rewards from their regulators, while less organized groups can be rendered quiescent with non-tangible, symbolic rewards. Edelman asserts that regulators and regulatees often develop symbiotic relationships. Regulators are usually mandated to regulate a particular activity in the interest of the public. Once the regulatory structure is in place, however, its very existence presents the public with a symbol of protection. The general public is, by its nature, relatively unorganized and incapable of monitoring or assessing the array of outputs produced by its regulatory protectors. Thus the erection of a regulatory entity changes the setting in which questions about the behavior of newly regulated enterprises are asked.[6] To quote Edelman:

Once it is assumed that an agency assures service and fair rates for consumers, protection of the industry against loss or destruction becomes a tactic in the protection of the industry's clients as well. A rate increase that would be rather obvious exploitation of these clients in a setting of economic infighting unrestrained by government is magically converted into help for the customers as well as the industry. Where the agency's functioning constitutes legitimizing of a claim on the national product, the same functioning symbolically involves both adversary parties as supporters of the claim.[7]

Here the regulator and the regulatee need and sustain one another. Groups outside this relationship may make new demands for favorable decisions, but their success may be limited to symbolic, "nontangible values." This may be all the regulatory structure needs to render its organized opposition quiescent. In fact, Edelman argues that such symbolic rewards may actually transform opponents into defenders of the very system of law which permits the organized to pursue their interests effectively.[8] He points to the example of antitrust policy where its very existence has forestalled efforts to halt the growing concentration of corporate capital in the United States. Demands for the break-up of monopolies were always channeled into the largely symbolic arena of antitrust policy. There, liberals could point to the existence of the antitrust laws and demand their enforcement.[9] Those who worried about the growth of monopoly capitalism possessed antitrust policy as their only immediate avenue for action.

Thus, regulatory structures often become symbiotic affairs embracing regulators and regulatees. The latter receive material benefits, while the public receives symbolic reassurances that it is being protected. The public can be accordingly rendered quiescent. Reform movements emerging from the public and pressing new demands on regulatory structures may themselves be rendered quiescent through symbolic rewards. In some cases this latter process can co-opt those who wish to alter a regulatory structure or, perhaps even more importantly, capture their arguments.[10]

If Edelman is correct in asserting that there is often a symbiotic relationship between the regulators and regulatees, and that groups making claims on such relationships "may be rendered quiescent by their success in securing nontangible rewards," then we would expect the responses to NOW of both regulators and regulatees to contain symbolic rewards that rendered NOW quiescent.

NOW's initial demands were aired before the FCC, sitting *en banc*, on January 3, 1973. Wilma Scott Heide, president of the organization, undertook to raise the commissioners' collective consciousness through a stream of evocative feminist symbols.[11] She reversed the traditional symbols for women and men and focused forcefully on the biology-is-destiny argument. For example, she stated that because of the male's "vagina-envy, he learns to bind his genitals, and learns to feel ashamed and unclean because of his nocturnal emissions."[12] The shocked commissioners sat numbly through the balance of Heide's remarks. Clearly NOW's objectives, as expressed by Heide, seem radical for an organization whose primary objective was women's entry into the mainstream of American society.

To understand the revolutionary nature of some of NOW's objectives, we need to recall Edelman's postulate that the public extensively relates to politics through symbols.[13] The broadcast media are a major source of these symbols. The symbols broadcast about women stem from the interrelationship of politico-economic factors, audience reactions, and regulation, a kind of social system in itself.[14] These symbols have been highly discriminatory in that "women just do not exist to the same degree that men do; that they occupy a restricted sex-defined sphere; that they serve primarily as auxiliaries to men; and that all this is as it should be."[15] It follows from the above that these symbols operate, to some degree, as a form of social control.

The thrust of this control legitimately concerned NOW. As one commentator noted two years after Heide's address to the FCC, women have been exploited and victimized by the media, as employees of the media and as a class generally.[16] Further, the cultural implications for women of this exploitation and victimization have been distinctly repressive.[17] For a dominated class, the cultural "after-effects" of this control mechanism may be perceived as serious enough to characterize the struggle for control of the broadcast media as one of primary importance.[18] The broadcast media disseminate symbols and strip and frame their content, a content discriminatory to a dominated class such as women.

Essentially, the feminist objectives pronounced by Heide expressed disdain for the indicted social system and proclaimed NOW's intention to overtake the system by capturing its symbols. The strategy enunciated was to gain control of the media's dissemination of these symbols. At NOW's national conference in 1974, Joyce Snyder, co-chair of NOW's Media Reform Task Force, clearly stated the tactics brought into play: "We will educate government and the entire communications industry as to how they can best serve the public interest by including federal policies in their decision making processes."[19]

NOW was somewhat successful in its quest. Its success is perhaps partly indicated by Storer Broadcasting Company's 1973 suggestion to the FCC that sexist referents be deleted from the Commission's rules and policies on license renewal. The FCC agreed to Storer's proposal.[20] On the other hand, Jo Freeman contends that the interaction between a social movement and policy is dynamic. The movement influences policy, and policy influences the movement.[21] If Freeman is correct, we would expect that NOW affected the symbiotic relationship between the regulator and the regulatees but that, despite its radical intent, NOW was in turn affected by the relationship.

THE FCC

The FCC operates under a vague congressional mandate contained in the Communications Act of 1934. The Commission presents the classic example of a regulatory body established at the behest of the regulatees. It is also a classic example of the type of agency Edelman had in mind when he described the development of symbiotic relationships between regulator and regulatee. The Commission has come to identify the public interest in a way that does not greatly distinguish it from the collective interest of the established firms in the industry. The Commission oversees the material interests of the industry it serves while providing symbolic reassurance to the public that its interest is served.[22] The Commission even affirms its goal to protect the public in the very decisions it issues to protect established broadcasting firms. As Edelman writes:

It is not uncommon to give the rhetoric to one side and the decision to the other. Nowhere does the FCC wax so emphatic in emphasizing public service responsibility, for example, as in decisions permitting greater concentration of control in an area, condoning license transfers at inflated prices, refusing to impose sanctions for flagrantly sacrificing program quality to profits and so on.[23]

The Commission's ability to perform tasks in this fashion has probably been aided by its amorphous statutory mandate.[24] The Commission has also given itself substantial latitude by avoiding, to a greater extent than many federal commissions, pronouncements of overall doctrines or policies. As Judge Friendly has noted, the agency can use this flexibility to skip back and forth among its own precedents in an impressive display of quasi-judicial creativity.[25]

The Commission deals with an industry unlike others subject to government regulation. The television industry is composed of hundreds of stations established in local and sometimes regional markets. These stations operate in the context of definable communities and are publicly and officially designated as service providers to their communities. It is this relationship that forms the core of the FCC's regulatory power over television. The commission awards a scarce good, market access, to private firms by rationing use of the local and regional public airwaves among them. Yet these same stations buy most of their more extensively watched programming from an oligopoly of three dominant national networks. The FCC can influence the "big three" but only through its regulation of the hundreds of local affiliates.

The present analysis is based on the FCC rules and procedures that were in effect from the mid-sixties to the mid-seventies, and is strictly limited to the rules and procedures existing during that period. Under those procedures, once a station received its FCC license it faced renewal every three years. Renewal tended to be automatic if papers were in order.[26] Stations had to keep a file on each year's problems, and on community needs and the station's programming efforts to respond to them. The file had to be kept open to the general public, and copies of its contents made available at reasonable cost to those who requested them in person.[27]

The public could file testimony with the Commission during the life of a station's license or when a station applied to the Commission for renewal. A station had to make such application at least three months before its license expiration. This gave interested parties a chance to contest the station's bid for renewal. Two weapons the public could then and can now employ against licensees are informal and formal complaints. An informal complaint is a request that the FCC undertake an investigation of a station's programming practices to ascertain if the licensee has or has not served in the "public interest." Informal complaints can be filed against a station at any time. Formal complaints are much more serious and are filed during the license renewal period or when a station applies for a change in its status. A formal complaint is a request to the FCC to deny a license renewal application. Citizens who filed formal complaints had no right to an evidentiary hearing under existing procedures, and the Commission seldom granted such hearings.

In the past, citizen groups seldom used Commission complaint procedures to challenge local station programming. Television stations' practices were almost always upheld by the Commission. This situation began to change with a landmark 1966 decision by the U.S. Court of Appeals for the District of Columbia, which overturned an FCC procedure whereby only those with a demonstrable economic stake in the outcome of a case were allowed to intervene in the hearings. The decision compelled the Commission to allow the Office of Communications of the United Church of Christ to challenge the license renewal of WLBT of Jackson, Miss. The court held that the church could challenge WLBT on the ground that the station had discriminated against black viewers who comprised about 45 percent of the city of Jackson.[28] As Erwin Krasnow and Lawrence Longley note, "The court held that responsible community organizations such as 'civic associations, professional societies, unions, churches, and educational institutions or associations' have the right to contest license renewal applications."[29] The court's decision was unanimous, and in his opinion Judge Burger argued that "providing legal standing to those with such an obvious and acute concern with license proceedings as the listening audience is essential in order that the holders of broadcasting licenses be responsive to the needs of the audience without which the broadcaster could not exist."[30]

In complying with the court, the FCC allowed the church to participate in WLBT's renewal proceeding. However, the Commission still found for the station licensee. The court overruled the Commission in 1969 and ordered the FCC to consider new applications for the Jackson franchise. The FCC assigned an interim license for WLBT to a new firm, pending the outcome of application hearings.[31]

The Church of Christ decision opened the door for other citizen groups to use the FCC license review process to pressure stations on the latter's fidelity to the Communications Act's public interest requirement. This open door also meant that the FCC was increasingly called on to make new determinations of what the "public interest" actually is. The newly opened license renewal policy threatened to alter, albeit modestly, the close, symbiotic relationship the industry and the FCC had incrementally developed and reinforced. The Church of Christ decisions were the second major judicial decisions in the 1960s affecting this relationship. In 1965, in *Red Lion Broadcasting Co. v. FCC*, the Supreme Court had upheld the FCC's "fairness doctrine." The high court declared in the majority opinion that "it is the right of the viewers and the listeners, not the right of the broadcasters, which is paramount."[32] Various citizen groups had joined this litigation by filing amici briefs. Altogether, these decisions gave citizen groups access to the regulatory process and also an additional weapon in the "fairness" test to assess programming content.[33]

It should be noted, however, that the FCC was far from ending its service relationship to the television broadcast industry. The citizen groups demanded diversity in programming and more attention to their particular social and cultural concerns. The FCC encouraged diversity only in news and public affairs programming. The Commission has continued to regard cultural programs as entertainment and has not required broadcasters to air representative, multi-faceted programs. As will be noted below, citizen groups made inroads into the FCC-licensee symbiosis but did not change its essential character. That was accomplished by the impact of changing technology and shifts in political coalitions within the broadcast industry itself.

The 1970s were characterized by extensive and often highly visible campaigns, by citizen groups both nationally and locally, to influence local programming and FCC policy through the license renewal process. NOW's leaders determined that the best way for the organization to affect the media was through the regulatory process. Over time a behavioral pattern developed. Local NOW chapters would confront a station's management around license renewal time. One especially vulnerable area for many stations proved to be their hiring practices. The FCC eventually began to scrutinize licensee employment patterns as important data in determining whether a station had operated in the public interest. In 1976, in *NAACP et al. v. FCC*, the Supreme Court approved without reservation regulations by the FCC requiring broadcasters to seek out minorities and women for employment.[34] The Court justified this as necessary in order for the FCC to ascertain that the obligations of the Communications Act were being fulfilled. Citizen groups, among them NOW, embraced this policy test and endorsed the notion that hiring practices were highly correlated with programming. Employment studies were important components of NOW actions against local stations throughout the 1970s.[35]

The broadcasting industry apparently felt threatened by these developments and appealed to the White House for assistance. The Nixon administration, while refusing to meet with citizen groups, scheduled a meeting for the president with thirty representatives of the broadcasting industry. According to NOW's national newsletter, *Do It NOW*, "the results of that meeting indicated that the Administration planned to introduce legislation which would further curtail citizens' rights to influence the media."[36]

NATIONAL ORGANIZATION FOR WOMEN

NOW presents an unusual case of a grassroots organization that grew from the top down and moved with increasing purpose rather than becoming status-quo-oriented. At its founding, NOW was a national organization only.[37] Later, its activists realized that local chapters were important to the achievement of its organizational goals. By 1974 NOW had 700 chapters in the United States. After establishing them, a layer of relatively ineffective regional units was established as well. NOW suffered the usual organizational growing pains: scanty resources, a proliferation of priorities, the need to coordinate and direct its activities. In 1975, prior to a divisive conference, its national board had split between two contending factions: the descendants of the original power elite and the "Majority Caucus," which held a minority of votes on the board, but took the name *Majority*, imitating a tactic used by Lenin to clothe a minority faction in majority legitimacy. After the election at the 1975 conference, the caucus controlled the board. Although NOW's original statement of purpose had not mentioned the word *feminist*, and although the dissension culminating at the 1975 conference was primarily a power struggle, the conflict produced an organizational sense of feminist commitment.[38]

NOW's feminism was in process before 1975. When its 1974 conference was constituted from the Image of Women and the Broadcast Media Task Forces, one Media Reform Task Force, Joyce Snyder (co-chairperson of the Media Reform Task Force with Kathleen Bonk) announced that "NOW believes the present treatment of women by the media is a calculated effort to stabilize the status quo and retain power by keeping women subjugated, urging them to buy unnecessary objects and promulgating a feeling of female inadequacy and powerlessness."[39] Her statement reflected the tone of Heide's feminist presentation to the FCC seventeen months earlier. Snyder's statement also outlined open-endedly the scope of NOW's media reform action, including commercial television. She described a formidably issue-oriented endeavor. Among the issues highlighted were the fairness doctrine, truth and accuracy in advertising, sexist bias in news reporting, license renewal legislation, and a complete analysis of new television shows with women leads.

One characteristic distinguishing NOW from most other media reform organizations was the bond, albeit imperfect, between the national and local levels of the organization.[40] Most other groups either had a national organization only or were distinctly localized. The role of local NOW chapters in the endeavor largely centered on the employment practices of the broadcast media and on women's programming. Many chapters took on ambitious monitoring projects. For instance, in 1975 the San Francisco NOW chapter monitored 228 half-hour local news broadcasts and the hiring practices of four San Francisco television stations. While chapters were free not to undertake these projects, those that did set up a local task force like that on the national level. Not all chapter members participated on a given task force, but those who did were notably active. The national task force was to coordinate these projects and address itself to national-level activities, for example, by appearing at public hearings conducted by the FCC. The national NOW office in Chicago kept up a steady stream of paper communications to the local chapters. It made available an inexpensive FCC action kit to assist the chapters in their efforts. The kit contained negotiating strategies on employment and programming for use when dealing with broadcast stations, and a model agreement. It explained where to find a radio or television station's employment records, and how to challenge a license renewal if such an extreme measure was warranted. It listed license renewal dates and action timetables for each state.

Many media reform organizations relied heavily on one dynamic leader for inspiration and goal fulfillment.[41] NOW was not one of these. Despite intra-organizational dissension, national-level media reform activities brought forth, in addition to Bonk and Snyder, consistently committed and visible women such as Toni Carabillo and Karen DeCrow. Further, significant local activists such as Carol DeSaram and Anne Ladky became involved in nationally important actions. This circulation of activists virtually guaranteed continuing organizational support for the media projects and provided the projects with a wealth of human resources. The Media Reform Task Force had a low budget, because NOW was not wealthy and because it addressed a wide range of issues, all requiring money to support projects around them. Yet NOW's activists—and its 504 (c) (4) I.R.S. status, which permitted lobbying—kept NOW in the forefront of media reform organizations. The circulation of activists also helped to overcome a structural problem. The organization's national task forces were not formally integrated with the national board; and communications from task force to task force could be poor.

NOW often joined forces with other organizations. One very ambitious undertaking—a request in 1975 that the FCC examine the hiring policies and practices of 295 broadcasters and sixteen broadcast headquarters—found NOW aligned with the Chinese for Affirmative Action, the National Association for the Advancement of Colored People, the National Black Media Coalition, the National Citizens Committee for Broadcasting, the National Council of La Raza, the National Latino Media Coalition, and the National Urban League. NOW, however, frequently found itself excluded from organizations composed of relatively establishment women in or near the broadcasting industry. NOW's feminist analysis probably put off some of these groups, although their members were not always reticent to pay NOW dues. Ironically, where establishment women saw NOW as too radical, radical women saw NOW as too conservative, because of its often systemic approach to problem solving. Absent this irony, NOW would have had access to more activists to accomplish what it set out to do in broadcast media. Even so, NOW president Aileen C. Hernandez told a 1971 conference, "It *must* be a sign of our phenomenal success that we are described: *By some—too radical, By some—too conservative.*"[42]

DISCUSSION

Thus, NOW undertook a series of actions against the television industry in the name of media reform, but with radical intent. (See Appendix 1 to this chapter for a selected chronology of NOW actions.) The means that NOW chose were decidedly reformist. It filed or threatened to file informal complaints at license renewal time for bargaining purposes. Station management typically agreed to portions of NOW's demands. Thereafter, the management filed the station's agreement with NOW as part of its license renewal application; and NOW took no further action. Some of these stations established women's advisory councils. Often women's programming appeared on the station in question. Women's programming was designed to present positively the image of women, to bring women into program decision-making, and to integrate them into broadcast media, as well as to emphasize experiences and issues important to women, and to men. NOW played a leading role in developing the definition of women's programming. From the station's standpoint, the women's programming was not necessarily a commercial success. Although the station might fund a program's development, sponsors for these programs were not abundant. Incidental changes that occurred in conventional entertainment programming were equally compromised.

No concrete evidence demonstrates that television's portrayal of women across the seventies became feminist. One study examined all prime time programs on the three major networks during a week in November, 1975, and reported frequencies from one-third of the population. It concluded that no sex discrimination was to be found.[43] The programs in the sample included "Sanford and Son," "All in the Family," "Welcome Back Kotter," and "Mash." With all respect to Jean Stapleton and Alan Alda, based on programs such as these, few feminists would have agreed with the conclusion drawn in the study cited above. In a survey of all (thirteen) prime time television programs featuring women leads in the summer of 1977, Deborah Haskell found women pictured in less traditional occupations and roles than those in which woman had been pictured in the past: The women interacted with men and asserted themselves. The selectivity of the research prohibited broad generalizations about adjustments in the image of women on television.[44] The programs surveyed ran the gamut, from "Maude" and "Mary Tyler Moore" to "Policewoman" and "Charlie's Angels." The former programs probably pleased the feminist viewer; it is unlikely that the latter two did.

In the equal employment area, some unspectacular changes occurred. The status of women at WRC-TV, Washington, D.C., provides a typical case. Table 7-1 demonstrates that over a five-year period women lagged substantially behind men in concrete opportunities.[45] Based on this data, the FCC ignored an Equal Employment Opportunity Commission finding of sex discrimination and dismissed a petition by a coalition of women's groups, including NOW, to deny WRC its license renewal.

In the three-year period after a license renewal, occasional follow-ups by NOW on station performance yielded unsatisfactory results. When NOW attempted to take further action, based on follow-up findings, these attempts were not very successful. Nor were more drastic efforts, such as filing a formal complaint, seeking a hearing before the FCC, or trying to prevent a change in the ownership of a station. As the action period extended, NOW focused most often on hiring practices, equal employment opportunity, and affirmative action. The assumption was that more women within the stations' employment structures would produce a more favorable portrayal of women on the screen. The assumption was not dramatically born out. A letter printed in *Media Report to Women* suggests the sorts of disappointments that were forthcoming:

Dear Ms. _____

I have just presented your case and your presentation to Mr. _____ [Director of Programming], who reviewed everything quite carefully before sending me his reply and rationale. For the for[e]seeable future there is no conceivable way we can consider a second "women's program" for the simple reason that, regardless of competition in funding the *Woman Alive!* series,* the corporation is simply not committed to another program in this area.

Mr. _____ does not feel that it would be either wise or necessary to do any budgeting because even if you did find your outside funding, the station's time slots (even in the afternoon) are already firmly spoken for.

I am sorry to have to put this decision to you so bluntly, but since you have been pursuing this idea so vigorously for so long, I feel you are entitled to a direct answer to all the questions you posed yesterday.

By the way, he did reply to your last letter, and is sorry you never received it. Perhaps it went astray. . . . It was a pleasure to meet you yesterday, and I shall look for you on Channel __.

Ms. _____
Program Planning[46]

Woman Alive! began as a pilot on the Public Broadcasting Service, June 19, 1974. It was funded by a grant from the Corporation for Public Broadcasting to KERA-TV, Dallas/Fort Worth. *Ms.* magazine consulted on its production.

Table 7-1. Women's Employment Opportunities at WRC-TV, 1970–
1975

	Number of Managers		Salaries	
	1970	1975	1970	1975
Male	24	25	up to 30,000	$14,900–$38,000
Female	1	7	$12,000	$17,600–$30,000

	Manager	Administration	Supervisor
Average amount females' annual salaries are below males' salaries by position	$3,702	$1,283	$7,500

Although a few women who acquired jobs during this period were antifeminist, there is no reason to believe that many or even most of them were. More likely, many had priorities other than feminist change, per se. These women sought to advance their careers in an employment area that had previously excluded them; and they addressed themselves accordingly, alone and through their own organizations. As junior employees, some may have identified to an extent with their senior counterparts. This identification may have influenced some to discount feminist pressure on the social system they had entered. Others may have perceived that they had to discount feminist pressure if they were to retain their jobs. While their job performance must have pleased their superiors on many occasions, it did not automatically revolutionize the attitudes of managers, programmers, and so on.

One finding strongly buttresses the contention that women who received television jobs during the time that pressure was being exerted for their inclusion were not the source of change in the attitudes of managers and programmers. The portrayal of gainfully employed women and coverage of employment discrimination over ten years (1968-1978) of evening news coverage was scanty and contradictory in its message. An exhaustive content analysis by William Adams and Suzanne Albin, based on the entire population of agenda items on these programs, may even have overestimated what coverage there was. To quote the authors:

Over this ten year period, all three networks added together devoted a grand total of one hour 52 minutes 30 seconds to stories about women in the work force and sex discrimination in employment. To put this into perspective, this amount of coverage barely exceeded the time given to Paris and international fashions or clothing (one hour 29 minutes).[47]

The FCC became increasingly stubborn in its treatment of NOW's demands. It has not been established that the FCC singled NOW out in a discriminatory fashion. A broader survey of the women's liberation movement's media reform activities would be necessary to test that hypothesis. It is clear, however, that as the decade wore on, NOW's accomplishments were modest compared to the ambitious endeavor outlined by Snyder in 1974. The question is why NOW's success was truncated. The answer to that question lies in the nature of the relationships among the FCC, the television stations, and NOW.

Historically, the FCC is not by any stretch of the imagination to be considered an eager regulator. Its systemic intent has been at best confused. The regulated stations have been willing accomplices in cutting short whatever potential the FCC once had. NOW, for all intents and purposes, reinforced the FCC's procedures. To be sure, NOW reinforced those procedures negatively. Yet, however displeased NOW was with the FCC, NOW willingly participated in its procedures and hence implicitly endorsed them as sound in principle. Indeed, in 1974 Snyder pronounced those procedures sound when she announced that NOW would educate regulator and regulatee on the inclusion of federal policies—many forthcoming through the FCC.

NOW did not literally intend this result. Its organizational behavior, however, demonstrated a mixed message. On the one hand, NOW's reform activities were characterized by coherent organization and pressure exercised through established contact points. The activists did their homework, rallied their resources impressively, and worked under the banner of a visible, prestigious organization. Because the organization had become somewhat decentralized, the chapters operated as individual pressure groups within well-defined local units.

On the other hand, NOW's members also sought to capture a social system's symbols through protest ranging from picketing to Heide's address before the FCC. Motivation here sprang from a shared perception that women were subordinated to a dominant social grouping, white males. From the standpoint of the social system believed by NOW to be representing white males, NOW acted on a distorted perception of reality, however carefully the results of its monitoring were presented. The organization responded quickly to the broadcast image of women as a symbol of women's oppression. Its political activities yielded relatively few tangible results, considering the objective underlying those activities. Further, the activities pursued were not explicitly designed to achieve the objective. NOW was notably silent about strategy and tactics better suited to the objective at stake. Instead, NOW intensely encouraged its mass membership to pursue the means at hand.

Edelman described these two patterns of interest group behavior in public regulatory politics. "Pattern A" displays "a relatively high degree of organization—rational, cognitive procedures—precise information," plus small numbers, a favorably perceived strategic position, and an interest in specifically defined tangible resources.[48] NOW fit this pattern. NOW's national and local task forces were small, organized, and well mobilized. The task forces had specific objectives for their reform efforts and had formulated recommendations to accomplish them. The NOW reformers were confident in their efforts and skilled in using the public regulatory process.

"Pattern B" is characterized by protest activity aimed at status improvement. Here the strategic position is perceived as unfavorable, the numbers are large, and the organization is poor. Responses are symbolic; and publics are quiescent.[49] NOW was financially weaker than its regulatee adversaries, but was the largest mass-based women's organization in the country. Throughout the seventies, NOW increasingly addressed the oppression of women by men, documenting the drastic need to improve the status of women, and also to remedy the unfavorable strategic position of women's organizations vis-à-vis male-dominated institutions.

The distinction between these two sets of behavioral patterns corresponds to a difference in "politics as a spectator sport and political activity as utilized by organized groups to get quite specific, tangible benefits for themselves."[50] The distinction also corresponds to the difference between condensation and referential symbols. The latter assist in ordering and manipulating a situation; the former in evoking something which may not yet exist but potentially might.[51] How was it that NOW involved itself in this perceptually confusing situation?

NOW sought out both incremental solutions in the form of material resources, and specific symbols. It requested the tangible but limited results that typically follow on process politics. And it demanded the right to the mythic symbolic rewards that follow the overthrow of an established system. It received increments in the form of limited women's programming, negligible changes in employment patterns, and ostensible but not feminist change in some traditional entertainment formats. Symbolically, it forced the FCC to listen to its demands, although not to hear them. And it backed the stations into ritualized negotiating stances and agreements that appeared to be capitulative. In these regards, Edelman's observed behavioral patterns are born out, although Edelman does not appear to anticipate their simultaneous juxtaposition.[52]

Further, both hypotheses presented here are supported. The responses to NOW of regulator and regulatees contained symbolic rewards such as women's programming and increased employment of women. These in effect defused NOW's radical intent, leaving the organization with less to demand in that regard. At the same time—for example, by limiting its scope of action—NOW affected and was affected by the symbiotic relationship between regulator and regulatees. The symbiotic relationship became increasingly tense, as the FCC was forced to define the public interest more precisely and as the television stations were forced to demonstrate their

adherence to that interest. The FCC had to apply another set of account-
ability standards to the stations, which raised the stations' operating
expenses, among others. Ultimately, this tension between regulator and
regulatee appeared to dissipate, as the FCC and the television stations
balked at any additional pressure from NOW for change. As the tension
dissipated, NOW was drastically modifying its challenge by pursuing
prescribed processes for attaining change. The organization was tracked
into standard equal opportunity procedures. Those procedures were not
designed to yield the radical change originally envisioned by the organization, because the new women employees had career objectives of
their own.

On the one hand, we must see NOW as having been successful, because it
achieved both incremental solutions and symbolic rewards, for example,
selective hiring of women and, simultaneously, the high visibility of those
women on the screen and in publicity generated by their hiring. Another
level of analysis is, however, indicated. We cannot be sanguine about
NOW's successes, because by agreeing to accept material and symbolic
awards, NOW achieved nothing more. It also limited its ability to achieve
more. NOW managed to place women in the social system under consideration. There, those women were destined to be either accepted or rejected by
the very system that NOW set out to overcome. NOW assumed that it
could infuse a fixed system with radical vision. It took an unfortunate
shortcut through established processes to achieve a symbolic victory in
what was then a big symbolic enterprise. Given the nature of the enterprise,
the symbolic victory was highly visible. Television argued, on the basis of
its visible capitulation, that the problem of sex discrimination was virtually
solved and that no further vigilance was indicated. The FCC agreed; and
NOW faced a steadily closing door.

Today, there are forthcoming serious limitations to what might be achieved
in this area. The unregulated development of cable television is one of
them.[53] Lest any media reform organization jump on a bandwagon to regulate this industry, we urge that it think twice upon NOW's experience.[54] An
anti-regulatory groundswell may be evolving. Hence, regulation of cable-
casting may not be simple to achieve. To be avoided is the temptation to
take a shortcut in achieving regulation by turning to the traditional concept
of public interest broadcasting. The traditional concept concerns not
"equality of actual use" but equality of opportunity.[55] In more ways than
one, this concept is not amenable to concrete opportunities, the kind that
yield concrete results. This time a long cut is preferable to a short one.

NOTES

1. *Report to the U.S. President of the National Commission on the Observance
of International Women's Year* (Washington, D.C.: Government Printing Office,
July 1, 1976), chap. 2. For an early brief history of women's efforts in this area see

Freedom of Information Center Report No. 289, "Liberating the Media" (School of Journalism, University of Missouri at Columbia, September 1972).

2. Martin H. Seiden, *Who Controls the Mass Media? Popular Myths and Economic Realities* (New York: Basic Books, 1974), chap. 2.

3. See Samuel Eliot Morison, Henry Steele Commager, and William E. Leuchtenburg, *A Concise History of the American Republic* (New York: Oxford University Press, 1977), p. 706.

4. See Gaye Tuchman, *Making News: A Study in the Construction of Reality* (New York: Free Press, 1978), chaps. 1, 9. See also her chap. 7, "The Topic of the Women's Movement."

5. *Media Report to Women*, January 1, 1975.

6. Jacob Murray Edelman, *The Symbolic Uses of Politics* (Urbana, Ill.: University of Illinois, 1974), pp. 22-73.

7. Ibid., p. 59.

8. Ibid., p. 40.

9. Ibid.

10. Ibid., pp. 22-44.

11. See ibid., p. 6.

12. See Barry Cole and Mal Oettinger, *The Reluctant Regulators: The FCC and the Broadcast Audience*, rev. ed. (Reading, Mass.: Addison-Wesley, 1978), p. 93, quoting *Television Digest*, January 8, 1973.

13. Edelman, *Symbolic Uses of Politics*, p. 102.

14. Melvin L. DeFleur and Sandra Ball-Rokeach, *Theories of Mass Communication*, 2d ed. (New York: McKay, 1970), p. 166.

15. Jean C. McNeil, "Feminism, Femininity, and the TV Series: A Content Analysis," *Journal of Broadcasting* 19 (Summer 1975): 259-71.

16. Cynthia Fuchs Epstein, "Media as Mechanism: Consequences for the Cultural Understructure of Exclusion," paper presented to the Symposium on Women and the News Media, Institute for Scientific Analysis, San Francisco, 1975.

17. See Gaye Tuchman, "Women and the Creation of Culture," in *Another Voice: Feminist Perspectives on Social Life and Social Science*, ed. Marcia Millman and Rosabeth Moss Kantor (Garden City, N.Y.: Anchor Press, 1975). See also Karin Dorring, *Frontiers of Communication: The Americas in Search of Political Culture* (Boston: Christopher Publishing House, 1975).

18. See Herbert I. Schiller, *Communication and Cultural Domination* (White Plains, N.Y.: International Arts and Sciences Press, 1976), pp. 68, 71.

19. *Media Report to Women*, July 1, 1974.

20. *Media Report to Women*, December 12, 1973. Storer may have anticipated that San Diego NOW was about to challenge its interest in a transfer of the ownership of KCST-TV.

21. Jo Freeman, *The Politics of Women's Liberation* (New York: McKay, 1975), p. 232.

22. Edelman, *Symbolic Uses of Politics*, pp. 58-60.

23. Ibid., p. 39.

24. Erwin G. Krasnow and Lawrence D. Longley, *The Politics of Broadcast Regulation*, 2d ed. (New York: St. Martin's Press, 1978), pp. 15-19.

25. Henry J. Friendly, *The Federal Administrative Agencies: The Need for Better Definitions of Standards* (Cambridge, Mass.: Harvard University Press, 1962), pp. 53-73.

26. See Cole and Oettinger, *Reluctant Regulators*, appendix B, pp. 321-32, for samples of the forms involved.

27. Ibid.

28. Krasnow and Longley, *Politics of Broadcast Regulation*, p. 44.

29. Ibid.

30. *Office of Communication of the United Church of Christ v. F.C.C.*, 359 F.2d 994, 1002 (C.A.D.C., 1966).

31. *Office of Communication of the United Church of Christ v. F.C.C.*, 425 F.2d 543 (C.A.D.C., 1969).

32. Quoted in Fred W. Friendly, *The Good Guys, the Bad Guys, and the First Amendment: Free Speech v. Fairness in Broadcasting* (New York: Random House, 1976), p. 74. *Red Lion Broadcasting Co. v. F.C.C.*, 395 U.S. 372 (1969).

33. Krasnow and Longley, *Politics of Broadcast Regulation*, pp. 44-45.

34. Ibid., pp. 45-52.

35. Cole and Oettinger, *Reluctant Regulators*, pp. 166-70.

36. *Do It NOW*, March 1973.

37. Much of the information in this section is forthcoming either from *Do It NOW*, NOW's national newsletter, or from co-author Sarah Slavin's participant observation in NOW up to 1976.

38. See Ruth Zaleon, "Feminism vs. the System," *Do It NOW* 9 (April 1976): 7.

39. *Media Report to Women*, July 1, 1974.

40. Anne W. Branscomb and Maria Savage, "The Broadcast Reform Movement: At the Crossroads," *Journal of Communication* 28 (Autumn 1978): 27.

41. Ibid.

42. "Revolution: From the Doll's House to the White House," keynote address to opening session of national NOW conference by Aileen Hernandez, outgoing president, Chicago, September 4, 1971.

43. S. Holly Stocking, Barry S. Sapolsky, and Dolf Zellmann, "Sex Discrimination in Prime Time Humor," *Journal of Broadcasting* 21 (Fall 1977): 947-57. But see "Window Dressing on the Set: Women and Minorities in TV. A Report of the U.S. Commission on Civil Rights," August 1977. However rigorous the content analysis, it will not establish whether a discriminatory effect has taken place. The same principle holds for NOW's monitoring projects. See Lawrence W. Lichty and George A. Bailey, "Reading the Wind: Reflections on Content Analysis of Broadcast News," in *Television Network News: Issues in Content Research*, ed. William Adams and Fay Schreibman (Washington, D.C.: School of Public and International Affairs, George Washington University, 1978), pp. 112-13.

44. Deborah Haskell, "The Depiction of Women in Leading Roles in Prime Time TV," *Journal of Broadcasting* 23 (Spring 1979): 171-76. But see "Window Dressing on the Set: An Update. A Report of the U.S. Commission on Civil Rights," January 1979, appendix A. The commission found "that the portrayal of women and minorities in prime time TV drama did not improve in the years 1975 through 1977, and in some ways their portrayal suffered" (p. 60).

45. More extensive examples may be found in *Media Report to Women*, January 1, 1974; February 1, 1974; and April 1, 1975. See also aggregate data presented on March 1, 1976, gathered by the Office of Communications, United Church of Christ. See also "Window Dressing on the Set: An Update," appendix C, pp. 87-94.

46. *Media Report to Women*, March 1, 1975.

47. William Adams and Suzanne Albin, "Public Information on Social Change:

TV Coverage of Women in the Workforce,"*Policy Studies Journal* 8 (Spring 1980): 717-33.

48. Edelman, *Symbolic Uses of Politics*, p. 36.

49. Ibid.

50. Ibid., p. 5.

51. Ibid., p. 6.

52. For a report on a similar juxtaposition see Joyce Gelb and Alice Sardell, "Organizing the Poor: A Brief Analysis of the Welfare Rights Movement," *Policy Studies Journal* 3 (Summer 1975): 346-54. Like Edelman, Michael Lipsky, "Protest as a Political Resource," *American Political Science Review* 62 (September 1968): 1144-58, does not foresee the simultaneous juxtaposition of quests for tangible resources and symbolic rewards.

53. See Branscomb and Savage, "Broadcast Reform Movement," pp. 31-32.

54. The Women's Institute for Freedom of Press scheduled as part of its fifth annual convention, April 1983, Washington, D.C., a workshop on the use of cable television for women's channels and women's programming, including the formation of coalitions toward this end.

55. Benno C. Schmidt, "Access to the Broadcast Media: The Legislative Precedents," *Journal of Communication* 28 (Spring 1978): 63.

Appendix 1

Selected NOW Media
Reform Actions, 1972–1977

Spring 1972: NOW filed a petition to deny a license renewal to WABC-TV, New York City, based on allegations of employment discrimination, failure to meet community programming needs, and presentation of a prejudiced view of women's roles.

Spring 1973: Seven organizations including NOW filed a claim with the FCC against WRC-TV, Washington, D.C., seeking either an evidentiary hearing or a finding favoring women on WRC's employment practices and programming content, and based on a prior favorable EEOC holding.

NOW's Legal Defense and Education Fund launched a public service advertising campaign that was endorsed by the Advertising Council. By the following year the campaign had acquired a media value of over $3 million. It consisted of six print ads, two thirty-second full color television commercials, and several radio spots.

Fall 1973: Chicago NOW charged that WBBM-TV had not met the FCC's licensing standards in its hiring practices and programming.

Detroit NOW, in coalition with other Detroit area groups, settled with WXYZ-TV and petitioned the FCC about WJBK-TV.

November 1973: NOW became a member organization of the Advisory Committee of National Organizations for the Corporation for Public Broadcasting.

December 1973: After a presentation by NOW Vice President for Public Relations Toni Carabillo about the media's treatment of women's image, the National Association of Broadcasters agreed to revise its radio code.

February 1974: NOW's Public Information Office in New York City announced that it was compiling a list of feminist programming for broadcasters' use.

April 3, 1974: NOW testified to the Senate Commerce Committee's Communications Subcommittee against the appointment of Luther Holcomb to the FCC.

Early spring, 1974: San Diego NOW filed a petition with the FCC to deny transfer of ownership of KCST-TV from Western Telecasters to Storer Broadcasting, because Storer-owned stations discriminated against female employees.

May 20, 1974: Storer filed with the FCC an agreement reached with San Diego NOW to supplement an agreement previously negotiated (October 1973) with ethnic minorities in the viewing area of its station, KCST-TV, San Diego.

May 22, 1974: Agreement entered between WGN of Colorado, Inc., licensee of KWON-TV, and Colorado Coalition of Women and Minorities, which included NOW.

May 1974: A report about the national broadcast media, listing achievements of NOW chapters and the FCC Task Force, became available in the national office.

May 25-27, 1974: NOW formed a new Media Reform Task Force to replace the former Image of Women Task Force and Broadcast Media (FCC) Task Force.

June 1974: The FCC had not yet decided whether to conduct a hearing on NOW's petition to deny WABC-TV its license renewal (see spring 1972).

June 24, 1974: KPRC-TV, Houston, reached an agreement with Houston NOW, which was filed by KPRC as a formal addendum to its license renewal application.

Summer 1974: NOW testified against HR12883, before the Senate Subcommittee on Communications, regarding the extension of the length of licenses from three years to five.

August 1, 1974: Rochester, Minn., NOW and the Business and Professional Women's Organization entered a complaint against the *Post-Bulletin* for identifying women by their husband's name.

Fall 1974: Los Angeles Women's Coalition for Better Broadcasting filed with the FCC petitions to deny license renewal to owners of four L.A. television stations: KTLA, KTTV, KCOP, KNXT.

Barbara Brusco, New York City NOW member and Columbia Pictures stockholder, filed with the FCC charges of employment and content discrimination and nonrepresentation of women on the board of directors against Columbia Pictures.

October 29, 1974: Agreement reached between four Los Angeles television stations and the L.A. Women's Coalition that became part of the stations' application for license renewal. Coalition took no further action (see fall 1974).

November 1974: Fresno, Calif., NOW filed formal petitions with the FCC to deny license renewals to KMJ-TV and KFSN-TV, and a formal objection to KJEO-TV's application.

January 16, 1975: NOW Media Task Force petitioned the FTC about deceptive advertising practices by manufacturers of vaginal sprays.

January 24, 1975: The U.S. Court of Appeals for the District of Columbia Circuit ordered the FCC to take action on claims by NOW and others that WRC-TV and WABC-TV were guilty of sex discrimination in programming and employment.

February 1975: NOW Media Task Force asked that the FTC require National Airlines to substantiate its advertising claim: "I'm going to fly you like you've never been flown before."

April 30, 1975: Metromedia filed with its application for license renewal to operate WNEW-TV, New York City, a supplementary agreement reached in negotiation with the Image Committee of the New York City NOW chapter.

June 1, 1975: One half-hour television magazine-type program on KPRC-TV, Houston, had found no sponsors (see July 1, 1974).

Early August, 1975: The NBC-TV network president and the vice president for program met with NOW to discuss its complaint about lack of positive image of women and agreed to consider NOW's recommendations during an NBC re-study of its policies.

September 5, 1975: The FCC ruled that presidential and political candidate press conferences qualify for the fairness doctrine exemption. Shirley Chisholm and NOW appealed.

September 27, 1975: Boston NOW began a boycott of products that were advertised by promoting sexist stereotypes. Its first target was WISK detergent, because of its "Ring Around the Collar" ad campaign.

February 18, 1976: The FCC ruled that despite the EEOC's finding of discrimination at WRC-TV, its own re-examination of station employment indicated sufficient improvement to hold WRC in compliance with FCC-EEO regulations, and to turn down a petition by women's organizations, including NOW, to deny broadcast license renewal to WRC (see spring 1973).

July 1976: Informal complaint filed against eight television and twenty-one radio stations in Los Angeles, asking the FCC to initiate a major investigation of employment practices.

July 9, 1976: Seven women's organizations in Los Angeles appealed to the U.S. District Court of Appeals, Washington, D.C., to overturn an FCC decision denying them a hearing on their case that KNXT-TV (Los Angeles) should not have its license renewed.

Fall 1976: Media monitoring project undertaken by San Diego County NOW, with the assistance of the North County and East County chapters.

March 1, 1977: Media Monitoring Task Force of Colorado NOW filed an informal objection with the FCC against thirty-two broadcasters for sex bias.

April 11, 1977: U.S. Court of Appeals, Washington, D.C., ruled that the FCC did not need to grant a hearing on charges of employment discrimination, violation of the fairness doctrine, and inadequate ascertainment of women's problems, re WABC-TV and others (see spring 1972). The appeal was based on rejections of petitions by the FCC in 1975 and 1976.

June 1977: Eight national organizations requested the FCC to examine the employment policies and practices of 295 broadcasters and 16 broadcast headquarters which had either no women in full-time employment in the top four job categories or no minority persons full-time in geographic areas having at least 5 percent minority people.

Public Intervenors and the Public Airwaves: The Effect of Interest Groups on FCC Decisions

ONE of the most common criticisms of regulatory commissions is that they are overly sensitive to the needs of the industry which they were created to oversee and insufficiently responsive to the needs of the public they were established to serve.[1] Some critics attribute the failure of regulatory commissions to make their decisions "in the public interest" to the lack of nonclientele participation and ever present industry participation in the policy-making process. Based on the belief that these bodies would benefit from alternative inputs beyond that of their clientele industry, Circuit Court Judge Warren Burger ruled in 1966 in *United Church of Christ* v. *FCC* that private citizens may be given the opportunity to intervene in Federal Communications Commission proceedings.[2] As a result of this and subsequent decisions, intervenor participation has expanded during the 1970s to include consumer organizations, environmentalists, minority groups, and public interest law firms which represent collective interests before regulatory bodies and at all levels of government. While intervention by a broad range of groups has become a more important force in regulatory policy-making, the effectiveness of these groups as alternative inputs which influence regulatory decisions is unclear. The impact of intervenors on these decisions will be examined where the intervention controversy begins, at the Federal Communications Commission (FCC).

The intervention issue is connected with the broad delegation of authority by Congress to the regulatory commissions to oversee a given area of the economy. As government power over private welfare has expanded, congressional mandates have become broader and more vague. One particularly common mandate is the "public interest" standard which requires the agency to act "in the public interest, convenience, or necessity."[3] The main approach that the courts use to deal with the problem of broad delegation of authority is the emphasis on the existence of procedural safeguards rather than clear policy standards. Based on the Administrative Procedure Act of 1946, the courts suggest that an agency must follow fair adjudicatory procedures and provide affected parties with the opportunity to be heard before it adopts rules.[4] The notion underlying this procedural approach is that in order for an agency to adhere to the congressional mandate that its decisions be "in the public interest," the agency must consider the views of all affected interests. The resulting policy will be in the public interest because it will be a compromise based on the input that the agency received from these groups.[5] The assurance of representation for all affected interests thus is the key to the procedural approach.

Critics of this approach maintain that agencies are not sufficiently responsive to all affected groups. Over the years, they have developed a close relationship with the industries they regulate. This is true of the FCC, particularly in the area of its broadcast license decisions, in which the Commission rarely denies renewal to an incumbent station.[6] The close relationship between regulatory bodies and their clientele industry is based on compatible interests and goals. The regulatory commissions desire to avoid adverse rulings by "sovereigns" that exert political, legislative, or judicial control over them.[7] One of the major means by which sovereign review of agency actions occurs is interest group appeal of agency actions, either through the courts or through direct pressure on congressmen. Thus, in order for the agency to maximize its probability of success, it should be responsive to the demands of the interest groups most likely to appeal its decisions, usually the regulated industry itself. First, clientele industries often are intensely interested in the decisions of the commission, because they are directly affected by commission regulations. Second, they are for the most part well organized and have sufficient resources to enable them to seek recourse in the external political arena. The broadcast industry, for instance, is represented by the National Association of Broadcasters, the three national networks, and more specialized trade associations. In contrast, the general public may have more total resources than the clientele industry, but it is not as well organized; consequently, it is unlikely to seek recourse in the external political arena. Thus, a natural partnership emerges between the Commission and its clientele group. The Commission provides the industry with regulations which it believes will promote industry performance. The industry gives the Commission information about important aspects of its sector of the economy, and political support throughout the Commission's dealings with its sovereigns.

One critique of this thesis focuses on the idea that alternative inputs beyond that of the clientele group are unlikely to emerge. Private organizations which seek to promote diffuse collective interests are hard to form and maintain, according to Mancur Olson, because of the lack of material incentives and the high communication cost involved.[8] Nevertheless, reform movements during the 1960s and 1970s have helped to open government agencies to interests other than those of the private sector.

As part of this reform movement, increased intervention has been advocated to broaden access to the administrative decision-making process. Intervenors are third parties who are permitted to participate in formal proceedings because they have a legitimate interest in the outcome of a case. Intervenors attain their status primarily through meeting certain statutory requirements. These requirements vary from commission to commission, although in general the petitioner must demonstrate some interest in the outcome of a proceeding and meet certain filing deadlines.[9] The FCC, for example, requires that intervenors be "parties in interest," that is, they must be responsible representatives of the community in which the applicant is located who have specific objections, based on factual evidence, which indicate that "a grant of the application would be inconsistent with the public interest, convenience, and necessity."[10]

Traditionally, clientele groups, such as broadcasters claiming electronic interference or economic injury, were favored in granting intervenor status. Recently, however, the federal courts have ordered agencies to open their hearings to citizen intervenors. They have held that broadcasting listeners, conservationists, and beneficiaries of welfare agency operations, in the capacity of formal intervenors, can challenge regulatory actions as being contrary to the public interest.[11] As a result, users of transportation or communications facilities, the Department of Justice, state and local bodies, and business and trade associations regularly appear as intervenors.[12]

What implications does this reform movement have for the relationship between clientele and commission? Sabatier, in his study of public participation in the policy-making process of the National Air Pollution Control Administration, asserts that an active constituency may forestall or even prevent the decay of aggressive regulation, particularly if such a constituency is cultivated by the agency.[13] Similarly, Mazmanian and Nienaber found that citizens' groups, through public participation programs, had an appreciable effect on decisions of the Army Corps of Engineers. They state that public participation is an important element in the cycle of organizational change.[14] In addition, a House subcommittee report on federal regulation commented on the effectiveness of environmental groups in ensuring that the Environmental Protection Agency keep to statutory deadlines for implementing programs to protect the environment.[15]

Not all scholars are optimistic about the ability of these groups to encourage aggressive regulation. Some point to the resource disadvantage of public interest groups relative to that of the regulated industry. The costs of participation include legal fees, payment for expert witnesses, multiple copy requirements, transcript charges, salaries for staff members who identify and prepare for relevant formal proceedings, and expenses associated with commissioning research projects.[16] Citizens' groups are often less able to afford these costs than are clientele groups.

Others charge that permitting intervention by uninformed and irresponsible citizens' groups may only confuse the issues in what frequently are complex and highly technical proceedings. Sabatier stresses the importance of providing technical information and well-conceived arguments in overcoming clientele influence.[17] Landis, in his report to President Kennedy on the regulatory commissions, observed that regulatory commission contacts with the general public "are rare and generally unproductive of anything except complaint."[18] Cupps notes contentions that "the tone of [citizens' groups'] published research and political lobbying is arrogant, belligerent, and personally demeaning, and on occasion it has undermined the effectiveness of their efforts."[19] In addition, he points out the frequency of inaccuracies and unsubstantiated conclusions, problems that raise questions about the reliability of research by citizens' organizations. Friedman stresses that the ineffectiveness of consumer groups before the Food and Drug Administration may be based on "their lack of technical credentials for inclusion in the 'scientific network.'" These groups often are viewed as outsiders, without the expertise needed to communicate with the professionals within the agencies.[20] This lack of expertise could alienate decision-makers, causing them to take the industries' positions when faced with public opposition. Consequently, intervenors may actually have a negative effect on regulatory outcomes.

Increased intervention has also been attacked for causing excessive delays and costs for an already overburdened process. Many broadcasters believe that citizens' groups have no true concern for reaching a decision that represents the public interest through the process of accommodating different views. Instead, they are committed to lengthy hearings and administrative delays. Observers of the Federal Communications Commission note that through the threat of a petition to deny renewal of a license, citizens' groups can "blackmail" a broadcaster who desires to avoid a costly, time-consuming hearing procedure into accepting an expensive settlement.[21]

Thus, the effect of intervenors on regulatory policy is unresolved. Particularly important in evaluating the effect of intervenors is the way in which intervention is incorporated into the hearing process. This is a significant issue, because critics have focused on the aforementioned "barriers" which the process places in front of intervenors, such as filing and duplicating costs, format requirements, and the necessity of legal representation. The direct effect of intervenors on broadcast regulatory decisions of the Federal Communications Commission will be examined here, as will the influence of aspects of the broadcast hearing procedure on the relationship between intervention and commission decision-making.

METHODS

In order to investigate the effect of intervenors on FCC broadcast decisions, data have been collected from opinions published in the *Federal Communications Commission Reports, Pike and Fisher's Radio Regulation,* and Miscellaneous Orders for the years 1973, 1976, and 1979. These years have been selected because, according to McLauchlan, intervention activity did not stabilize until the 1970s.[22] More important, the choice of these years permits examination of the effects of intervenors on FCC decisions under three different presidential administrations, during which three different chairmen served.[23] Only memorandum opinions and orders, orders, and letters from the Commission itself have been considered; although the Commission decides only a small proportion of the total number of cases that the agency receives, these cases represent important policy issues in which pressure groups are likely to be most interested.

The dependent variable is the outcome of a Commission vote on a broadcasting adjudicatory case. The outcomes may be divided into three categories: decisions favoring the main party's arguments; those opposing the main party's arguments (thereby supporting the intervenor's stands); and conditional decisions. Conditional decisions are defined as those in which the main party is required to pay a fine, awarded only a short-term renewal, or granted renewal subject to certain specifications such as submitting periodic employment reports.[24]

The major independent variable is the presence or absence of intervenor participation. For the purpose of this study, an intervenor is defined as a party which brings a petition or complaint to the F.C.C. There are four types of participants in formal adjudicatory proceedings: those who file complaints, informal objections, petitions to deny, and petitions to intervene.[25] Not all of these participants may meet the legal definition of an "intervenor." However, each of them engages in intervention activities by bringing additional information to the Commission. They are, therefore, intervenors in a behavioral sense. This broad approach was used by William McLauchlan in his empirical study of intervenors and the FCC.[26]

INTERVENOR PARTICIPATION AND FCC DECISIONS

As previously noted, qualitative studies of participation in administrative proceedings have suggested that intervenors have no impact on agency decisions because of their lack of resources and expertise.[27] They may even have a negative effect on agency decisions according to Cupps and Friedman, who charge that intervenors' presentations to regulatory bodies are often belligerent in tone, unsupported by empirical evidence, and filled with inaccuracies.[28] In his quantitative study of decision-making at the FCC, McLauchlan found an unstable pattern of intervenor influence. In 1971-1972 the percentage of licenses granted was lower in the cases where intervenors were present, but in 1973-1974 such requests were more likely to be granted when intervenors participated than when they did not.[29]

According to Table 8-1, intervenors have no positive effect on FCC decisions; in fact, intervention appears to have a negative impact on

Table 8-1. Outcome of Broadcast Decision by Presence of
         Intervenors

Decision	Intervenors Not Present	Intervenors Present
For broadcaster	26.7%	56.5%
Against broadcaster	47.6%	29.8%
Conditional	25.7%	13.7%
(Total N)	(584)	(460)

regulatory outcomes. When intervenors participate, the odds are 4.12 to 1 that the FCC will support the broadcaster rather than oppose him.[30] In cases without intervention, however, the FCC is not any more likely to grant than to deny a broadcaster's request (the odds are about 1 to 1). Nor does the negative impact of intervenors differ notably by year, as it did in McLauchlan's study (see Table 8-2). In 1976 and 1979, the Commission was still more likely to support the broadcaster when intervenors participated than when they did not participate.[31] Thus, when intervenors are present, the FCC frequently votes in favor of the broadcaster, but when they are not present, the FCC is just as likely to object to a broadcaster's argument as to support it.

Before examining the influence of specific aspects of the hearing process on intervenor participation, further investigation of the types of impacts that intervenors may have is in order. For instance, it is possible that intervenors may change the outcome even though the broadcaster's request is not completely denied. The Commission may only partially grant a broadcaster's request, by attaching conditions to the decision, in an effort to find a compromise between the broadcaster's and intervenor's positions.[32] This idea is not supported by the data, however (see Table 8-2). The odds are almost 2 to 1 that the FCC will completely support the broadcaster rather than award him a conditional grant in the face of intervenor participation. In contrast, when intervenors are not present, the odds of a conditional decision are higher than those of a "pro broadcaster" outcome (1.78 to 1). In terms of the type of condition imposed on the broadcaster, fines and—to a much lesser extent—short-term renewals and reporting requirements (for instance, updates on the extent of minority employment) are more likely to be demanded of broadcasters when intervenors are not present at the hearing (see Table 8-3). If a broadcaster is assessed a fine, the odds are almost 20 to 1 that no intervenors will be present. Similarly, the odds of receiving a short-term renewal or a reporting requirement are 1.50 to 1 and 1.90 to 1 respectively when there is no intervenor participation. The FCC, then, may often rely on conditional decisions in its effort to eval-

Table 8-2. Outcome of Broadcast Decision by Presence of Intervenors by
Year

Broadcaster	Decision for Broadcaster	Decision Against Broadcaster	Conditional	Totals
1973				
Not present	24.2%	53.6%	22.2%	(252)
Present	44.8%	14.4%	40.8%	(174)
1976				
Not present	30.7%	27.6%	41.7%	(163)
Present	52.3%	33.3%	14.4%	(195)
1979				
Not present	26.6%	58.0%	15.4%	(169)
Present	55.2%	32.4%	12.4%	(145)

Table 8-3. Type of Conditional Decision by Intervenor Participation

Type of Condition	Intervenors Not Present	Intervenors Present	(Totals)
Fine	95.2%	4.8%	(125)
Short-term renewal	60.0%	40.0%	(20)
Reporting require- ment	65.7%	34.3%	(137)
Additional hearings	51.7%	48.3%	(58)
Other	36.0%	64.0%	(75)

uate the claims of broadcasters. However, the Commission tends not to
utilize the conditional grant approach in the face of intervenor input. Perhaps the Commission feels the need to present a solid argument to the
intervenors so that they may have a clear understanding of the outcome of
the hearing which will prevent them from appealing the decision to the
courts or Congress.

Another impact which intervenors may have involves creating dissatisfaction within the Commission. Although intervenors did not alter the total
outcome, they may have persuaded a minority of the Commission that their
claim was just. As a test of this notion, cases have been grouped according
to whether or not they were decided unanimously or nonunanimously. As
Table 8-4 indicates, nonunanimous decisions occur more frequently in those
cases where intervenors participate (with odds of 1.54 to 1), while

Table 8-4. Unanimous and Nonunanimous Broadcast Decisions
Presence of Intervenors

Decisions	Intervenors Not Present	Intervenors Present
Unanimous		
For broadcaster	24.0%	54.1%
Against broadcaster	51.7%	29.7%
Conditional	24.2%	16.1%
(Totals)	(495)	(353)
Nonunanimous		
For broadcaster	33.8%	63.8%
Against broadcaster	26.5%	30.5%
Conditional	39.7%	5.7%
(Totals)	(68)	(105)

unanimous decisions are made more often when intervenors are not present
(with odds of 1.40 to 1). Thus, even though intervenors do not have a direct
positive effect on regulatory outcomes, they are at times able to convince
some of the commissioners of the validity of their argument. On the other
hand, since the FCC is a relatively inconspicuous decision-making body
compared with the Supreme Court, for example, it is unlikely that a nonunanimous decision by the FCC would have a significant policy impact.[33]

An additional way to evaluate the effect of intervenors on regulatory
outcomes is to isolate cases where more than one intervenor participated.
One might expect that the Commission would find it more difficult to
support the broadcaster in the face of participation by a number of different
intervenors, because such participation might indicate to the Commission
that claims against broadcasters are broad-based, not just representative of
an isolated group of viewpoints. As shown in Table 8-5, in cases where
more than one intervenor participated the odds are about even (1.28 to 1)
that the Commission will rule in favor of the broadcaster in the presence of
more than one intervenor, compared with odds of 5.57 to 1 for cases in
which only one group intervened. This finding suggests that while the
Commission is less likely to support the broadcaster in the face of multiple
intervenors (compared with single intervenor participation), multiple intervenors still are not able to convince the Commission to rule against the
broadcaster.

Public Intervenors and the Public Airwaves 157

Table 8-5. Outcome of Broadcast Decisions by Presence of Multiple Intervenors

Decision	No Intervenors	One Intervenors	Multiple Intervenors
For broadcaster	26.7%	62.2%	31.0%
Against broadcaster	47.6%	26.6%	44.0%
Conditional	25.7%	11.2%	25.0%
(Totals)	(584)	(376)	(84)

THE HEARING PROCESS

Thus, the question remains: Why do intervenors have a negative effect on FCC decisions? Green, in his evaluation of hearing procedures in nuclear licensing, maintains that the license proceeding is structured in a way that impedes effective public participation.[34] Three aspects of the process have been identified in the literature: the type of main party, the type of issue, and the type of intervenor.

In terms of the type of main party at which the intervenor's complaint is directed, the literature suggests that regulated industries are not always unified in their efforts to influence regulatory decision-making. For instance, Krasnow and Longley note that the broadcasting lobby has been weakened by the emergence of specialized trade associations which represent different types of broadcasting industries. Decision-making bodies, then, do not respond uniformly to all the interest groups with which they interact. Their decisions frequently reflect the special interests of the larger, well-established enterprises, in part because of the financial profitability and political ties that these industries have. Television stations, for example, generally have an advantage over radio stations in terms of finances and frequency of past adverse FCC political decisions. Cole and Oettinger note that large profit margins are not uncommon in the television industry, but that radio (and some VHF television) stations often report losses or slim profit margins. In addition, radio stations are more likely to be sanctioned by the FCC; from 1972 to 1976, forty-five radio stations received short-term renewals in punishment for past deficiencies, compared with only five television stations.[35] Thus, one might expect intervenors to be more likely to have a positive effect on FCC broadcasting decisions if the main party is a radio station rather than a television station.

Gellhorn, Cramton, Gormley, and McLauchlan have stressed the importance of the nature of the issue in the proceeding as a factor that may affect the relationship between intervenors and Commission decisions.[36] Gellhorn and Cramton maintain that intervenors are more interested in and informed about hearings that involve broad policy issues.[37] Similarly, Gormley demonstrates empirically that "grassroots advocates" deal little with technical issues and are more involved with general policy questions which pit one class of consumers against another.[38] However, McLauchlan contends that while intervenors more readily participate in a hearing which concerns general policy issues, they may actually be more effective in proceedings which are narrow and technical in nature, because they are required to present a tighter case in these proceedings.[39] Consequently, one would expect a higher proportion of intervenor participation in cases involving broad policy issues than in those involving technical communications issues. On the other hand, intervenors should be more likely to have a positive effect on FCC decisions dealing with technical issues than on those dealing with general communications issues.

The negative relationship between intervention and FCC decisions might also be explained by the type of intervenor. In light of the interests and expertise of broadcasters, one might expect them to be more successful as intervenors than are citizens' groups. However, citizens' groups may intervene more frequently than would broadcasters because these groups are more likely to be dissatisfied with the "broadcaster-orientation" of Commission policy. Consequently, the relationship between intervenor participation and Commission decisions may be explained by the higher proportion of citizens' group intervenors. Such a finding would suggest that the Commission is still, to some extent, "captured by its broadcasting clientele," but that nonclientele groups could potentially become effective participants by employing some of the same approaches to intervention taken by the broadcasting industry. The effects of the main party, the issue, and the type of intervenor will be evaluated simultaneously, since these aspects of the process may be highly interrelated. For example, the type of intervenor participating may be associated with the nature of the issue in the hearing. Citizens' groups tend to be attracted to broad policy questions, while broadcaster intervenors may be most interested in the impact of modifications that the FCC may grant a licensee on its ability to present programs to its audience without electrical interference. Logit regression has been employed to assess the effect of each independent variable, holding the others constant, on the odds of the dependent variable (Commission decisions). First the appropriate logit model will be determined using a stepwise procedure that attempts to locate the most parsimonious model which still fits the data, as determined by a likelihood ratio chi square goodness of fit test.[40] The estimated coefficients for the independent variables will then be interpreted in terms of their impact on the odds of the Commission supporting or opposing the broadcaster.

Fitting the Model

The variables in this multivariate analysis have been defined as follows. Commission decisions (referred to as V) are divided into "pro broadcaster" and "anti broadcaster" categories, with conditional decisions included in the latter category, under the assumption that conditional decisions imply that the broadcaster's position was not completely supported, a categorization particularly relevant for commissions such as the FCC whose policies are clientele-oriented. The intervenor variable (G) consists of broadcasters, citizens' groups, and no intervenors.[41] The type of issue variable (I) includes technical communications issues (license transfers, waivers of rules, violations of rules, and construction permits), general policy issues (employment, programming, and concentration of control), and mixed issues (for hearings which include both technical and general issues). Finally, the television/radio distinction (M) has been chosen to represent the type of main party. These variables have been cross-classified into a four-way contingency table for the initial step in the procedure (see Table 8-6). Then, several models were fit in order to locate the most parsimonious one which still fit the data. In keeping with Knoke and Burke's suggestion, the approach used here began with the simplest model—the one which fit the one-variable marginal table for the Commission's decisions—and successively added increasingly complex interaction terms until an acceptable fit was obtained which could not be improved significantly by adding more terms,[42] that is, one with a low likelihood chi square and high p-value. These models are presented in Table 8-7.

The first question asked was whether intervenor input and commission decision are independent. The likelihood ratio test for this hypothesis, comparing the difference in the likelihood ratio chi squares for model 1 and model 2, was examined to determine whether or not the addition of the intervenor term results in a significant improvement in fit. The likelihood ratio chi square for the difference between model 1 and model 2 ($157.84 - 59.84 = 98.00$ with $17 - 15 = 2$ degrees of freedom) is significant at $p < .05$. Thus, we can reject the null hypothesis and conclude that there is a significant relationship between intervenor participation and Commission decision.

The next aspect of the process to be added to the equation is the effect of the main party variable on Commission decisions. The hypothesis contrasts model 3, with the main party-Commission interaction term included, with the reduced model (model 2), which does not contain this term. The difference between the two models is 3.66 with one degree of freedom, significant at $p. < .05$, so the null hypothesis that Commission decision is independent of the type of main party is rejected and the main party-interaction term will be added to the model.

In model 4, the interaction between the type of issue and Commission decision has been added. The likelihood ratio chi square test for the null

Table 8-6. Outcome of Broadcast Decisions by Type of Intervenor, by
         Type of Issue, and by Type of Main Party

Type of Intervenor	Main Party	Decision for Broadcaster	Conditional Against
No intervenor			
Technical	Radio	74	218
	TV	28	60
General	Radio	4	85
	TV	2	8
Mixed	Radio	13	19
	TV	10	5
Broadcaster			
Technical	Radio	34	34
	TV	22	15
General	Radio	7	3
	TV	2	3
Mixed	Radio	13	5
	TV	3	7
Citizen's groups			
Technical	Radio	24	10
	TV	13	4
General	Radio	29	31
	TV	22	20
Mixed	Radio	26	18
	TV	25	16

Table 8-7. Models for Data in Table 8-6

Model	Fitted Marginals	DF	G^2	P
1	V, MIG	17	157.84	0.0000
2	VG, MIG	15	59.84	0.0000
3	VG, VM, MIG	14	56.18	0.0000
4	VG, VM, VI, MIG	12	34.11	0.0000
5	VGI, VM, MIG	8	11.97	0.1527
6	VIG, VMG, MIG	6	9.32	0.1527

hypothesis that the term should be dropped is 22.07 with two degrees of
freedom, which indicates that model 4 differs significantly from model 3

with $p < .05$. Therefore, there is a significant relationship between the type of issue and the Commission decision.

While model 4 includes all the two-way interactions between Commission decision and each of the three independent variables, with a likelihood ratio chi square of 34.11 with twelve degrees of freedom, it still does not adequately fit the data. Thus, a three-way interaction term must be added to the equation in order to estimate more accurately the appropriate model for the data. Model 5 contains a term for the joint relationship of type of intervenor and issue with Commission decision; this term indicates that the effect of intervention on Commission decisions depends on the type of issue involved. The likelihood ratio chi square statistic for this model, 11.97 with eight degrees of freedom, signifies that it provides an acceptable fit for the data. In addition, it significantly improves the fit over that of model 4 at $p < .05$,[43] but its chi square value does not differ significantly from that of the more complex model, model 6.[44] Thus, model 5 meets the criterion of being the most parsimonious model which still fits the data.

Interpreting the Model

The model indicates that relative to the categorizations of the variables in the model, the effect of different classes of intervenors on FCC decisions depends on the nature of the issue involved. It does not depend on the type of broadcaster at which the complaint is directed. Similarly, the influence of the main party on the vote is independent of the type of intervenor at the hearing and the kind of issue involved.

In its loglinear form, model 5 can be written as

$$F(ijk) = \theta + \lambda_v + \lambda_g + \lambda_i + \lambda_m + \lambda_{vg} + \lambda_{vi} + \lambda_{vm} + \lambda_{gi} + \lambda_{gm} + \lambda_{im} + \lambda_{vgi} + \lambda_{mig}$$

which, in its logit form, reduces to

$$\Phi^v(ijk) = \beta^v + \beta^{vg} + \beta^{vi} + \beta^{vm} + \beta^{vgi}$$

where Φ^v is the log of the expected odds on Commission decision and each β represents the average of the logits (18) of Commission decision across all levels of a particular independent variable or interaction. The β's can be interpreted similar to the additive coefficients in ordinary regression; that is, the change in the log odds of Commission decision for a unit change in one of the parameters (holding the others constant) is *beta*. Table 8-8 gives the values for the odds ratios and their *beta* equivalents in model 5. To illustrate the meaning of these parameters, the following equation has been written for citizen group intervenors participating against television broadcasters on a technical communications issue. The dependent variable has been

Table 8-8. λ and β **Parameters for Model** *[VGI] [VM] [MIG]*

Term	λ	β
λ(2)	0.07	0.13
λ(2)G̲(1)	-0.22	-0.45
λ(2)G̲(2)	-0.31	-0.62
λ(2)G̲(3)	0.53	1.06
λ(2)I̲(1)	-0.11	-0.21
λ(2)I̲(2)	0.30	0.59
λ(2)I̲(3)	-0.19	-0.38
λ(2)M̲(1)	0.06	0.12
λ(2)M̲(2)	-0.06	-0.12
λ(2)G̲(1)I̲(1)	0.18	0.36
λ(2)G̲(1)I̲(2)	-0.36	-0.73
λ(2)G̲(1)I̲(3)	0.18	0.37
λ(2)G̲(2)I̲(1)	-0.16	-0.32
λ(2)G̲(2)I̲(2)	-0.07	-0.13
λ(2)G̲(2)I̲(3)	0.23	0.45
λ(2)G̲(3)I̲(1)	-0.02	-0.04
λ(2)G93)I̲(2)	0.43	0.86
λ(2)G(3)I(3)	-0.41	-0.82

Note: V (2)= a decision against the broadcaster. G (1) = a broadcaster intervenor; G (2) = a citizens' group intervenor; G (3) = no intervenor; 1 (1) = a technical issue; 1 (2) = a general issue; 1 (3) = a hearing which involves both types of issues. M (1) = a radio station main party; M (2) = a television station main party.

coded such that the odds of an "anti broadcaster" vote are the object of explanation.

$$\Phi V_2 = 1.34V_2 - .118V_2M_1 - .616V_2G_2 - .214V_2I_1 - .318V_2G_2I_1$$

The first term is the log odds of an "anti broadcaster" decision; the FCC appears to be more likely to arrive at a decision that is not completely favorable to the broadcaster. The second term suggests that the odds that the Commission will rule against a television station (as compared with a radio station) are reduced ($\beta = -.118$). In interpreting the third term, all coefficients for the type of intervenor variable must be considered, because it is a polychotomous variable. Thus, citizens' group participation reduces the odds of an "anti broadcaster" decision ($-.616$) to a larger degree than does broadcaster intervention ($-.446$); in contrast, the odds of an "anti broadcaster" decision are increased (1.062) when intervenors are not present at the hearing. Regarding the fourth term, the odds of the Commission opposing the broadcaster on a general policy issue are increased (.394), whereas they are reduced on a technical communications issue ($-.214$).

In interpreting the intervenor and issue effects, however, the interaction between the two must be considered as well. First, in hearings where no intervenors are present, a unit change in the three-way interaction term reduces the odds of an "anti broadcaster" decision on a technical communications issue ($\beta = -.04$) and increases the odds for a general policy issue ($\beta = .858$). Second, when citizens' groups participate in hearings that deal with technical communications issues, the odds of an "anti broadcaster" decision ($\beta = -.318$) are reduced to a greater extent than when they participate in hearings that deal with broad policy questions ($\beta = -.726$). This finding is important because it indicates that intervenors may have an effect on FCC decisions, depending on the type of intervenor and issue involved.

From this logit regression analysis it can be concluded that the three aspects of the hearing process isolated earlier (the type of main party, the issue, and the intervenor) generally have no effect or enhance the negative relationship between intervenor participation and FCC decisions. However, two significant findings which do have an impact on this relationship did emerge in the logit model. First, the association between intervention and FCC decisions is independent of the main party at which the intervenor's complaint is directed; on the other hand, this association is not independent of the type of issue involved in the hearing. Second, the FCC is likely to rule against the main party when broadcasters intervene on a technical communications issue; otherwise, the main party usually wins, regardless of the type of intervenor and issue involved.

CONCLUSIONS

While intervention was suggested by reformers as a means of opening up the regulatory decision-making process to groups beyond that of the clientele industry, critics expressed doubts as to the effectiveness of this reform in terms of policy outputs. They maintained that intervenors probably would not have much impact on policy outcomes because of their lack of resources, expertise, and familiarity with the political process by which regulatory policy is made. Thus, intervention is unlikely to alter the close relationship between the commission and the clientele group.

The results presented in this study tend to support the views of those who are less than optimistic about the impact of intervenors on regulatory policy. Intervenors at the FCC, as suggested in the earlier hypothesis, have no positive direct effect on broadcast decisions; in fact, they actually appear to have negative impact on Commission decisions, in that the FCC tends to side with the broadcaster when intervenors are present at the hearing. Even if conditional grants, as opposed to complete denials of the broadcaster's request, are considered, the Commission is still more likely to favor the broadcaster when intervenors participate in the process. Intervenors do appear to have some influence in this process, in that they are likely to convince a minority of the Commission of the validity of their claims. However, the policy significance of nonunanimous decisions by the FCC is probably minimal, given the relative inconspicuousness of this body in the political arena.

In an effort to find an explanation for why intervenors have a negative effect on FCC decisions, this analysis has focused on the influence of key aspects of the decision-making process: the type of main party, the issue, and the intervenor. Given the interdependent nature of these variables, a logit regression approach was used to separate out the independent effects of each variable on the relationship between intervention and FCC decisions. The hypothesis that the type of main party has an impact on the relationship between intervenor input and Commission decisions was not supported by the data. The type of issue involved, however, does influence the interaction between intervenors and the FCC. McLauchlan's theory that intervenors are more often successful in proceedings which involve technical communications issues was upheld for broadcaster intervenors, but not for citizens' groups; in fact, citizens' groups, regardless of the issue, were unable to obtain favorable rulings from the FCC. This finding may indicate that "clientele capture" still exists to some degree at the FCC; despite the expansion of intervenor participation, only clientele group intervention appears to have an impact on broadcasting decisions. Thus, intervention may provide merely another means for clientele group input to reach the Commission, rather than an avenue for alternative sources of information to be heard.

NOTES

1. U.S., Congress, Senate, Committee on Governmental Affairs, *Public Participation in Regulatory Agency Proceedings*, Committee Print, 95th Cong., 2d sess., 1977, chap. 1; James Q. Wilson, ed., *The Politics of Regulation* (New York: Basic Books, 1980), pp. ix-xi.

2. 359 F. 2d 1003 (D.C. Cir. 1966).

3. See *Federal Radio Commission v. Nelson Bros.* 289 U.S. 266 (1933).

4. See Kenneth Culp Davis, *Administrative Law* (St. Paul, Minn.: West Publishing Co., 1973), pp. 288-413.

5. See Richard B. Stewart, "The Reformation of American Administrative Law," *Harvard Law Review* 88 (June 1975): 1667-1813; and David B. Truman, *The Governmental Process: Political Interests and Public Opinion* (New York: Alfred A. Knopf, 1951).

6. Barry Cole and Mal Oettinger, *The Reluctant Regulators: The F.C.C. and the Broadcast Audience* (Reading, Mass.: Addison-Wesley, 1978), p. 200. For instance,

out of the approximately three thousand licenses up for renewal in 1976, only eight were not renewed. For an example of an instance in which the FCC was reproached for denying renewal, see Erwin G. Krasnow and Lawrence D. Longley, *The Politics of Broadcast Regulation*, 2d ed. (New York: St. Martin's Press, 1978), chap. 8; Louis Jaffe, "WHDH: The FCC and Broadcasting License Renewals," *Harvard Law Review* 82 (1969); Hyman H. Goldin, "Comment: 'Spare the Golden Goose': The Aftermath of WHDH in License Renewal Policy," *Harvard Law Review* 83 (March 1970): 1014-36; William H. Wentz, "Comment: The Aftermath of WHDH: Regulation by Competition or Protection of Mediocrity," *University of Pennsylvania Law Review* 118 (1970): 368-409; and Henry Geller, "A Modest Proposal for Modest Reform of the Federal Communications Commission," *Georgetown Law Journal* 63 (February 1975): 76-721.

7. See Roger Noll, *Reforming Regulation* (Washington, D.C.: Brookings Institution, 1971), p. 40. On the notion of sovereigns, see Anthony Downs, *Inside Bureaucracy* (Boston: Little, Brown, 1967).

8. Mancur Olson, *The Logic of Collective Action*, rev. ed. (New York: Schocken, 1971).

9. See David L. Shapiro, "Some Thoughts on Intervention Before Courts, Agencies, and Arbitrators," *Harvard Law Review* 81 (February 1968): 721-72; and U.S., Congress, Senate, *Public Participation in Regulatory Agency Proceedings*, pp. 47-49.

10. "Federal Communications Commission: Public and Broadcasting: A Procedure Manual," *Federal Register*, vol. 39, no. 173, part III (September 15, 1974), pp. 3228-32291.

11. *Office of Communication of the United Church of Christ v. FCC*, 359 F. 2d 994 (D.C. Cir. 1966); *Scenic Hudson Preservation Conference v. FPC*, 354 F. 2d 608 (2d Cir. 1965), cert. denied, 384 U.S. 941 (1966); and *National Welfare Rights Organization v. Finch*, F. 2d 725 (D.C. Cir. 1970).

12. Howard S. Boros, "Intervention in Civil Aeronautics Board Proceedings," *Administrative Law Review* 17 (Fall 1964): 5.

13. Paul Sabatier, "Social Movements and Regulatory Agencies: Toward a More Adequate and Less Pessimistic Theory of 'Clientele Capture,' " *Policy Sciences* 6 (1975): 310-17.

14. Daniel Mazmanian and Jeanne Nienaber, *Can Organizations Change? Environmental Protection, Citizen Participation, and the Corps of Engineers* (Washington, D.C.: Brookings Institution, 1979).

15. U.S., House of Representatives, Committee on Interstate and Foreign Commerce, Subcommittee on Oversight and Investigations, *Federal Regulation and Regulatory Reform*, Subcommittee Print, 94th Cong., 2d sess., 1976, p. 12.

16. Ernest Gellhorn, "Public Participation in Administrative Proceedings," *Yale Law Journal* 81 (January 1972): 388-400; and Roger Cramton, "The Why, Where, and How of Broadened Public Participation," *Georgetown Law Journal* 60 (February 1972): 525-50.

17. Sabatier, "Social Movements and Regulatory Agencies," pp. 310-42.

18. Report on Regulatory Agencies, n. 30, quoted in Erwin G. Krasnow and Lawrence D. Longley, *The Politics of Broadcast Regulation*, p. 64.

19. D. Stephen Cupps, "Emerging Problems of Citizen Participation," *Public Administration Review* 37 (September/October 1977): 482.

20. Robert Friedman, "Representation in Regulatory Decision Making: Scientific,

Industrial, and Consumer Inputs to the F.D.A.," *Public Administration Review* 38 (May/June 1978): 218.

21. Joseph A. Grundfest, *Citizen Participation in Broadcast Licensing Before the FCC* (Santa Monica, Calif.: Rand Corporation, 1976), p. 65.

22. William P. McLauchlan, "Research Proposal to Study Public Participation in Administrative Proceedings," unpublished manuscript, Purdue University, 1979, pp. 8-9.

23. These include Dean Burch and Richard Wiley (the Republican chairmen under the Nixon and Ford administrations, respectively) and Charles Ferris (the Democratic chairman during the Carter presidency).

24. Differences among these types of conditional decisions also will be examined, although the groups will be treated as one category for most of the analysis.

25. "Federal Communications Commission: Public and Broadcasting," pp. 3228-32291.

26. William P. McLauchlan, "Agency-Clientele Relations: A Study of the Federal Communications Commission," *Washington University Law Quarterly* (1977): 357-406.

27. Gellhorn, "Public Participation in Administrative Proceedings," pp. 359-404; Cramton, "The Why, Where, and How of Broadened Participation," pp. 525-50;

28. Cupps, "Emerging Problems of Citizen Participation," pp. 482; Friedman, "Representation in Regulatory Decision Making," p. 213.

29. William P. McLauchlan, "Agency-Clientele Relations," p. 290.

30. Odds ratios may be interpreted as probabilities. For instance, odds of four to one correspond to an 80 percent probability of an event occurring.

31. The odds comparing "pro broadcaster" to "anti broadcaster" decisions are 3.64 and 4.44 for the experimental groups in 1976 and 1979 respectively, and .74 and 1.73 for the control groups in these years.

32. McLauchlan, "Agency-Clientele Relations," p. 298.

33. On the policy impact of nonunanimous decisions by the Supreme Court, see Stephen L. Wasby, "The Communication of the Supreme Court's Criminal Procedure Decisions: A Preliminary Mapping," in Sheldon Goldman and Austin Sarat, eds., *American Court Systems* (San Francisco: W. H. Freeman, 1978), p. 556.

34. Harold P. Green, "Public Participation in Nuclear Power Plant Licensing: The Great Delusion," *William and Mary Law Review* 16 (Spring 1974): 508-14.

35. Cole and Oettinger, *Reluctant Regulators*, pp. 26, 194.

36. Gellhorn, "Public Participation in Administrative Proceedings," pp. 359-404; Cramton, "The Why, Where, and How of Broadened Participation," pp. 525-50; William T. Gormley, "Impacts of Public Advocates on Public Utility Regulatory Policy," unpublished manuscript, University of Wisconsin, 1980, pp. 19-36; and McLauchlan, "Agency-Clientele Relations," pp. 290-92.

37. Gellhorn, pp. 359-404; Cramton, pp. 525-50.

38. Gormley, "Impacts of Public Advocates on Public Utility Regulatory Policy," p. 36.

39. McLauchlan, "Research Proposal to Study Public Participation in Administrative Proceedings," pp. 8-9.

40. See Stephen E. Fienberg, *The Analysis of Cross-Classified Categorical Data* (Cambridge: MIT Press, 1978); and James A. Davis, "Hierarchical Models for Significance Tests in Multivariate Contingency Tables: An Exegesis of Goodman's

Recent Papers," in Herbert L. Costner, ed., *Sociological Methodology* (San Francisco: Jossey-Bass, 1974), pp. 189-231.

41. Jerry A. Hausman and David A. Wise, in "A Conditional Probit Model for Qualitative Choice: Discrete Decisions Recognizing Independence and Heterogeneous Preferences," *Econometrica* 46 (March 1978): 403-26, demonstrate that for this kind of variable, a conditional probit analysis provides more accurate predictions for the conditioned categories which in this case consist of citizens' group intervenors and broadcasters. Thus, the estimates for these categories may be somewhat conservative. Nevertheless, the Commission appears to react differently enough to citizens' groups and broadcaster intervenors (that is, the errors in prediction are close to being uncorrelated), so that the estimates are relatively accurate.

42. David Knoke and Peter J. Burke, *Log-linear Models*, Sage University Paper Series on Quantitative Applications in the Social Sciences, series no. 07-001 (Beverly Hills and London: Sage Publications, 1980), p. 38.

43. The difference in chi squares is 22.14 with four degrees of freedom.

44. The difference in chi squares is 2.62 with two degrees of freedom.

PART THREE

Directing
Communications
Policy

9

Technological Innovation in the Communications Industry: An Analysis of the Government's Role

> . . . he who wants . . .
> Order without disorder
> Does not understand the principles
> Of heaven and earth.
> He does not know how
> Things hang together.
>
> *Chuang-tzu*

THE central question facing American government in the twilight of the twentieth century is how to manage the economy. A strong economy was what made the tremendous expansion of social programs during the 1960s possible. A weak economy is what makes the Reagan administration's military build-up so problematic today.

Few economists would disagree that productivity is a key to a healthy, modern economy. The total annual hours worked in a nation can remain constant and yet that nation can have an ever increasing gross national product—provided that the productivity rate in its industries continues to rise. But what drives productivity?

In an early and famous study, Robert Solan concluded that over 80 percent of the growth in output per man hour from 1906 to 1949 in the United States was due to technological progress. In a more recent and comprehensive study Edward Denison of the Department of Commerce has argued that economic growth in the United States has been due in very considerable part to technological change. He concludes that it contributed about 12 percent of the growth in real output during 1909-29, and about 20 percent of this growth during 1929-57. Also, he estimated that it should contribute about 25 percent of this growth during 1969-80.[1] Because it is difficult to separate the effects on growth of technological change from those of investment in physical capital, these estimates are rough. Nevertheless, the fundamental point remains: technological change drives productivity.

For this reason, government policymakers have an abiding interest in promoting invention. During the past two decades, policy analysts, economists, social scientists, historians, and government managers have devoted much study to how government can stimulate innovative activity. Until only quite recently, most of this work has been concerned with the description of the process of innovation at a high level of aggregation or abstraction. Little consideration has been paid to the study of the specific innovation outputs of industries and firms. Yet, an understanding of what influences innovation in an industry or firm seems essential if public policy is to be successful in increasing the production of useful technology in specific areas.

Working on the assumption that more sector-specific microanalysis is needed, the focus here will be on the relationship between technological innovation in the communications industry and government action. For purposes of this analysis, the communications industry consists of point-to-point services (telephone) and point-to-many-point services (broadcast).

Why focus on this particular industry? The simplest answer perhaps is that, at the present time, the variety and intensity of federal intervention in this sector are shifting dramatically. These conditions make the need to better understand the effects of such intervention on technological innovation especially acute. Another reason for focusing on the communications industry involves the issue of productivity. The growth rate of productivity in this industry has been the highest in the U.S. economy (see Table 9-1).

Consider the case of American Telephone and Telegraph (AT&T). Productivity gains for the Bell System in the 1970s were more than three times those of the private domestic economy. In 1956 it took 133 people to service 10,000 telephones; in 1981 it took 60. But there is an important paradox worth noting: high-technology industries with good productivity gains tend to be the industries with the best prospects for expanded employment. In short, they create new jobs in the economy.

The following section takes a look at the technological innovation that lies behind this productivity record. More specifically, it presents a model of the process by which new technology comes to market. Before considering the questions of why and how government intervenes in the process, we need to clarify the nature of the process itself. The next step in our analysis will be to explore the economic justifications and policy tools for this intervention. The final section will present two broad policy recommendations and suggest some wider implication of the analysis.

THE PROCESS OF TECHNOLOGICAL INNOVATION

Technological innovation can be defined as the entire sequence of activities through which scientific and technical knowledge is translated into a

Table 9-1. Productivity Growth Rates in the U.S. Economy 1968–
1978

Industry	1972 SIC Code	Productivity
Communications	48	5.84
Manufacturing	20-39	2.34
Transportation	40-47	2.02
Wholesale trade	50-51	1.64
Electric, gas and sanitary services	49	1.59
Finance, insurance and real estate	60-67	.99
Retail trade	52-59	.76
Business services	73	.69
Agriculture, forestry and fishing	01-09	.68
Government & government enterprise	NA	.56
Health services	80	-1.44
Construction	15-17	-2.28
Mining	10-14	-2.29

Note: Productivity is defined as gross product originating per hour worked. "Gross product originating" represents constant dollar value added and represents the industry's contribution to real GNP. SIC = Standard Industrial Classification.

Source: Adapted from U.S. Department of Commerce, Bureau of Industrial Economics, *1981 U.S. Industrial Outlook*, p. XXIV.

physical product that is used widely in society. This definition encompasses more than any list of communications hardware such as that in Table 9-2 might suggest. It tells us that every invention requires that someone, somewhere initiate a scientific or technical idea; acquire the necessary additional knowledge; transform the idea into a useful product; and then successfully produce and market it.

Because technological innovation is complex, and varies from industry to industry, those who investigate it are not entirely agreed upon how best to divide the process into stages.[2] Fortunately, much of this difference of opinion is semantic rather than substantive; and the following discussion, which identifies eight stages, is not radically different from the alternative ways to identify the emergence of a new technology.

A Conceptual Model of Technical Progress

Study of technological innovation offers government policymakers help in many ways. Specifically, it tells them about the time, the critical factors,

Table 9–2. Developing Technologies Significant to the Communications Industry

Pulse Code Modulation--System invented in 1938 which, instead of transmitting the analog waveform of human voice, converts that waveform into its digital equivalent.

Packet switching--A network in which data items are stored in minicomputers and then transmitted to the next part of the network in blocks, which are called "packets". Arguably the most significant development in communications since geostationary satellites.

Large scale integration (LSI)--Effective explotation of the first two technologies had to await the development of the silicon large scale integrated circuit. Today gallium is being developed as a material for chips that are faster than silicon but more practical than the ultrafast Josephson junctions (which must operate near absolute zero).

Geostationary platforms--A proposed configuration for future communications spacecraft which incorporates large, multibeam antennas. Perhaps the only way to expand satellite communications capabilities substantially.

Millimeter-wave radio--Radio in frequencies in the band above the microwave band and capable of relaying a greater quantity of information.

TV receivers for data broadcasting.

Cable TV.

Computer--Controlled switching.

Intelligent telephones--With voice answerback (that is, storage of the human voice in a machine) and pushbuttons, ordinary telephones become potential computers.

Picturephone.

Scramblers.

Mobile radio.

Optical fibers--The transmission of concentrated light pulses through minuscule glass fibers which can carry a thousand times as much information as a copper wire pair.

Lasers--Laser communications systems have the potential of carrying several million telephone calls at once and, unlike radio receivers, are practically impervious to interference from a nuclear explosion.

Source: A survey of inventions reported in the trade press and compiled by the author.

and other considerations useful in influencing technical progress. Data collected over several decades on technical innovations in the communications industry are uneven, yet there are enough commonalities to suggest patterns of experience.

Scientific Suggestion or Discovery. One of the central features of modern technologies, and the industries that have sprung up around them, is that they are based on theoretical knowledge or, in short, science. Industries such as steel, motor, electricity, telephone, and aviation are all "nineteenth-century" industries in that they were created by "talented tinkers" who worked independently of contemporary science.[3] For example, Samuel Finley Breese Morse was a portrait painter who caught the fever of electrical experimentation. Through trial-and-error empiricism, he was able to obtain a patent for the telegraph in 1840.

In contrast, the modern semiconductor industry has a scientific base: in 1950, William Shockley published *Electrons and Holes in Semiconductors*, a book that presented the theory of semiconductor devices. Ralph Bown's foreword to that book gives an eloquent account of the scientific base for semiconductor technology:

> If there be any lingering doubts as to the wisdom of doing deeply fundamental research in an industrial laboratory, this book should dissipate them. Dr. Shockley's purpose has been to set down an account of the current understanding of semiconductors. . . . But he has done more than this. He has furnished us with a documented object lesson. For in its scope and detail this work is obviously a product of the power and resourcefulness of the collaborative industrial group of talented physicists, chemists, metallurgists and engineers with whom he is associated. And it is an almost trite example of how research directed at basic understanding of materials and behavior, "pure" research if you will, sooner or later brings to the view of inventive minds engaged therein opportunities for producing valuable practical devices.[4]

Thus, at the root of most significant technological innovations today are the suggestions of scientists or engineers, the discoveries of new phenomena, or the recognition of an opportunity. This third source seems to have occurred in the case of semiconductor devices cited above.

Proposal of a Concept. By combining existing techniques and knowledge, researchers put forward a theory or design concept that ultimately is workable enough to become the basis of the technology that is first introduced into operational use. Perhaps the classic example of such a proposal is the communications satellite. In the October 1945 issue of *Wireless World*, Arthur C. Clarke, scientist and science fiction writer, published an article entitled "Extra-Terrestrial Relays." Clarke proposed artificial earth satellites with transmitters and receivers orbiting high above earth and relaying messages between remote locations on the surface of the globe.

Verification. Continuing with the communications satellite example, the question immediately raised by Clarke's proposal was a simple one: Would it work? On 11 January 1946, the U.S. Army Signal Corps conducted an experiment that confirmed the validity of Clarke's design concept. Under the code name Project Diana (named for the ancient moon goddess), engineers bounced 112-MHz radar signals off the moon and detected them on earth. This first extraterrestrial communication in history indicated that these frequency ranges were potentially useful for transmitting over great distances through the earth's atmosphere, but it did not demonstrate very conclusively or directly an application to a useful purpose.

Laboratory Demonstration. In this stage, the first primitive model of the technology concept in a useful form appears. The launching of Sputnik in

October 1957 and Explorer I several months later quickly dispelled whatever doubts remained about the feasibility of communications satellites. In the language of communications research and development, the demonstration often appears as the laboratory "breadboard" model.

Before we can say that the next stage has begun, numerous trials of alternative configurations, materials, and scale occur. The criteria for successful assessment of this stage are two-fold. First, a truly significant invention will use its new combination of scientific and engineering principles to relieve or avoid major constraints inherent in the previous technology. For example, in the case of the transistor radio, "elimination of the heated cathode of a vacuum tube allowed portable radio size and weight to be reduced while offering longer battery life and greater reliability." The second criterion is embodiment merit, that is, the "assessed value of the physical form given to an inventive concept." This means that even the most creative invention requires substantial additional engineering to be complete. George R. White and Margaret B.W. Graham, who formulated both these criteria state further that

it was such an embodiment opportunity that the Japanese radio manufacturers seized when they made the pocket transistor radio. They reinforced the size and weight advantages the transistor offered by miniaturizing the ferrite antennae, loudspeakers, and tuning capacitors as well. . . . The main embodiment concern is to minimize dilutions of the value of the inventive concept while maximizing enhancements.[5]

Field Trial. Eventually the technical concept leaves the laboratory bench and the process continues on a life-size scale in the field.

In the communications sector, prototypes in several stages of testing are recognizable. In recent experiments, conventional telephones have become part of a teleprocessor, including an electric typewriter keyboard and a video screen similar to that of television. For the first time, it was clear that videotex—the generic name for such information retrieval systems—was no longer the stuff of science fiction. For example, in 1980 AT&T gave several dozen families and a handful of businesses in Albany, New York, an experimental telephone device that allowed them to obtain in seconds, on a video screen, the telephone number of any of the area's 400,000 subscribers without leafing through forty telephone books or dialing information.[6]

This experiment illustrates the ways in which companies actively try to design the most economical way to introduce into America's communications system what heretofore had been an interesting oddity. Even though there are no profits as yet, and sales are minuscule, dozens of major U.S. corporations are already investing nearly $100 million in developing and testing videotex systems. One estimate counted eighty-three experiments in 1981 going on around the world with the total investment amounting to one-quarter of a billion dollars. As Ben B. Smylie, General Manager of Field Electronic Publishing, said about the videotex experiment his company was running in Chicago, "You've got to go out there and get your nose bloody—get some field experience."[7]

Commercial Introduction. This stage marks the point at which the technology is accepted as a valid, operating system. As the following example shows, the start of this stage may overlap the field trial stage. In December 1978, AT&T began field trials that were to indicate that cellular transmissions compared favorably to land-line telephone service. (This new concept of mobile radio service involves dividing a large urban area into cells. Certain frequencies are assigned to the use of vehicles that happen to be in that cell. As a vehicle moves from one part of town to another, its call is automatically switched from one cell to the next without interruption. An electronic processor keeps tabs on users' locations and radio signals.) While AT&T continues to test this system, it has progressed to the point of having 1,300 customers.

Widespread Adoption. This stage, like the last one, is not clearly defined. Essentially, it marks the time at which the innovation has achieved widespread use in society. By the mid-1980s it is estimated that more than one million of Japan's 30 million registered vehicles will carry mobile telephones. Does that constitute "widespread adoption?"

The adoption of most new communications technologies is slow at first; then the market growth rate becomes massive. The main reason for this growth pattern is probably that the first subscribers have few people to call. Why have a Picturephone set if there are few other sets in the community? Similarly, few people wanted to have a television when that technology was first introduced. At the time, the industry for making programs had not been built up. Thus, the widespread adoption of television came about a decade after the introduction of the first television service. The slope of the curve when television did take off was amazingly steep.[8]

Proliferation. The term *proliferation* as used here carries two meanings. First, it can refer to the adaption of the technological device to purposes other than its original one. For example, although over 80 percent of fiber-optic installations are used by the telephone and cable television industries, the technology has increasingly been adapted to the intrasystem wiring of computers and nuclear power plants, and the internal wiring of weapons systems and aircraft. Second, proliferation can refer to the adaptation of the technical principle to other functions. For example, radar microwave technology now is used in home cooking ovens.

Refining the Model

Order and simplicity are important first steps toward the understanding of a subject. The eight-stage model of technological innovation presented above meets those objectives. But in order to do justice to the spirit of the whole process of innovation, there are at least four specific aspects that should be emphasized as well.

Length. The full process of technological innovation—from the conception of an idea to its introduction into the market—may take between one and three decades. (See Table 9-3.) An issue frequently addressed is whether innovation time lags have been increasing or decreasing over the years. But a review of the literature fails to reveal conclusive evidence for either position. Moreover, Langrish et al. argue that it is impossible to observe anything but relatively short time lags for recent innovations.[9] Our perspective when looking at these innovations allows us to identify only those which have already been introduced into the market, although there may be inventions that have already been conceived but which will bear fruit only after the study.

To test this proposition, consider the record of holography. In the late 1960s this revolutionary form of photography, which uses laser light to faithfully render the three-dimensionality of an object, was being hailed as one of the most exciting developments in modern optics. Among the many commercial applications it was to have offered were holographic movies and three-dimensional television. But unlike the laser, which is now starting to find its way into fiber-optic communications links, holography still remains essentially in the laboratory stage. The case is not uncommon. The entire process of technological innovation may be filled with delays, false starts, and technical, economic, and social pitfalls.

Or consider the history of the multiple-beam antenna which can transmit and receive signals from several satellites at once. Production has been technologically possible for a long time. Comsat built a demonstration model of its Torus antenna in 1973. But not until 1981 did Comsat bother to carry the technology forward to the next stage, field trial. The reason for the delay seems to be that the market was not deemed ready for multiple-beam antennae during the 1970s.

Components. A second detail about the process to be noted is that innovations are actually composed of many components or subsystems. Each of these merits careful, individual analysis. A prime example of this clustering of technologies into one major innovation is the "home/office of the future." The future home will probably be a giant electric "appliance" plugged into a nationwide communications network (such as the previously described videotex). The most important components are already available in the telephone and the television receiver. In the future, specialized terminals will combine microprocessors with conventional hardware to perform not only information retrieval but other more complex chores. Meanwhile, upcoming communications services, made possible by commercial satellite and microwave systems, will accelerate the drive toward the fully automatic office of the future. The concept received impetus from

Table 9-3. Process of Technological Innovation for Radio

Stage	Date	Event
1	1846	Michael Faraday's experimental observations lead to discovery of electrial induction.
2	1873	James Clark Maxwell presents the theory of electromagnetic energy.
3	1886	Heinrich Hertz confirms Maxwell's theories by sending and receiving radio waves.
4	1894	Oliver Lodge demonstrates a method of selective tuning for wireless communications.
5	1896	Marconi, after refinement of equipment, receives first patent on wireless transmission.
6	1897	Marconi establishes a company in England to exploit commercial applications of wireless.
7	1901	Wireless spreads to marine use.

the introduction of word/text processors in the mid-1970s. But full realization of this concept will require the integration of many sophisticated components.[10]

Merging. When two or more technologies are linked to form one, the result is richer than the sum of its parts. Instances of such linkage or cross-fertilization in the communications sector are plentiful. The contribution that satellites and lasers are making to the communications revolution has already been noted (see Table 9-2). But surely the most significant confluence of technologies in the last generation is the merging of conventional communications technology with computers and semiconductors.

Although a comprehensive chronology of computers might begin with the calculating machines built by Pascal (1642), Leibniz (1671), and Babbage (1822), the history of the modern computer begins about 1941, when it became linked to electronics. The marriage to electronics accounts for two of the most important features of the modern computer—tremendous gains in performance characteristics and declines in costs. Electromechanical relays, hand-wired plugboards, and manually set switches—the main alternatives in 1941 to electronic circuitry—simply would not have provided an adequate basis for such improvements in speed, reliability, and costs of operations.

Until 1940 developments in electronics took place at a fairly moderate pace. The pace quickened during World War II and began to explode in the late 1950s with the introduction of the first transistors, which were invented in the late 1940s. In these, the current connecting electrodes flows through solid materials known as semiconductors rather than through bulky vacuum tubes. Transistors are typically made of silicon, the most economical semiconductor. Integrated circuits, invented in 1959, contain many interconnected transistors on a piece of silicon. Since 1959 integration has proceeded so fast that the number of transistors per piece of silicon has doubled yearly. By 1980, the semiconductor industry was producing 1,000 to 100,000 components on a pea-sized chip of silicon. In research laboratories, chips carrying anywhere from 100,000 to a million transistors are being produced experimentally.

In the 1970s computer technology began to become deeply intertwined with communications technology. Indeed, the most rapidly growing area of electronic communications is the transmission of digital information. Digital circuits, which use on-off pulses of electricity, are the heart of the modern computer. Most other electronic devices, such as radios and television sets, rely on the other type of circuit, analog, in which electricity varies continuously in strength and amount.

Fundamental to data communications networks are modems. A modem, or data set, converts digital signals to analog (voice grade) signals, then reconverts them to digital signals at the other end of the communications line. These devices enable companies to send computer-generated data from one location to another through standard telephone lines. Distributed data processing—essentially networks of small and medium-size computers connected by transmission links—allows the transfer of much more data between dispersed points at lower costs.

But even plain old telephone service (POTS, in the industry jargon) is going digital: voice signals are compacted and compressed to put more calls on a channel. Today about 40 percent of the trunks in the Bell System employ digital transmission, and the majority of independent suppliers of switching equipment in the United States are installing only digital equipment in new offices. In a communications terminal, a microprocessor (essentially, a complex type of integrated circuit that can contain on a single chip the equivalent of the central processor of a minicomputer) can convert signals to a digital form, reduce redundant information, process incoming signals to extract desired information, and serve as a local computing center. Such developments have posed a major problem for those, such as the Federal Communications Commission (FCC), who must decide where communications—a regulated activity—ends and where the unregulated computer market begins.

Risk. The fourth and final refinement to the conceptual model of innovation presented earlier is this: many factors besides technical feasibility will influence the progress and direction of a technology. For example, the office of the future will require the development of new techniques for managing offices. Whole organizations will have to be restructured to make the best use of new machines and services.

Based on his 1971 study of innovation in radio, W. Rupert Maclaurin suggested five factors that influence the process of innovation: advances in sciences underlying industry; the engineering act that is closely attuned to these scientific advances; organization of the industry; capital freely available for radical new developments; and entrepreneurs with requisite innovative skills.[11] Viewing the process from the perspective of the early 1980s, two additional factors may be added which make innovation an even riskier enterprise.

The first is market conditions. Evidence by Edwin Mansfield suggests that the hardest task in creating a successful product is not invention, which requires only technical virtuosity; rather, it is marketing, which requires a different sort of astuteness. Mansfield's studies indicate that R&D projects in the American private sector produce successful products only 12 to 20 percent of the time, depending on the company. The failures occur not mainly in research—most projects achieve their technical goals—but in marketing.[12] The case of three-dimensional television makes the point. The technology has reached a point where it could begin to be used in the United States; indeed, it is already thriving in several nations (Japan and Australia, for example). But marketing uncertainty hobbles the television industry: are viewers willing to buy adapters, glasses, or new television sets for three-dimensional reception?

The second new factor making innovation riskier is government actions. More specifically, the federal government today chooses the goals of communications research, funds that research, and controls the final product. Arguably, this factor is even more significant than market conditions. In any event, government intervention requires a closer look.

JUSTIFICATION AND MEANS
FOR GOVERNMENT INTERVENTION

One theme already stressed is that the process of technological innovation is extremely complex. Implicit in that theme is the idea that proper management of the process requires close attention. Most economists who study innovation would probably agree. But given the complexity of the process, some might also think that government should not interfere directly in the marketplace. But all economists do recognize certain conditions, known as market imperfections, that may necessitate government intervention. An examination of four such imperfections or market failures and of the policy tools available for correcting those imperfections follows.

Why Intervene?

Incomplete Appropriability of Benefits. According to Kenneth J. Arrow, society will fail to allocate an optimal amount of resources to inventive activity even under perfect competition. Since it is never possible to predict the output to be produced by a given combination of inputs, inventive activity is inherently a risky process, and devices that will permit the shifting of risks have been only imperfectly developed. Consequently, society under-invests in such risky enterprises. Furthermore, there is an inherent conflict in government attempts to create property rights in information,. for example, through the patent system. On the one hand, a patent system strengthens a company's incentive to engage in research, but on the other hand such a system prohibits full utilization of information that has already been produced.[13]

To understand why there may be under-investment in civilian technology, one must recognize that private rates of return may not equal social rates of return. As is evident from repeated case studies and detailed investigation of the innovative activities of major firms, private companies often cannot appropriate all of the social benefits from an innovation. A good example is the improvement in television receivers for better spectrum utilization. It has been recognized that it would be possible to place television broadcast stations closer together geographically, if television receivers were better able to reject signals on channels adjacent to the channel being watched and were less susceptible to other forms of interference from television signals on various other channels near the desired channel. But receiver manufacturers have little incentive to provide sets, at a higher cost, because such improved receivers are not necessary given the current placement of television broadcast stations. The result is a problem that the marketplace cannot solve by itself, even though cable television has provided ample evidence of people's desire for more channels of television service. Accordingly, the FCC funds research in this area.[14]

Public Goods. This justification for government intervention is similar to the concept of incomplete appropriability of benefits. But the distribution of external benefits differs. Public goods are benefits enjoyed by nearly everyone, in contrast to the distribution of benefits (in the form of profits) among companies trying to exploit the innovations developed by one company.

To the extent that communications R&D does promote industrial productivity, economic prosperity, national security, and trade surpluses, government intervention is needed to assure a satisfactory amount of communications research. Private firms do not produce public goods in adequate quantities because (1) such goods are "nonrival" so that one person's use of them does not diminish someone else's enjoyment, or (2) they are "nonexclusive" so that those who choose not to pay cannot be barred from their enjoyment. National security is a category of public goods particularly important to public policy. For example, some observers argue that aid to the American steel industry is necessary because steel is vital to national security. This kind of argument, applied in other countries, is one reason why 45 percent of world steel capacity is government owned.[15]

Similar arguments can be made for public policies to promote the communications industry,—namely that communications technology has critical military applications. Like Austerlitz and Gettysburg, the Yom Kippur War of 1973 changed strategic doctrine in a way that no serious military power could afford to ignore. While the Israeli army lost hundreds of tanks and planes in a few weeks against its less sophisticated opponents, its gunboats were sinking or disabling two-thirds of the Egyptian fleet. The difference lay in the black boxes that jam radar and intercept or deceive communications, and are collectively called "electronic warfare." Israeli gunboats had the latest technology; Israeli tanks and planes did not.[16]

Externalities. The costs to society as a whole associated with private economic activity generally differ from private costs. Therefore, market decisions based on private calculations do not necessarily yield outcomes that are socially desirable. Such externalities or spillovers often justify public policy measures having significant effects on the communications industry. Such measures are discriminatory in the sense that some industries are affected more than others. For example, while control of environmental pollution and worker safety has caused a serious financial burden in many industries, its impact on the communications industry has been relatively mild.

This might change in the future, however. Radio waves are the invisible cables of the vast communications systems in the United States. We are surrounded with radio emitters, from low-power walkie-talkies to strong industrial sources. If the human eye were sensitive to radio waves, it would be able to see the relay networks that carry telegrams and long-distance phone calls as dim shafts of light stretching from the roof of one tall building to another or the radiation that carries television programs from a broadcast tower. Some have called this electronic smog, the prime pollutant of the emerging information age.

Whenever an electric current runs through an antenna, it radiates waves of electric and magnetic force. Intense exposures to a radio-frequency source can burn the skin and underlying tissue. Scientific opinion on the effect of lower doses, however, remains divided. One recent experiment showed that a power density twenty times lower than the current U.S. occupational guideline altered the behavior and blood chemistry of laboratory rats. In light of these and other findings, the federal government's National Institute for Occupational Safety and Health has proposed mandatory safeguards stricter than the voluntary measures now recommended.

Natural Monopoly. A natural monopoly exists when the production of a good or service is characterized by increasing returns to scale, that is, when per-unit production costs decrease as the firm becomes larger. Consequently, the largest firm in the industry should also be the most efficient, that is, it should have the lowest cost per unit of output. Such a firm has the ability to underprice competing firms and drive them out of business. The surviving firm then becomes a monopolist, the sole producer of the good or service. If unregulated, it may pursue price and research objectives that are not considered desirable from the public's viewpoint.

The primary attribute of natural monopolies, and the reason they are allowed to exist, is that they can supply the entire market with a product more cheaply than can any combination of smaller firms. Local telephone service is a classic example of a natural monopoly. The value of telephone service is a function of the number of people with whom a subscriber can talk. A single firm can interconnect large numbers of local subscribers at lower cost because the presence of more than one firm would require wasteful duplication of facilities.

Changing circumstances can call into question the designation of certain industries as natural monopolies. Interstate telecommunications is a case in point. The sharp increase in demand for data transmission services has exceeded the single-firm economies of scale of microwave transmission. A monopoly is not needed for efficient point-to-point specialized services.[17] Similarly, satellite communications has sharply reduced scale economies when compared to long lines, and the microwave transmission medium— optical fibers—has such extensive economies of scale that it might restore the natural monopoly designation to the interstate telecommunications industry.[18]

Closely related to the preceding discussion is the regulation of natural resources. Exclusive control over an essential natural resource can be a source of monopoly power. Traditionally, an important justification for government intervention in the communications sector has been the interdependencies that result from the exploitation of the electromagnetic spectrum suitable for radio and television broadcasting. Government regulation, presumably, would help insure the efficient use of that quite limited natural resource. After all, early unregulated use of the airwaves resulted in a disruptive overlapping of signals. The FCC accordingly assigned wavelengths, broadcast power, and geographic areas served. Today, telecommunications executives and administrative officials, led by FCC Chairman Mark S. Fowler, are arguing that the expanding video market should be deregulated. They say that technological change—for example, eighty-channel cable systems and television sets that can send as well as receive information—has undermined the old rationale.

The rationale still seems to hold, however, above the earth. Worldwide demand for international satellite communications is growing rapidly. In the United States, at this writing, five domestic satellite companies are in operation and at least three others are contemplated. As a result of the increased demand for satellites, the portion of the geosynchronous orbit that can serve North America is becoming congested. Until new technology can be substituted for existing systems, the FCC will have to ration the remaining orbital slots.

Economists generally agree that monopoly power reduces production and allocative efficiency, but they are far less certain about its effect on the creation of new technology and other aspects of dynamic efficiency.

Strategies of Government Intervention

Options for government intervention in communications research can be grouped into seven broad categories:

Technology Push Actions

1. Education
2. Basic research and advanced development
3. Mission R&D program (leading to prototype)
4. Demonstration programs

Technology Pull Actions

5. Procurement
6. Tax relief
7. Regulation

The first four categories attempt to initiate change by directly creating new technology. Government programs such as these, which seek to induce change through new inventions, are referred to as "technology push." Categories 5 through 7 rely on designing market mechanisms or incentives to induce companies to create new products or modify existing ones. This process of induced change is referred to as "technology pull."

Technology Push versus Technology Pull

The technology push position tends to dominate most government policy toward technology. It is the position which many scientists and engineers tend to take. It is based on the assumption that, if the technology is made available through government funding of R&D, someone, somehow, will find a use for it.

The technology pull, or market demand, position tends to be most popular with economists. It is based on the assumption that market forces and consumer demand stimulate innovation. Consequently, public policy should concentrate on making markets more effective in order to stimulate innovation. Proponents of this position would say, in short, "necessity *is* the mother of invention." Let us take a closer look at each approach.

One of the most persistent and important characteristics of American R&D is the diversity of institutional sources of support. Most funding of R&D comes from federal and industrial sources, each providing approximately the same proportion of funds (about 48 percent) in recent years. Measured in constant dollars, national R&D spending in 1981 amounted to about $69 billion. Despite the diversity of funding sources, most research (about 71 percent) is performed by industry. Slightly over 10 percent of R&D expenditures by industry is for communication.

Table 9-4 shows that civilian agencies provided only $71,190,000 in fiscal 1981 to communications research. But as indicated earlier, the Department of Defense is quite interested in communications technology. Defense related expenditures can be broken down roughly into two categories: (1) "Communications Research, Development, Testing, and Engineering," which includes programs specifically oriented toward communications functions and processes (for example, the Minimum Essential Emergency Communications Network and the Joint Tactical Information Distribution System); and (2) "Other," which includes programs primarily oriented towards command-and-control functions and processes (for example, Post-Attack Command and Control System and Airborne Warning and Control System [AWACS]). The first category totaled $733.3 million in 1981; the second category totaled $61.2 million. In addition, the DOD Science and Technology Program sponsors exploratory development in communications technology. The fiscal 1981 request included $25.5 million. Thus, the total DOD Communications R&D program for fiscal year 1981 was $820 million.[19]

While government funding is a popular and much discussed public policy tool for encouraging private research, it is not the only one. Nor is it necessarily considered the most important tool. This conclusion emerges from a 1980 survey of 101 American companies carried out by Yankelovich, Skelly and White, Inc., for the Sperry Corporation.[20] The survey of business executives' opinions about technological innovation found three factors perceived to have affected innovation in the 1970s. Direct government actions—particularly regulations (cited by 66 percent) and tax policies (53 percent)—were seen as having been the primary deterrents to innovation. The economic environment, characterized by inflation and shrinking capital markets, was also frequently cited. To the extent that these conditions are to a large degree the result of economic policy, they represent important, albeit indirect, ways in which the federal government hinders technological innovation. The only factors that the executives frequently cited as having encouraged industries to innovate were foreign competition (54 percent) and rising energy costs (48 percent).

Table 9–4. Civilian Communications R&D Funding, FY 1981
(Dollars in Thousands)

NASA	$29,900
Department of Transportation	16,700
Department of Commerce	9,000
Postal Service	7,500
FCC	100
NSF	4,000
Department of Justice	550
Department of the Interior	20
HEW	3,000
ICA - Internation Communication Agency	140
FEMA - Federal Emergency Management Admin.	280
Total	$71,190

Source: U.S. Congress, House Committee on Science and Technology, *Communications Research and Development* (Washington, D.C.: Government Printing Office, 20 May 1980), p. 50.

Three of the most important ways in which government can adopt a technology pull position are procurement, taxation, and regulation.

Procurement. There is some difference of opinion between those who claim that military and space funding of communications components (particularly semiconductors and high speed computers) was essential to their development and those who see only the market provided by the Pentagon and the National Aeronautics and Space Administration (NASA) as having been important. The following is a fair summary of the latter view:

The Department of Defense has clearly had a major influence on electronics technology but not in the direct way one might initially expect. Substantially, none of the major innovations in semiconductors has been a *direct* result of defense sponsored projects. . . . How, then, has the Department of Defense influenced the generation of new technology? Defense procurement and sponsorship of R&D has stimulated the civilian electronics industry to introduce new products more rapidly and has led to dramatic increases in the performance and reliability of electronic components and dramatization of the urgency of these demands through direct funding for research and development.

New entrants have been found to most often be the innovators of major product advances in the electronics and computer industries. The crucial influence of defense programs on electronics technology has been in their role as sponsors of new firms and ventures.[21]

A similar pattern of early large-scale government support through contracts is evident in the computer industry.

Further, government procurement appears to have helped accelerate the diffusion process (Stage 7), that is, it has facilitated the widespread commercial adoption of new technology. As the firms increased their production—to meet the substantial government market—learning economies were realized and costs fell. In a few years, the price was low enough to allow penetration of the consumer market. The large space-defense market also produced a "demonstration effect." For example, without the demonstration effect of space-defense computer systems, the combination of unfamiliarity and skepticism among business executives would have been a significant barrier to commercial sales.

Today, the federal government is the biggest single user of telecommunications equipment and services in the United States. The telecommunications inventory is over $50 billion. Use, of course, implies procurement; and the government's annual bill for these purchases is about $10 billion. Naturally, this gives government enormous potential marketplace leverage—which can be used to advance the state of the art and reduce costs.

Taxation. Tax credits for R&D could benefit the communications industry enormously. While this proposition has always been true, it became extremely significant in the early 1980s. In the first place, the Reagan administration has chosen to pull government out of most commercial-development ventures. To its way of thinking, a vigorous expansion of R&D should take place in the private sector. In the second place, the semiconductor industry, which is the backbone of modern communications technology, has been growing so rapidly that some firms have been hard pressed to generate sufficient cash flow to keep up with internal needs. The capital needs of the semiconductor industry for the 1980s have been estimated at $25 billion to $35 billion, compared to $5 billion for the 1970s.[22]

These trends may be offset by actions taken by Congress in 1981. Congress enacted a 25 percent tax credit for certain corporate research expenditures higher than the average during the previous three years. It also allowed companies to depreciate capital equipment used in R&D over three years rather than ten.

Most costs associated with R&D—in the communications industry or any other—can now be deducted in the year they occur. But R&D typically amounts to only a small fraction (10 to 20 percent) of the expenses associated with bringing a new product to the market. Thus, tax policies in the United States are not a very strong stimulus for innovation. In contrast, the Japanese government gives a tax credit of 20 percent for increases in

R&D spending, as well as a variety of sector-specific tax breaks (for example, to firms developing computer software).

Accelerated depreciation of communications equipment would help the telephone industry move more rapidly to give consumers some of the new communications products and services discussed here. In the telephone industry, the average depreciation-rate period (that is, the time over which a firm recovers its investment) is sixteen years. In contrast, the computer industry has a capital recovery period of about five years. State regulatory commissions often specify a useful life as long as thirty-three years for central office switching equipment. Clearly, with today's rapidly changing technology, the economic life of such computerized equipment is considerably less than a third of a century. The upshot of these depreciation schedules in the communications industry is that replacing old technology with new occurs at a rate slower than the optimum. A more generalized policy for encouraging R&D investment, designed to stimulate the venture capital markets which are important for many communications firms, became effective on 1 January 1982: R&D tax shelters.[23]

Regulation. While governments in countries like Japan and France work closely with industry to foster innovation, the United States government has adopted a relatively adversarial relationship towards business, subjecting it to thousands of complex regulations issued by dozens of federal agencies. On balance, these regulations increase uncertainty and make technological advance more difficult. Moreover, corporations based on older technologies will use the laws to fight threatening new technologies. (They have not forgotten what Western Union did to the Pony Express!)

Thus, television broadcasters lobbied successfully until 1970 to stop the spread of cable television (CATV). In 1966 they even managed to persuade the FCC to require that, in the top 100 markets (about 89 percent of all television sets), cable television operators had to prove that importing distant signals would not harm any existing or future television stations. Meanwhile the telephone companies worked to prevent CATV from engaging in two-way communications.

Similarly, government regulation has retarded the use of satellite technology for domestic communication. Telstar, the first successful communications satellite, was launched in 1962, and thereafter international satellite traffic grew rapidly. Yet not until 1975 was the first American domestic satellite launched. The reason for the delay was the fear that satellites could bypass established telephone trunks, carrying toll traffic at much lower cost.

The profits of regulated firms like AT&T are often computed by multiplying the allowed rate of return times the firm's rate base, that is, the depreciated value of its capital stock. Consequently, AT&T has tended to reject the most efficient innovations if they are low capital and has chosen instead less efficient high capital alternatives that expand its rate base. That alternative is referred to as "high capital" when adoption of a particular technology requires heavy expenditures for new plant and equipment. In 1968 such considerations led AT&T to select the TAT-5 transatlantic cable over less costly satellite technology.[24]

Legal and regulatory actions seeking to block new service offerings carry an intangible cost. They add uncertainty to the firm's decision to invest in a new research project. Gerald W. Brock writes:

> Regulation helped maintain AT&T's market dominance against the threats of technological change and antitrust action during the 1934-1956 period. In the case of microwave, the inherently slow procedures of regulation prevented new entrants from exploiting the profitable opportunity caused by the simultaneous advent of new technology and a new source of demand. . . .
> The [FCC's] decision to grant experimental licenses required potential entrants to take the risks of developing a new technology without assurance that they would be granted the legal right to continue in business if their technology proved to be commercially feasible. The new companies could have been expected to move rapidly to take advantage of the excess demands for communications services after World War II if there had been no FCC restrictions. With only experimental licenses and the knowledge that AT&T had the ability and the incentive to at least delay the granting of regular licenses, the new companies had no incentive to invest significant amounts in building microwave networks.[25]

The purpose of patent laws is to encourage innovation by insuring that inventors will be rewarded for their efforts. AT&T used these laws, however, to build a kind of patent wall of protection around itself. The massive research efforts of Bell Laboratories not only led to important technology but also restricted the activities of companies in other fields. AT&T followed a policy of seeking patents on all alternative methods—not just the one that seemed most useful. This huge effort had a chilling effect on R&D elsewhere: it was impossible for smaller companies to be certain that they were not infringing on a Bell patent. The justification for regulation is simple. It should maximize benefits to the consumer. But federal policy has not always abided by this principle, as the foregoing examples should make clear.

A New Regulatory Environment. Though hard to measure, the atmosphere of a regulated environment seems likely to reduce incentives for management to investigate and introduce new types of technology. In any event, since 1968 that atmosphere has begun to change. New policies and rules are not only making the communications industry more competitive, but also giving birth to new, multibillion dollar industries.

In 1968, in the Carterfone decision, the FCC ruled that a customer who wishes to connect a device (for example, a mobile radio system) to the telephone network should be able to do so. This landmark decision gave rise to the "interconnect industry" which provides the consumer with everything from decorator telephones and telephone answering machines to computer terminals and modems. Significantly, after the decision Bell revealed that it had ready its own inexpensive and easy to use interfacing device. "One can reasonably infer that for years, possibly decades, the System had exaggerated the technological case against foreign attachments and had neglected research and development on such devices."[26]

In 1969 the FCC permitted Microwave Communications, Inc. (MCI) to construct a common-carrier microwave system from St. Louis to Chicago. This landmark decision gave rise to the "specialized common carrier industry" which provides microwave communications links for specialized markets.[27]

In 1970 the FCC permitted CATV operators to import distant signals and substitute commercials on them. This ruling gave a boost to the cable television industry.

In 1971 the FCC formulated its "open skies" policy which allowed for the use of commercial transmission within the United States.

In 1982 the Department of Justice and AT&T agreed to a plan whereby AT&T would divest itself of two-thirds of its assets (mainly local telephone operations). In return, the company will be free for the first time to enter any market its management wishes. This plan means increased competition for the interconnect industry, the specialized common carrier industry, the cable television industry, and the value-added network (VAN) industry. (A VAN is a network in which existing transmission links are used in a new way that enhances their value to the end users. New corporations like Telenet and Graphnet add computers to existing links to provide new transmission service, such as data networks which move bursts or packets of data rapidly and inexpensively from one subscriber to another.)

To sum up the technology push versus technology pull debate: Which is more important for innovation in the communications industry—the supply of new technology or the market demand for new technology? While this debate can not fairly be compared to the one in *Gulliver's Travels* about which end an egg should be opened from, it is fundamentally a false debate. In reality, neither strategy should totally be neglected. After all, it has been demonstrated how pre-1968 policies tended to reduce market pull and probably reduced the total innovative effort in the communications industry. But government funding did in fact help stimulate the semiconductor industry, especially in its early stages. Moreover, semiconductor electronics provides a classic example of how new knowledge can lead to demand where none had existed.

Therefore, it is preferable to pose the question this way: What is the optimal blend between demand push and market pull strategies in a given industry?

TWO POLICY RECOMMENDATIONS

Fund Infrastructure—Not Technology

Direct government support for technology is generally more effective in the early stages of technological innovation, rather than in the later stages when the technology nears commercialization (see Figure 9-1). There are a number of reasons why the rule seems valid. Government funding of basic research (Stages 1 and 2) is relatively effective because of the uncertainty and inappropriability of benefits facing companies conducting such activities. Not surprisingly, support of basic research by industry is only about 16 percent of the total national effort.[28]

While federal funding for basic research grew steadily throughout the 1960s, it declined in constant dollars from the late 1960s through the mid-1970s, falling at an average annual rate of about 2 percent in the period from 1969 to 1975. These decreases occurred at a time of general cutbacks in defense and space programs closely related to communications technology. In 1976 federal support of basic research began to expand again and by 1980 had increased in constant-dollar funding by 22 percent over the 1976 level.

When government funding begins to move beyond basic research and centers on more applied research and development, certain distortions in motivation begin to appear. Specifically, the private reward structure changes from trying to develop new products and processes that can be exploited profitably in the marketplace to getting R&D contracts and pleasing government sponsors (with advances that may be technically impressive but not socially useful).

Government-funded R&D is usually less flexible because it is directed by a contract. New discoveries made in the course of research cannot quickly be capitalized, especially if they require deviating from established procedures (they usually do). Further, government funding might reduce the level of private funding and bias project selection (according to the whims and self-interest of elected officials). Finally, because federal funding of R&D is one of the few areas in which spending levels are not committed to long-term legislative mandates, it tends to be reduced whenever pressure for budgetary reduction becomes great. The benefits of R&D usually come only in the future, so reductions in spending often have no immediate effect on the flow of benefits. This feast and famine funding creates inefficiencies in the way human resources and research equipment are used.

Corporate expenditures for R&D have been a long-standing part of communications industry policy. Company funds for R&D had averaged about 3.6 percent of sales for the last two decades, the highest of all industries. As previously noted, federal policy has been to stimulate innovation through end-product procurement. Given the outstanding results of U.S. communications research, this strategy seems justified.

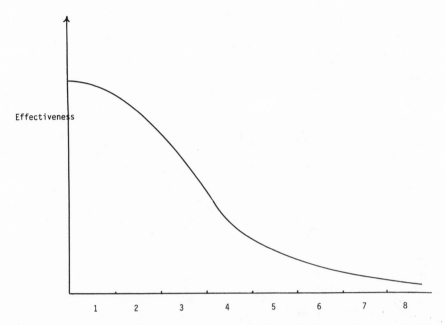

Figure 9-1. Effectiveness of Government Funding of Technological Innovation (Hypothesized)

Arguably, then, as a technology moves from research through the development and demonstration stages, the private sector can expect to capture more benefits from its investment; consequently, it should be less in need of federal monies. Still, government support for communications R&D seems warranted in three special instances. One is national security telecommunications. Another is high-risk, long-delayed payoff technologies whose application would have a social benefit. Many aspects of satellite communications fall into this class. The third is future services for which no present market exists but for which a future one can be foreseen because of social benefits. The office of the future might fall into this class. The more appropriate government role is in supporting the infrastructure for R&D. But what is meant by infrastructure?

Albert H. Rubenstein's concept of "imbedded technology" seems useful here. It refers to the skills, knowledge, people, and organizational capabilities which have been dominant factors in the past and current position of U.S. leadership in many fields. Imbedded technology, Rubenstein maintains, "constitutes a necessary condition for this leadership position and without it the country would be unable to fulfill the potential provided by R&D results, including patents."[29]

In the communications industry, basic supporting technologies vary, but breadboarding, maskmaking, wiring, and instrument modification have played prominent roles. "The arts involved in actually designing and producing a product predicted by theory or getting a new, patented process to work efficiently and economically are generally not transmitted through textbook instruction. . . . These are learned behaviors which can be transmitted by various means but which require time, personal interaction, and much trial and error."[30]

What can public policymakers do to enhance this kind of know-how which will play a decisive role in the coming global shake-out in telecommunications technology? Table 9-5 suggests a number of actions that the federal government might undertake. Perhaps the most conspicuous is to increase the size of the technical workforce, particularly the supply of electrical engineers, computer scientists, and technicians. (Japan now graduates significantly larger numbers of electrical engineers than the United States—one-third more for 1977—the reverse of the situation at the beginning of the 1970s, and a foreboding sign.)

Focus on Industries—Not Technologies

Simon Kuznets, the Nobel Prize-winning economist, has argued that any rapidly growing industry ultimately slows down as the cost-reducing advantages of its basic technology are exhausted. The nation's economy thus depends on new inventions to spur new, high-growth industries that continuously replace older, less efficient ones. How these sunrise industries can benefit the nation is nicely illustrated by the example of the Intel Corporation. Founded in 1968 with an initial investment of $3 million, Intel has grown to the point that its sales in 1980 were about 10 percent of the U.S. semiconductor industry. During the 1970s the company paid over $244 million in taxes; its employees, another $146 million. In the same decade, Intel purchased $466 million of goods and services to expand its capital plant. Its employment grew from 500 to 16,000.[31]

Today, a great deal is being written about Japan. But one point seems not to have received adequate attention—namely, the total and complete subordination of Japanese technology policy to economic growth policies. The Japanese have allowed low-technology and inefficient industries, which have often been propped up in the developed Western countries, to die. The aim of the Ministry of International Trade and Industry (MITI) is not to reduce competition among Japanese firms but to create the strongest possible companies with the greatest competitive potential. "Perhaps the nearest American analogy," Ezra F. Vogel writes, "is the National Football League or the National Basketball Association. League officials establish rules about size of team, recruitment and rules of play that result in relatively equally matched teams of great competitive abilities. They do not interfere in internal team activity or tell a coach how to run his team,

Table 9-5. Some Suggested Government Actions to Enhance the U.S.
Position with Respect to Imbedded Technology (IT)

Share the cost of training of technicians and other IT specialists.
Provide tax credits for labor savings on IT investments.
Increase sharing of IT capabilities by Federal labs.
Ease licensing and waiver of IT's covered by government-owned patents.
Increase access to Federal laboratories for testing of products and
      materials by industry.
Stimulate action on technology transfer by Federal agencies which give
      primarily lip service to it (despite policy directives to participate).
Include development of IT capabilities and products explicitly as part
      of federally financed or federally performed R. & D.
Subsidize trade magazines which specialize in IT in addition to professional
      journals which specialize in scientific and technical information (STI).
Expand the technology transfer agent programs that were tried by various
      agencies (e.g. NSF, NASA, Department of Commerce) and design them so
      that they will be more self-sustaining and more effective.
Count IT spin off as part of the social and economic benefits explicitly
      when evaluating cost-effectiveness of a government-sponsored R.&.D.
      program.
Identify and target needs for IT in different fields.
Use government influence (through regulations, procurement, tax laws,
      direct support) to encourage investment in IT by industry.
Provide support for use of retired executives to transfer IT skills and
      knowledge and to provide formal training.
Conduct or support technical audits of IT in individual companies and
      industries on a confidential basis.
Provide incentives to larger firms to assist small firms (including some
      of their supplier firms) in developing independent IT capabilities.
Support research and experimentation on IT.
Direct more attention to the IT aspect of the R.&.D. Innovation process,
      in addition to the current heavy focus on the R.&.D. aspects.
Consider IT skills when establishing immigration preferences.
Consider IT skills when considering export and technology transfer reg-
      ulations and individual export contracts.

Source: Albert H. Rubenstein, "The Role of Imbedded Technology in the Industrial
Innovation Process: in U.S. Congress, Joint Economic Committee, *Special Study on
Economic Change*, vol. 3 (Washington, D.C.: Government Printing Office, December
1980), p. 412.

although they do try to provide information that would enable him to
improve."[32] They have stressed the commercialization of technology in
contrast to the creation of specific inventions. Indeed, the Japanese
government provided only about 2 percent of the R&D funds used by the
private sector in 1977. The U.S. figure for the same year was 35.3 percent.
Government funding aside, Japanese companies enjoy certain built-in
strategic advantages in their drive for technological leadership. They have a
lower cost of capital, and a corporate management that focuses on long-
range product goals rather than quarter-to-quarter profit pressure. Joint
research ventures provide another Japanese advantage.

It is beyond the scope of this study to lay out a blueprint for an industrial
policy in the United States. But the specific components of a policy that
would enhance innovation in the communications sector should not go
unnoted. First, it is vital that all stages in the innovative process be coupled.
This means that scientists should talk to engineers, who should in turn talk
to production people—and everyone should listen to the marketing people.

Texas Instruments no longer even uses the term *basic research*, but rather talks of *total technical effort*, a phrase which embraces a good deal, including some aspects of marketing.[33] The idea of coupling helps explain why research done in good industrial laboratories has some advantages over that done in academic institutions and national laboratories. In this respect, Bell Laboratories is exemplary. In 1980 its members published about twenty-three hundred papers, most of which were peer-reviewed. Seven of its scientists have received Nobel Prizes. Interaction between scientists and engineers is good. Everyone understands the mission—providing new telecommunications technology—yet has remarkably broad latitude.

The idea of coupling also suggests that government should be more open to vertical integration of firms. Most Japanese television-makers produce their own semiconductors; at least in theory, semiconductor development can be closely coupled to the needs of the consumer division. At the same time, consumer goods provide a ready-made market for new semiconductor devices, removing much of the risk from their development. Yet antitrust laws have often made it difficult for American firms to take advantage of these synergies.

Companies like IBM, CBS, and AT&T—which seem dangerously large relative to the United States—are not quite so awesome in the context of the world economy. Indeed, many foreign firms are government-owned, benefit from massive government research financing, or belong to larger combines. A French electronic company like Thomson-CSF or a company belonging to the Mitsubishi group simply has more lines of credit and stubborn government backing than an American firm with the same sales. Antitrust action by the U.S. government against IBM, which began in 1969, has cost that company millions of dollars. Some observers argue that those monies might have been better spent keeping America number one in computers. In any event, today IBM faces increasingly effective competition from Fujitsu and Hitachi—supported with subsidies and administrative direction from the Ministry of International Trade and Industry.

In 1982 Fujitsu had $424 million in short-term bank loans at rates around 7 percent; meanwhile, IBM was borrowing at 14 percent. And such figures lead us to a second component in an innovation-oriented industrial policy: public policies to encourage a more rational pattern of investment. Today, the federal government seems to assume that capital markets automatically allocate resources to their most productive uses. But the assumption is erroneous: government tariffs, quotas, subsidies, loans, and tax loopholes create a hodgepodge of benefits that have little to do with technological innovation or productivity. For example, the government gives $455 million in tax breaks to the timber industry but none at all to the semiconductor industry. Again, international comparisons are striking. Governments in

Japan and Sweden attempt to explicitly identify areas of future industrial growth based on new technologies. In Japan, financing for investment in industries such as optical fibers, robotics, and high-speed computers comes from MITI in collaboration with the Ministry of Finance and the Japan Development Bank.

CONCLUDING OBSERVATIONS

The innovative rate in the United States during the 1970s was not uniform across industries. How are the differences explained? To repeat an earlier point: any rapidly growing industry ultimately slows down as the cost-reducing advantages of its basic technology are exhausted. This seems to be clearly the case with the paper, food, industrial machinery, and tire and rubber industries. But once these slowdowns occur, the economy then depends on new inventions to spur new, high-growth industries that continuously replace older, less efficient ones. This point, which was first raised by Simon Kuznets, seems to be appreciated more by public policymakers in Japan than by those in the United States.

Slowdowns in the chemical, drug, fuel, and personal/home care industries are perhaps best explained in terms of the funds and effort that had to be diverted from R&D to comply with the spate of federal regulations that occurred during the 1970s. But regulations can also spur innovation, as in the case of the automobile industry.

Innovation in the communications industry, which was high during the 1970s, shows no signs of flagging. The simplest explanation is that microelectronic technology accounts for the high innovation rate in this industry. But a more thoughtful explanation would run something like this:

A constant and prolific merging of technology generates the breakthroughs in the communications industry. These technological breakthroughs, in turn, are blurring industrial boundaries. The old industrial paradigm assumed that communications is communications and that computing is computing. Today, it no longer makes sense to try to separate them into orthogonal components. Neither does separating communications from the semiconductor, electronics, information processing, office equipment, newspaper, and aerospace industries. As industrial boundaries blur, regulation becomes difficult and often unnecessary.

The government response to this multiple interindustrial rivalry has been to move toward deregulation. Evidence presented here and elsewhere suggests that less regulation means more competition, which itself leads to more innovation. In a competitive environment, a high technology firm cannot afford to follow a conservative research policy. Thus, public policy aimed at deregulation tends to provide positive feedback to the rate of industrial change. (See Figure 9-2.) If this analysis is correct, the

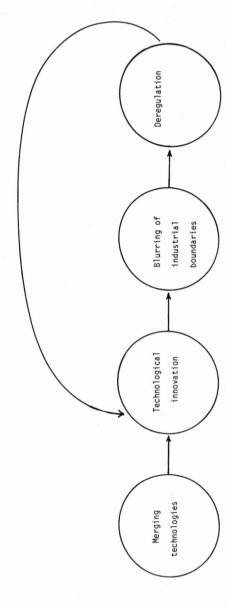

Figure 9-2. Dynamics of Technical and Industrial Change

implications are rather interesting. In today's communications industry we might be witnessing a new paradigm of industrial change and market rivalry.

By the late 1980s the outlines of a similar pattern of industrial change might begin to appear in the area of biomedical technology, with recombinant DNA serving as the technological catalyst, as did the semiconductor in communications. We might also begin to witness market rivalry based more on "systems" than "products." For instance, machine tool manufacturing might be replaced by a "production systems industry" (which will provide versatile, intelligent manufacturing and control equipment, incorporating programmable robots and artificial intelligence).

If this paradigm becomes reality, what should the public policy response be? The complexity and flux which are the warp and woof of the model make centralized, comprehensive planning exceedingly difficult. Yet "free enterprise," as defined by conventional wisdom, does not seem an entirely satisfactory alternative. This is a serious dilemma, which will no doubt solicit extended debate. During the course of this debate, perhaps the master planners will come to see the virtue of self-organizing systems and the free market advocates will grow less suspicious of coordination. Perhaps all can grow to appreciate the coming bliss of instability.

NOTES

1. Robert Solan, "Technological Change and the Aggregate Production Function," *Review of Economics and Statistics* (August 1957). Edward Denison, *The Sources of Economic Growth in the United States* (New York: Committee for Economic Development, 1962); and his paper in Tigran Khachaturov's *Methods of Long-Term Planning and Forecasting* (London: Macmillan, 1976). For a summary of existing knowledge in this area, see Edwin Mansfield, "Contribution of R and D Economic Growth in the United States," *Science* 175 (4 February 1972), p. 477. See also Nathan Rosenberg, "Thinking about Technology Policy for the Coming Decade," in U.S. Congress, Joint Economic Committee, *U.S. Economic Growth from 1976 to 1986: Prospects, Problems and Patterns* (Washington, D.C.: Government Printing Office, 1977).

2. For an overview of the various models of technological innovation, see Edwin Mansfield et al., *Research and Innovation in the Modern Corporation* (New York: Norton, 1971), chap. 6; and Mary Ellen Mogee, "The Process of Technological Innovation in Industry: A State-of-Knowledge Review for Congress," in U.S. Congress, Joint Economic Committee, *Research and Innovation: Developing a Dynamic Nation* (Washington, D.C.: Government Printing Office, 29 December 1980), pp. 171-256. The eight-stage model used in this article follows roughly that presented in James R. Bright, "The Process of Technological Innovation—An Aid to Understanding Technological Forecasting," in James R. Bright and Milton E. F. Schoeman's *A Guide to Practical Technological Forecasting* (Englewood Cliffs, N.J.: Prentice-Hall, 1973), pp. 3-12.

3. This idea is developed by Daniel Bell in his essay, "The Information Society,"

which appears in Tom Forester's *The Microelectronics Revolution* (Cambridge, Mass.: MIT Press, 1981), pp. 501-4.

4. William Schockley, *Electrons and Holes in Semiconductors* (New York: Van Nostrand, 1950).

5. George R. White and Margaret B. W. Graham, "How to Spot a Technological Winner," *Harvard Business Review* (March-April 1978), pp. 146-52.

6. David Burham, "Tests Point Way to Use of Home Teleprocessors," *New York Times*, 28 April 1980.

7. Quoted in *Business Week* (29 June 1981), p. 74.

8. See James Martin, *Future Developments in Telecommunications* (Englewood Cliffs, N.J.: Prentice-Hall), pp. 16-18.

9. J. Langrish et al., *Wealth from Knowledge: A Study of Innovation in Industry* (New York: Wiley, 1972).

10. See E. Bryan Crane, "The Wired Household," and Nicholas Mokoff, "Office Automation: A Challenge," in *IEEE Spectrum* (October 1979), pp. 61-69.

11. W. Rupert Maclaurin, *Invention and Innovation in the Radio Industry* (New York: Arno Press, 1971), pp. 241-65.

12. Edwin Mansfield et al., *Research and Innovations*, pp. 206-11. Distinguishing empirically between these types of failure raises an identification problem that Mansfield seems to ignore. Does an innovation fail because the market for it never emerges or because technological improvements are not of sufficient magnitude to make it possible to sell the product at a lower price? The Picturephone, which has been around for over a decade, is a case in point. One can argue that it has not caught on because the demand is not there; people may not want to look at each other when telecommunicating. But one can also argue that the device is still too expensive and that picture resolution or clarity remains poor, which means that charts and written texts cannot be transmitted.

13. Kenneth J. Arrow, "Economic Welfare and the Allocation of Resources for Invention," in the National Bureau of Economic Research's *The Rate and Direction of Inventive Activity: Economic and Social Factors* (Princeton, N.J.: Princeton University Press, 1962), pp. 609-25.

14. U.S., House of Representatives, Committee on Science and Technology, *Communications Research and Development* (Washington, D.C.: Government Printing Office, 20 May 1980), p. 27.

15. Office of Technology Assessment, *U.S. Industrial Competitiveness* (Washington, D.C.: Government Printing Office, July 1981), pp. 175-76.

16. See "SALT, SAMs, and Silver Bullets," *Forbes* (9 July 1979), pp. 33-36.

17. Leonard Waverman, "The Regulation of Intercity Telecommunicatons," in Almarin Phillips, *Promoting Competition in Regulated Markets* (Washington, D.C.: Brookings Institution, 1975).

18. U.S. General Accounting Office, *Government Regulatory Activity* (Washington, D.C.: Government Printing Office, 3 June 1977), p. 11.

19. U.S. Congress, House Committee on Science and Technology, *Communications Research and Development* (Washington, D.C.: Government Printing Office, 20 May 1980), p. 115.

20. Arthur H. White, "A Business Perspective on Technological Innovation," paper presented to a symposium for the International Business Press sponsored by Sperry Corporation, 1980.

21. James M. Utterback and Albert E. Murray, "The Influence of Defense Procurement and Sponsorship of Research and Development on the Development of the Civilian Electronics Industry," Center for Policy Alternatives at the Massachusetts Institute of Technology, Working Paper CPA-77-5, Cambridge, Mass., 30 June 1977, pp. 3-4.

22. J. F. Bucy, "Semiconductor Industry Challenges in the Decade Ahead," Institute of Electrical and Electronic Engineers Solid-State Circuits Conference, San Francisco, 13-15 February 1980.

23. For some early evaluations of R&D limited partnerships, see Hal Lancaster, "R&D Tax Shelters Catching Fire, But Potential Abuses Cause Concern," *Wall Street Journal*, 14 September 1981.

24. William G. Shepard, "The Competitive Margin in Communications," in W. E. Capron's *Technological Change in Regulated Industries* (Washington, D.C.: Brookings Institution, 1971), pp. 106-7.

25. Gerald W. Brock, *The Telecommunications Industry* (Cambridge, Mass.: Harvard University Press, 1981), pp. 194, 195.

26. Shepard, "The Competitive Margin," p. 111.

27. The words *in a particular market* are crucial here, since there is evidence to suggest that a combination that works well in one sector may not work well in another. See William J. Abernathy and Balaji S. Chakravarthy, "Government Intervention in Industry: A Policy Framework," paper presented to American Association for the Advancement of Science meeting in Washington, D.C., on 15 February 1978.

28. Unless otherwise noted, all the data in this section are taken from National Science Board, *Science Indicators 1980* (Washington, D.C.: Government Printing Office, 1981).

29. Albert H. Rubenstein, "The Role of Imbedded Technology in the Industrial Innovation Process," in U.S. Congress, Joint Economic Committee, *Special Study on Economic Change*, vol. 3 (Washington, D.C.: Government Printing Office, 29 December 1980), p. 387.

30. Ibid.

31. *Congressional Record* (10 July 1981): E3393.

32. Ezra F. Vogel, *Japan as Number One* (New York: Harper & Row, 1979), p. 72.

33. Ernest Braun and Stuart MacDonald, *Revolution in Miniature* (Cambridge, England: Cambridge University Press, 1978), p. 140.

JOEY REAGAN, THOMAS F. BALDWIN,
AND JOHN D. ABEL

10

The Impact of Mass Media Environments on Political Behavior

MOST of the research on media effects on political activity has focused on existing mass media. But emerging telecommunication services may alter the effects that mass media have on voting and other political behavior. It is especially important to consider these effects when public policy decisions affect the number of media outlets in a community.

The Federal Communications Commission, for example, has been considering rules to expand telecommunication services. "Must carry" rules for cable television systems require access to all local television signals. The lifting of cable importation restrictions means that local systems can offer more television signals that originate outside the community;[1] the consideration of a narrower bandwidth (from 10 kHz to 9 kHz) could increase the number of AM radio offerings;[2] additional regional television outlets may be provided by direct-to-home satellite broadcasting;[3] the number of local television outlets may be expanded through the use of VHF "drop-ins";[4] and television broadcasting at the neighborhood level may be introduced through low power stations.[5] Congress has attempted to preserve diversity among newspapers by exempting some failing newspapers from certain antitrust regulations through the Newspaper Preservation Act.[6]

Cable television provides the most significant example of major change in the availability of media outlets. It may be too early for the existence of cable television to affect voting and political activity, but it increasingly provides more information and greater diversity in some U.S. communities.

At the moment, there is very little localized cable news. Narrowcast news has only recently emerged; much more can be expected as a result of the promises of new franchise applicants in urban communities. Twenty-four-hour cable news channels, with much more time for political coverage, give people the opportunity to become better informed and more involved. In the summer of 1980 there was only one twenty-four-hour news channel, with limited penetration. There should be at least four channels under the expansion plans of Cable News Network (CNN) and the addition of two new services of the ABC and Westinghouse joint venture. Some of the news will be regional, and breaks will be provided for local news inserts.

It is possible that the rich diversity of cable will divert attention from local information. Television entertainment options during what used to be news time could seduce people away from news, or people may opt to watch the more engaging local news from the nearby, bigger towns. (This was discovered in a pilot study by Hill and Dyer.)[7]

In the future we can expect cable-delivered radio, television teletext and videotext, as well as broadcast teletext to bring much greater access to information to people in some communities. Cable is capable of providing gavel-to-gavel coverage of news events—city council meetings, school board sessions, court cases, nominating conventions, utility rate hearings, political speeches, and so on. Fringe political candidates will have unlimited access to television through public access channels. Through videotext and teletext, some people will have on-demand access to political candidate voting records and biographies or be able to make comparisons of candidates, issue by issue, on matters of interest. Government meeting agendas and the disposition of items will be continuously available. Statutes and ordinances may be accessed. Polling, with instant feedback, may be conducted through interactive television. Schools will be burdened with a responsibility to prepare new generations to use these additional tools effectively.

Over the next few years, access to new communication media and a much wider range of political information, as well as reduced reliance on existing mass media, suggests a need to reassess and continuously evaluate the impact of emerging communication technologies on the political process.

Although previous research has shown that mass media use is a positive predictor of voting and other political participation,[8] little research has explored the impact of altering the availability of media outlets. One study that did compare media availability was conducted by Chaffee and Wilson, who point out that the traditional model of media effects focuses on changes within individuals related to use of a medium that contains specific messages intended to change an individual's behavior.[9] However, they suggest that another valid research perspective is concerned with the structure of society; this perspective evaluates media effects at the level of the community as a system. It is important to determine how the total community reacts to the set of media available to the community. In their comparison of "media rich" (those with more than one newspaper) versus "media poor" communities, Chaffee and Wilson found that the richer communities have a greater diversity of political perceptions.

RESEARCH QUESTIONS

For public policymakers who have the ability to affect the number of media available to a community it is important to ask the following research questions:

1. Does political activity differ based on differences in media environment? Additionally, one needs to know the impact of new telecommunication technologies. Since only cable television has achieved major penetration into U.S. households[10] it is appropriate to focus on cable television.

2. Does political activity differ based on differences in cable television availability or cable subscribership? If there are differences in political activity in different media environments then the effects of cable television should be examined while controlling for the effects of the media environment.

3. Does political activity differ based on differences in cable availability or subscribership within similar media environments?

4. Do these differences vary depending on the type of media environment available?

METHOD—THE MEDIA ENVIRONMENT STUDY

In order to test questions like those raised above a national study involving personal interviews in seventeen communities was undertaken by the Department of Telecommunication at Michigan State University.[11] The seventeen cities were selected for their membership in mass media environment categories established by the number of daily newspapers, radio stations, and television stations originating in or within twenty miles of the city. Wherever possible, similar media environments contained both cabled and uncabled communities.

The cities selected were fit to the following categories: *Isolated*—one to two local radio stations, no television and no newspaper;[12] *Limited Service*—three to nine local radio stations, no television, and one daily newspaper;[13] *Full Service*—four to fifteen local radio and one to three local television stations, one daily newspaper; [14] *Saturated*—eleven to sixty-two local radio and four to twelve local television stations, and two or more daily newspapers.[15] These four media environments were used for the analysis.

Political Activity

Political activity was separated into two components: voting and political participation. Voting behavior was assessed by asking respondents whether they voted: (1) in the 1976 presidential election, (2) in the 1978 congressional election, (3) in the last local election. These three items were summed to form a scale measuring voting behavior (range: 0-3).

Political participation was also indexed. Respondents were asked: (1) whether they had tried to get a candidate on the ballot; (2) whether they had given money, attended rallies, or helped canvass for Democrats or Republicans; (3) whether they had tried to get an issue on the ballot; and (4) whether they had given any money, attended rallies, or canvassed for independents or minor parties. These four items were summed (range: 0-4).

Sampling within each city was done by Market Opinion Research (MOR), a survey research organization based in Detroit. MOR used a cluster sampling method. Personal interviews were conducted in the selected cities between June 17, 1980 and July 26, 1980. Only Buffalo, New York, and Eureka, Nevada, had interviews with less than 100 respondents (75 in each city). All other cities had 100 to 121 respondents each.[16]

RESULTS

Media Environment

The results for the four media environments are presented in Table 10-1. Both have significant differences (for voting $F = 11.96$, $p < 0001$; for political participation $F = 4.14$, $p < .01$; $df = 3,1824$ for both). Examination of the means shows mixed results. For voting, the Isolated environment shows the highest mean, with a sharp drop for the Limited Service environment, and a slight rise through the Full Service and Saturated environments. For political participation there is again a sharp drop in means between the Isolated and the Limited Service environments, but the Full Service and Saturated environments have the highest rates of political participation. *Post hoc* analyses (Scheffé tests) reveal that for

Table 10-1. Analyses of Variance for Voting and Political Participation by Media Environment

Dependent Variable	Environments					
	Isolated	Limited Service	Full Service	Saturated	F	p
Voting	2.13	1.62	1.65	1.75	11.96	<.0001
	(1.19)	(1.32)	(1.29)	(1.26)		
Political participation	.43	.27	.47	.50		
	(.77)	(.59)	(.85)	(.90)	4.14	<.01
N	345	200	559	724		

Note: Standard deviations in parentheses; degrees of freedom: 3,1824

voting, the Isolated environment has a significantly higher mean than the average of the means for the other three environments, while for political participation the average of the Isolated and Limited Service environments is significantly lower than the average for the other two.

Cable Television

Uncabled communities had a significantly ($p < .001$) higher mean for voting (1.94; $s.d. = 1.24$; $N = 728$) than did cabled communities (1.67; $s.d. = 1.29$; $N = 1100$). None of the other comparisons, for political participation or comparing subscribers versus nonsubscribers, was significantly different.

These analyses may not be very meaningful because of possible confounding effects from differences in other media available. Therefore, the cable analyses would be more meaningful if these factors were controlled.

Controlling for Environment

Only two media environments contained both cabled and uncabled communities: Isolated and Saturated. These communities were used as controls. Within these communities differences in voting and political participation were tested based on cable status and subscribership. Only in the Saturated environment were there significant differences ($p < .05$) with uncabled areas voting more (1.84; $s.d. = 1.24$; $N = 483$) than cabled areas (1.58; $s.d. = 1.29$; $N = 241$) and nonsubscribers (1.78; $s.d. = 1.25$; $N = 669$) voting more than subscribers (1.44; $s.d. = 1.39$; $N = 55$). None of the comparisons for political participation is significantly different.

At this point another confounding element emerges. The above analyses have mixed cabled and uncabled communities to test for differences based on subscribership. If differences are related to subscribership, such a relation should show up if one selected only cabled communities.

Controlling for Cable Status and Environment

This final analysis used only the cabled communities. In addition, the control based on environments is maintained. Thus, comparisons will be made only in communities with cable television *and* with similar mass media available.

Only one environment showed a significant difference ($p < .05$): Isolated. Subscribers (2.33; $s.d. = 1.01$; $N = 57$) were more likely than nonsubscribers (1.84; $s.d. = 1.29$; $N = 43$) to vote. There were no significant differences for voting in the other environments or for political participation.

DISCUSSION

Media Environments

There are differences in voting and political participation in different media environments. Voting may be high in the Isolated environment because there is more personal interest in local elections. The voters are likely to know the candidates and talk about the election to associates. The media in the rural and small town locations are less important to communication about elections when people have so many interpersonal contacts; while in the metropolitan areas, saturated with media, the election "hype" may be more pronounced. There are more media. Elections are well-suited to the character of big city media where contests and personalities are good subjects for news coverage. The big city media are slick in their coverage of elections. These media are better at generating interest because they have larger staffs and larger budgets and attend to the detail of making the election exciting. This could pique voter interest and activity.

Some of the same explanations may be given for the results of political participation across media environments. Here the isolated environment may have people who participate because of personal contact with candidates or party members. There may also be a single dominant party, which is comfortable to support actively.

In the Full Service and Saturated media environments, where media are impersonal and political parties somewhat removed from most citizens, it may be necessary more aggressively to develop political participation (for example, through canvassing) to touch people personally.

Cable Television

Mixed results were obtained for cable television. Overall, cabled areas and cable subscribers voted less than did non-cable viewers. This was true when controlling for media environment. However, when controlling for both cabled status and media environment in the Isolated environment, subscribers were more likely than nonsubscribers to vote.

As noted in the introduction, it may be too early to assess the effect of cable on political activity. But the results of this study suggest that cable subscribership has little impact except in those areas that have no local mass media (the Isolated environment). Perhaps the potential for cable, at the present time, is to provide mass media information channels where none exist. In those areas that already have local mass media cable television may merely provide redundant information. This, of course, may change with the emergence of more local dedicated information channels and with additional twenty-four-hour news services.

Policy Implications

The studies discussed here have shown that differences in media environment are related to differences in political activity or political awareness. Further, one of the new telecommunication technologies, cable television, possesses the potential—at least in communities with limited access to the mass media—to enhance voter turnout. Thus, availability of media plays some role in encouraging political activity.

One question that immediately arises is whether people living in sparsely populated areas and in the cores of major metropolitan areas will be denied that menu of new information services that other more economically attractive communities enjoy. How can those areas of the country that have little access to the media obtain the services that the "richer" communities possess? How can a national communication policy address these inequalities? Part of the answer to these questions lies in the ability of those who create communication policy to be well informed regarding these potential inequalities. These policymakers can encourage the development of other technologies, such as direct broadcast satellites and low power television stations, which can serve sparsely populated areas. The requirements of local cable franchise agreements—local origination and access channels, specialized imported channels, etc.—are an attempt to address the problem of providing media outlets to all parts of the community, even to small minorities.

Policymakers, whether national, regional or local, should be aware of the potential impact of media and media availability on political activity, and perhaps intervene to insure maximum access to a diversity of media outlets.

The results of this study indicate that the influences of media environment and new technologies on voting and political participation are strong enough to be considered a new variable among the factors that play a role in the political process. As media environments change dramatically over the next few years, their impact on political behavior will bear watching.

NOTES

1. Federal Communications Commission, 36 FCC 2d 143 (1972).
2. Federal Communications Commission, Docket Number 79164, 44 FR 39550 (1979).
3. Federal Communications Commission, Docket Number 80398 (1981).
4. Federal Communications Commission, FCC 80-505; 45 FR 73059; 48 RR 2d 585; 91 FCC 2d 233 (1980).
5. Federal Communications Commission, FCC 81-15; 48 RR 2d 1197; 84 FCC 2d 713 (1981).
6. 15 U.S.C. 1801, et. seq. (Suppl. 1971).

7. D. B. Hill and J. A. Dyer, "Cable Diversion to Distant Signal Local News Programs," *Journalism Quarterly* 58 (Winter 1981): 552-55.

8. See S. Kraus and D. Davis, *The Effects of Mass Communication on Political Behavior* (University Park: Pennsylvania State University Press, 1976).

9. S. H. Chaffee and D. G. Wilson, "Media Rich, Media Poor: Two Studies of Diversity in Agenda-Holding," *Journalism Quarterly* 54 (Autumn 1977): 466-76.

10. Cable penetration has reached about 25 percent while other technologies such as video recorders have entered only 2 percent of U.S. households. See M. R. Levy, "Home Video Recorders: A User Survey," *Journal of Communication* 30 (Autumn 1980): 77-80; A. C. Nielsen Co., *Nielsen Report on Television: 1981* (Northbrook, Ill.: A. C. Nielsen Management Services, 1981).

11. A full description of the development of the questionnaire, sampling, and methodology of the study can be obtained by writing the authors. The data used in this paper were gathered as part of "Mass Media Consumption and Function in Different Media Environments," funded by the National Science Foundation, grant #DAR-7910614; principal investigators: Dr. Thomas F. Baldwin and Dr. John D. Abel. In addition to the authors, the following persons worked on the project team: Jayne Zenaty, Rick Ducey, Janet A. Bridges, Genie Zerbinos, Tony Atwater, Ewart Skinner, Lonnie Moffet, Mohammad Suleibi, and Walter Matthews.

12. Buffalo, S.D.; Eureka, Nev.; Augusta, Arkansas; Tell City, Ind. (cabled).

13. McAlester, Okla.; Liberal, Kansas (both cabled).

14. Missoula, Mont.; Quincy, Ill.; Albany, Ga.; Manchester, N.H.; Cedar Rapids, Iowa (all with cable).

15. Mesa, Ariz. (cabled); Randallstown, Md.; Clovis, Calif. (cabled); Detroit, Mich.; Dallas, Tex.; Portland, Oreg.

16. Interviews were completed with 1,828 respondents. Almost half (48.8 percent) were male; 54 percent had annual household incomes at or above $15,000; 84.1 percent were white, 13 percent were black; 39 percent had at least some college education; 68 percent were married; 79.2 percent lived in a house, 5.6 percent in a mobile home, and 14.3 percent in an apartment; 71.0 percent owned their residence; and 19.2 percent lived in rural areas. The average age of respondents was 45.3 years.

Bibliography

Abel, John A., Charles Cliff III and Frederic A. Weiss. "Station License Revocations and Denials of Renewal 1934-1969." *Journal of Broadcasting* 14 (1970): 411-21.

Anderson, Kent. *Television Fraud: The History and Implications of the Quiz Show Scandals.* Westport, Conn.: Greenwood Press, 1980.

Baer, Walter S. *Cable Television: Franchising Considerations.* New York: Crane, Russak and Co., 1974.

Barcus, F. Earle and Rachael Wolkin. *Children's Television: An Analysis of Programming and Advertising.* New York: Praeger, 1977.

Barnouw, Erik. *The Golden Web: A History of Broadcasting in the United States, 1933-1953.* New York: Oxford University Press, 1968.

Barnouw, Erik. *The Image Empire: A History of Broadcasting in the United States since 1953.* New York: Oxford University Press, 1970.

Barnouw, Erik. *A Tower in Babel: A History of Broadcasting in the United States to 1933.* New York: Oxford University Press, 1966.

Barnouw, Erik. *Tube of Plenty: The Development of American Television.* New York: Oxford University Press, 1975.

Belendink, Arthur and Scott Robb. *Broadcasting Via Satellite: Legal and Business Considerations.* New York: Communications Research Institute, 1979.

Berner, Richard. *Constraints on the Regulatory Process: A Case Study of Regulation of Cable Television.* Cambridge, Mass.: Ballinger, 1976.

Bernstein, Marver H. *Regulating Business by Independent Commission.* Princeton, N.J.: Princeton University Press, 1955.

Bittner, John R. *Broadcast Law and Regulation.* Englewood Cliffs, N.J.: Prentice-Hall, 1982.

Brock, Gerald. *The Telecommunications Industry.* Cambridge, Mass.: Harvard University Press, 1981.

Cary, William L. *Politics and the Regulatory Agencies.* New York: McGraw-Hill, 1967.

Cherington, Paul W. *Television Station Ownership: A Case Study of Federal Agency Regulation.* New York: Hastings House, 1971.

Chester, Edward. *Radio, Television, and American Politics.* New York: Sheed and Ward, 1969.

Coates, Vary T., and Bernard Finn. *A Retrospective Technology Assessment: Submarine Telegraphy—The TransAtlantic Cable of 1866.* San Francisco: San Francisco Press, 1979.

Cole, Barry G., and Mal Oettinger. *The Reluctant Regulators: The FCC and the Broadcast Audience.* Reading, Mass.: Addison-Wesley, 1978.

Cowan, Geoffrey. *See No Evil: The Backstage Battle over Sex and Violence on Television.* New York: Simon and Schuster, 1979.

DeFleur, Melvin L., and Sandra Ball-Rokeach. *Theories of Mass Communication.* 2d ed. New York: McKay, 1970.

DeVol, Kenneth, ed. *Mass Media and the Supreme Court: The Legacy of the Warren Years.* 2d ed. New York: Hastings House, 1976.

Dordick, Herbert S., ed. *Proceedings of the Sixth Annual Telecommunications Policy Research Conference.* Lexington, Mass.: Lexington Books, 1979.

Edelman, Murray. *The Licensing of Radio Services in the United States, 1927-1947: A Study in Administration Formulation of Policy.* Urbana, Ill.: University of Illinois Press, 1950.

Edelman, Murray. *The Symbolic Uses of Politics.* Urbana, Ill.: University of Illinois Press, 1974.

Emerson, Thomas I. "Communications and Freedom of Expression." *Scientific American* (1972): 163-72.

Foley, Joseph M. "Broadcast Regulation Research: A Primer for Non-Lawyers." *Journal of Broadcasting* 17 (1973): 147-58.

Francois, William E. *Mass Media Law and Regulation.* 2d ed. Columbus, Ohio: Grid, 1978.

Franklin, Marc. *The First Amendment and the Fourth Estate: Communications Law for Undergraduates.* 2d ed. Mineola, N.Y.: Foundation Press, 1981.

Friendly, Fred W. *The Good Guys, the Bad Guys and the First Amendment: Free Speech vs. Fairness in Broadcasting.* New York: Random House, 1976.

Galloway, Jonathan F. *The Politics and Technology of Satellite Communications.* Lexington, Mass.: D. C. Heath, 1972.

Gibson, George H. *Public Broadcasting: The Role of the Federal Government, 1912-1976.* New York: Praeger, 1977.

Gillespie, Gilbert. *Public Access Cable Television in the United States and Canada.* New York: Praeger, 1975.

Gillmor, Donald M. and Jerome A. Barron. *Mass Communication Law: Cases and Comment.* 3rd ed. St. Paul, Minn.: West, 1979.

Ginsburg, Douglas H. and Jerome A. Barron. *Regulation of Broadcasting: Law and Policy Towards Radio, Television and Cable Communications.* St. Paul, Minn.: West, 1979.

Gormley, William T. "A Test of the Revolving Door Hypothesis at the FCC." *American Journal of Political Science* 23 (1979): 665-83.

Graham, James, and Victor Kramer. *Appointments to the Regulatory Agencies: The Federal Communication and the Federal Trade Commission, 1949-1974.* Washington, D.C.: Government Printing Office, 1976.

Grundfest, Joseph A. *Citizen Participation in Broadcast Licensing Before the FCC.* Santa Monica, Calif.: Rand Corporation, 1976.

Guimary, Donald L. *Citizens' Groups and Broadcasting*. New York: Praeger, 1975.

Hadden, Jeffrey K., and Charles E. Swann. *Prime Time Preachers: The Rising Power of Televangelism*. Reading, Mass.: Addison-Wesley, 1981.

Hamburg, Morton I. *All About Cable: Legal and Business Aspects of Cable and Pay Television*. New York: Law Journal Press, 1979.

Head, Sydney W. *Broadcasting in America*. 4th ed. Boston, Mass.: Houghton Mifflin, 1982.

Held, Virginia. *The Public Interest and Individual Interests*. New York: Basic Books, 1970.

Henderson, Madeline, and Marcia J. MacNaughton, eds. *Electronic Communication: Technology and Impacts*. Boulder, Colo.: Westview Press, 1980.

Johnson, Nicholas, and John Dystel. "A Day in the Life: The Federal Communications Commission." *Yale Law Review Journal* 82 (1973): 1575-1634.

Johnson, Nicholas. *How to Talk Back to Your Television Set*. Boston: Little, Brown, 1970.

Jones, William K. *Cases and Materials on Electronic Mass Media: Radio, Television and Cable*. 2d ed. Mineola, N.Y.: Foundation Press, 1979.

Kahn, Frank J., ed. *Documents of American Broadcasting*. 3d ed. Englewood Cliffs, N.J.: Prentice-Hall, 1978.

Kittross, John M. *Television Frequency Allocation Policy in the United States*. New York: Arno Press, 1979.

Kohlmeier, Louis M. *The Regulators: Watchdog Agencies and the Public Interest*. New York: Harper and Row, 1969.

Krasner, Stephen D. *Defending the National Interest*. Princeton, N.J.: Princeton University Press, 1978.

Krasnow, Erwin G., Lawrence D. Longley, and Herbert A. Terry. *The Politics of Broadcast Regulation*. 3d ed. New York: St. Martin's Press, 1982.

Landis, James M. *Report on Regulatory Agencies to the President-Elect*. Washington, D.C.: Government Printing Office, 1960.

LeDuc, Donald R. *Cable Television and the FCC: A Crisis in Media Control*. Philadelphia: Temple University Press, 1973.

Levin, Harvey J. *Fact and Fancy in Television Regulation: An Economic Study of Policy Alternatives*. New York: Russell Sage Foundation, 1980.

Lewin, Leonard, ed. *Telecommunications: An Interdisciplinary Study*. Dedham, Mass.: Artech House, 1979.

Lowi, Theodore. "American Business, Public Policy Case Studies and Political Theory." *World Politics* 16 (1964): 677-715.

Lowi, Theodore. *The End of Liberalism*. 2d ed. New York: Norton, 1978.

MacAvoy, Paul W., ed. *Deregulation of Cable Television*. Washington, D.C.: American Enterprise Institute for Public Policy Research, 1977.

McConnell, Grant. *Private Power and American Democracy*. New York: Knopf, 1966.

McGillem, Clare D., and William McLauchlan. *Hermes Bound: The Policy and Technology of Telecommunications*. West Lafayette, Ind.: Purdue Research Foundation, 1978.

Maclaurin, W. Rupert. *Invention and Innovation in the Radio Industry*. New York: Arno Press, 1971.

McMahon, Robert S. *The Regulation of Broadcasting: Half a Century of Government*

Regulation of Broadcasting and the Need for Further Legislation.
Washington, D.C.: Government Printing Office, 1958.

Magnant, Robert S. *Domestic Satellite: An FCC Giant Step Toward Competitive Telecommunications Policy.* Boulder, Colo.: Westview, 1977.

Minow, Newton N. *Equal Time: The Private Broadcaster and the Public Interest.* New York: Atheneum, 1964.

Mitnick, Barry. *The Political Economy of Regulation: Creating, Designing and Removing Regulatory Forms.* New York: Columbia University Press, 1980.

Mosco, Vincent J. *Broadcasting in the United States: Innovative Challenge and Organizational Control.* Norwood, N.J.: Ablex, 1979.

Nagel, Stuart S., ed. *The Legal Process from a Behavioral Perspective.* Homewood, Ill.: Dorsey Press, 1969.

Nelson, Harold L. and Dwight L. Teeter, Jr. *The Law of Mass Communications: Freedom and Control of Print and Broadcast Media.* 4th ed. Mineola, N.Y.: Foundation Press, 1982.

Neustadt, Richard M. *The Birth of Electronic Publishing.* White Plains, N.Y.: Knowledge Industries, 1982.

Noll, Roger G., Merton J. Peck, and John J. McGowan. *Economic Aspects of Television Regulation.* Washington, D.C.: Brookings Institution, 1973.

Noll, Roger G. *Reforming Regulation.* Washington, D.C.: Brookings Institution, 1971.

Owen, Bruce M. *Economics and Freedom of Expression: Media Structure and the First Amendment.* Cambridge, Mass.: Ballinger, 1975.

Owen, Bruce M. and Ronald Braeutigam. *The Regulation Game: Strategic Use of the Administrative Process.* Cambridge, Mass.: Ballinger, 1978.

Owen, Bruce M., Jack H. Beebe, and William G. Manning, Jr. *Television Economics.* Lexington, Mass.: Lexington Books, 1974.

Pool, Ithiel de Sola, ed. *The Social Impact of the Telephone.* Cambridge, Mass.: M.I.T. Press, 1977.

Porter, William E. *Assault on the Media: The Nixon Years.* Ann Arbor: University of Michigan Press, 1976.

Quiyk, Paul J. *Industry Influence in Federal Regulatory Agencies.* Princeton, N.J.: Princeton University Press, 1981.

Rivers, William L., Wallace Thompson, and Michael Nyhan, eds. *Aspen Handbook on the Media.* New York: Praeger, 1977.

Robinson, Glen O., ed. *Communications for Tomorrow: Policy Perspectives for the 1980s.* New York: Praeger, 1978.

Rosenblum, Victor. "How to Get into TV: The Federal Communications Commission and Miami Channel 10." In Alan F. Westin, ed., *The Uses of Power.* New York: Harcourt Brace Jovanovich, 1962, pp. 177-228.

Rourke, Francis E. *Bureaucracy, Politics, and Public Policy.* 2d ed. Boston: Little, Brown, 1976.

Rubin, Bernard. *Media, Politics, and Democracy.* New York: Oxford University Press, 1977.

Sabatier, Paul. "Social Movements and Regulatory Agencies: Toward a More Adequate and Less Pessimistic Theory of Clientele Capture," *Policy Sciences* 6 (1975): 301-342.

Schiller, Herbert I. *Communications and Cultural Domination.* White Plains, N.Y.: International Arts and Sciences Press, Inc., 1976.

Schmidt, Benno C. *Freedom of the Press vs. Public Access.* New York: Praeger, 1979.

Schwartz, Bernard. *The Professor and the Commissions.* New York: Knopf, 1959.

Seiden, Martin H. *Cable Television U.S.A.: An Analysis of Government Policy.* New York: Praeger, 1972.

Seiden, Martin H. *Who Controls the Mass Media? Popular Myths and Economic Realities.* New York: Basic Books, 1974.

Sigel, Efrem, ed. *Videotext: The Coming Revolution in Home/Office Information Retrieval.* White Plains, N.Y.: Knowledge Industry Publications, 1980.

Signitzer, Benno. *Regulation of Direct Broadcasting from Satellites.* New York: Praeger, 1976.

Simmons, Steven J. *The Fairness Doctrine and the Media.* Berkeley: University of California Press, 1978.

Sterling, Christopher H. and John M. Kittross. *Stay Tuned: A Concise History of Broadcasting.* Belmont, Calif.: Wadsworth, 1978.

Terreberry, Shirley. "The Evaluation of Organization Environments," *Administrative Science Quarterly* 12 (1968): 590-613.

Truman, David B. *The Governmental Process: Political Interests and Public Opinion.* 2d ed. New York: Knopf, 1971.

Wellborn, David M. *Governance of Federal Regulatory Agencies.* Knoxville: University of Tennessee Press, 1977.

Wicklein, John. *Electronic Nightmare: The New Communications and Freedom.* New York: Viking Press, 1981.

Will, Thomas E. *Telecommunications Structure and Management in the Executive Branch of Government, 1900-1970.* Boulder, Colo.: Westview Press, 1978.

Wilson, James Q. *Political Organizations.* New York: Basic Books, 1973.

Wilson, James Q. *The Politics of Regulation.* New York: Basic Books, 1980.

Zuckman, Harvey L. and Martin J. Gaynes. *Mass Communications Law in a Nutshell.* St. Paul, Minn.: West, 1977.

Index

About the Contributors

JOHN D. ABEL is Professor and Chairperson of the Department of Telecommunication at Michigan State University. He served as a Social Science Policy Analyst at the Federal Communications Commission in 1977-78 and as a Post-doctoral Fellow at Exeter University in England. As a consultant, he has conducted research for the Federal Trade Commission, the FCC, the Corporation for Public Broadcasting, multiple system cable operators and broadcast stations. Dr. Abel received his graduate degrees from Indiana University and has been on the faculty at Michigan State University since 1972. He has published over forty articles, papers, reports and chapters in books.

THOMAS F. BALDWIN is a Professor appointed jointly in the Departments of Telecommunication and Communication at Michigan State and is Chairman of the Mass Media Ph.D. Program. Dr. Baldwin is co-author of *Cable Communication*. He was director of the Rockford Two-way Cable project and a co-principal investigator in the Media Environment Study, both funded by the National Science Foundation.

C. ANTHONY BROH is an Assistant Professor of Political Science and a Faculty Associate of the Eagleton Institute of Politics at Rutgers University. He is currently doing research on the media's use of public opinion polls, regulation of commercial television, and news coverage of school desegregation. He is the author of *Toward a Theory of Issue Voting, Voting Behavior: The 1980 Election*, and several articles on voting behavior, political socialization, and communications policy.

JON S. CRANE is an Assistant Professor of Telecommunications in the Department of Communication, University of Minnesota-Duluth. He received his Ph.D. from the University of Massachusetts at Amherst. His current research interests are in Constitutional First Amendment theory and the regulation of radio, television, cable, and other means of commercial telecommunication.

JOHN J. HAVICK is an Associate Professor of Political Science at the Georgia Institute of Technology. His research interests include the mass media, communications policy, party politics, and program evaluation. He has published previously in such periodicals as the *Journal of Politics, Polity*, and the *American Journal of Political Science*.

FLORENCE HEFFRON is an Associate Professor of Political Science and Director of the MPA program at the University of Idaho. She is the author of *Administrative Regulatory Process* (1983).

JAN H. LINKER is currently a Research Associate with a syndicated research and consulting firm in Atlanta, Georgia. She received her Ph.D. in 1981 from the Department of Political Science at Emory University. Her dissertation was on the impact of interest groups on broadcast decisions at the FCC.

M. STEPHEN PENDLETON, Assistant Professor of Economics and Political Science, State University College at Buffalo, is a member of the SUCB urban studies faculty and of the Buffalo Urban Research Consortion. His research interests are currently focused on federalism and environmental policy.

JOEY REAGAN received his Ph.D. in mass media from Michigan State University in 1981. He is currently Assistant Professor of Communication at the University of Michigan where he teaches Video Production and Communication Theory. His research interests include the effects of media exposure on community integration and political activity, and the effects of new communication technology news services on traditional information media and news source selection and credibility.

SARAH SLAVIN, Assistant Professor of Economics and Political Science, State University College at Buffalo, is Managing Editor of *Women & Politics: A Quarterly Journal of Research and Policy Studies* and a member of the American Political Science Association Task Force on Women and American Government. Her research interests include women and American politics.

GROVER STARLING is a graduate of the U.S. Military Academy (1965) and holds a Ph.D. in government from the University of Texas at Austin (1972). He has served as the Chief of a Management Engineering Team in the Strategic Air Command and Director of Programs in Public Affairs at the University of Houston at Clear Lake City. He has been a consultant to several major corporations and federal agencies. He is the author of seven books, the most recent of which are *The Changing Environment of Business* and *Understanding American Politics*. Currently, Dr. Starling is Professor of Public Affairs in the School of Business and Public Administration at University of Houston at Clear Lake City.

MICHAEL J. STOIL is a Washington-based consultant in the fields of communications content and policy. Following six years of service with the Department of State, he has been employed by the National Governors' Association, Walter Hinchman and Associates, KAPPA Systems, Inc., and the congressional Office of Technology Assessment. He was appointed a member of the Virginia Public Telecommunications Board in 1982. In addition to his consulting activities, Dr. Stoil holds a full-time appointment on the faculty of Mount Vernon College and is the author of two books and several articles on the subjects of communications and satellite operations.

STEVE WEINBERG is an Assistant Professor at the University of Missouri School of Journalism. He is the author of the book, *Trade Secrets of Washington Journalists* (1981) and freelance articles in more than twenty magazines. He is a former Washington correspondent for magazines and newspapers.